Stories of Old-Time Oklahoma

Also by David Dary

The Buffalo Book: The Full Saga of the American Animal

True Tales of the Old-Time Plains

Cowboy Culture: A Saga of Five Centuries

Entrepreneurs of the Old West

Seeking Pleasure in the Old West

True Tales of Old-Time Kansas

More True Tales of Old-Time Kansas

Kanzana, 1854–1900: A Selected Bibliography of Books, Pamphlets, and Ephemera of Kansas

Lawrence, Douglas County, Kansas: An Informal History

Red Blood and Black Ink: Journalism in the Old West

Pictorial History of Lawrence, Douglas County, Kansas

The Santa Fe Trail: Its History, Legends, and Lore

The Oregon Trail: An American Saga

The Oklahoma Publishing Company's First Century: The Gaylord Family Story

(ed.) *A Texas Cowboy's Journal: Up the Trail to Kansas in 1868*

True Tales of the Prairies and Plains

Frontier Medicine: From the Atlantic to the Pacific, 1492–1941

Stories of Old-Time
Oklahoma

∼

David Dary

University of Oklahoma Press : Norman

Publication of this book is made possible through
the generosity of Edith Kinney Gaylord.

LIBRARY OF CONGRESS CATALOGING-IN-PUBLICATION DATA

Dary, David.
 Stories of old-time Oklahoma / David Dary.
   p. cm.
 Includes bibliographical references and index.
 ISBN 978-0-8061-4181-7 (cloth)
 ISBN 978-0-8061-4419-1 (paper)
 1. Oklahoma—History—Anecdotes. 2. Frontier and pioneer life—Oklahoma—
Anecdotes. 3. Pioneers—Oklahoma—Biography—Anecdotes. 4. Oklahoma—
Biography—Anecdotes. I. Title.
 F694.6.D37 2011
 976.6—dc22
                                                              2010049963

The paper in this book meets the guidelines for permanence and durability of the
Committee on Production Guidelines for Book Longevity of the Council on Library
Resources, Inc. ∞

Copyright © 2011 by David Dary. Published by the University of Oklahoma
Press, Norman, Publishing Division of the University. Paperback published 2013.
Manufactured in the U.S.A.

All rights reserved. No part of this publication may be reproduced, stored in
a retrieval system, or transmitted, in any form or by any means, electronic,
mechanical, photocopying, recording, or otherwise—except as permitted under
Section 107 or 108 of the United States Copyright Act—without the prior written
permission of the University of Oklahoma Press.

*Dedicated to the memory of
Kirk Bjornsgaard,
editor, writer, journalist, musician,
and friend.
He died too young.*

Contents

List of Illustrations   xi
Introduction   xiii

Part I   The Land, Rivers, Towns, and Wild Creatures

The Cross Timbers   3
Some Wild Creatures   7
Oklahoma Rivers   14
Naming and Pronouncing Oklahoma Towns   20
When Oklahoma Got Electric Lights   29
Oklahoma's Black Gold   32

Part II   On Trails and Rails

Early Trails   39
Military Forts   43
Trading Posts and Early Businesses   49
The Butterfield Overland Stage   54
Early Cattle Trails and Ranching   58
When the Railroads Arrived   63
"No Man's Land"   67

Part III   From Tipis and Lodges

Making Peace with the Plains Indians   73
Mountains Named for the Wichita Indians   76
"Gopher John," Black Seminole   80
Satanta, Kiowa Chief   84
Cherokee William P. Ross, Father of Oklahoma Journalism   88
Jane Austin McCurtain   91
Quanah Parker, Last Comanche Chief   94
Oscar Jacobson and the Kiowa Five   97

Part IV **Oklahoma Treasure Legends**
A Few Words about Treasure Legends 103
Spanish Legends 105
Why Pioneers Buried Their Treasures 108
Bryan County Treasures 110
Hidden Treasures 112
The Tres Piedras Legend 115
The Treasure Belle Starr Sought 120
The Legend of California Gold 122
He Did Not Know the Treasure Was There 125

Part V **Outlaws and Lawmen**
The Mystique of Oklahoma Outlaws 129
Bill Doolin, Oklahoma's Worst Outlaw 132
William Coe, Oklahoma's Least-Known Outlaw 135
Bass Reeves, the Most Feared U.S. Deputy Marshal 141
The Misadventures of Al Jennings 144
Bill Tilghman, Lawman 148
Al Spencer, Forgotten Outlaw 153
Pretty Boy Floyd, Bank Robber 156

Part VI **People, Events, and Things**
Will Rogers's Last Interview 163
Oklahoma Symbols and Emblems 169
David Payne, Boomer 174
Kate Barnard, First Woman Elected to State Office 178

The Night Boise City Was Shaken	182
Roscoe Dunjee, Oklahoma's Little Caesar	186
The Miller Brothers' 101 Ranch	189
The Man from Bugtussle	193
Oklahoma Inventors	196
Oklahoma Storms, Fires, Floods, Train Wrecks, and Other Disasters	199

Part VII Artists, Writers, and Entertainers

Washington Irving's Oklahoma Visit	209
Artists in Indian Territory	214
Angie Debo, Teacher and Writer	220
Woody Guthrie, Father of American Folk Music	224
Gene Autry, Yodeling Cowboy	228
Patti Page, the Singing Rage	234
Kay Starr, Salon Singer	238
Notes on Sources	243
Index	255

Illustrations

Oil gusher	34
Coach driven by John Butterfield, Jr.	54
Rock cut on the Missouri, Kansas, and Texas Railroad, 1872	64
Sod house	68
"Gopher John"	81
Satanta	84
William Porter Ross	90
Jane Austin McCurtain	92
Quanah Parker	95
The Kiowa Five with Oscar Jacobson	98
Belle Starr	121
Bill Doolin in death	134
William Coe's "Robber's Roost"	136
Bass Reeves	142
Al Jennings	146
Bill Tilghman	151
Pretty Boy Floyd	157
Will Rogers and Wiley Post	164
David L. Payne and other Boomers	176
Kate Barnard	179
Roscoe Dunjee	188
Geronimo and other Indian performers with the 101 Ranch	191

Carl Albert	195
Washington Irving	210
Angie Debo	221
Woodie Guthrie and Pete Seeger	225
Gene Autry	230
Patti Page	236
Kay Starr	240

Maps

Cross Timbers	4
Camp Holmes and Chouteau's Trading Post	51
Washington Irving's 1832 tour	212

Introduction

THIS IS A COLLECTION OF stories about people, events, and things in Oklahoma, the nation's twentieth-largest state in land mass, rich in natural resources, well-watered, and with a remarkably varied topography. Its history is colorful yet complex, something like a patchwork or crazy quilt that has evolved without much planning or design. During the nineteenth century, Oklahoma evolved haphazardly in a climate that often lacked integrity and honesty. There was much hypocrisy, outlawry, and greed, along with cultural and racial animosity. In addition, outside business interests exerted pressure to open Indian lands to white settlement.

Indians lived in Oklahoma long before Spanish and French explorers arrived. Next came traders. With the U.S. purchase of Louisiana Territory in 1803, American explorers and soldiers came to inspect the land. The federal government soon used much of modern Oklahoma as a place to send Indian tribes so that lands east of the Mississippi could be used by whites. In time, many other tribes were moved to what became known as Indian Territory.

Five tribes in particular—Cherokee, Chickasaw, Choctaw, Creek, and Seminole—were exiled to Indian Territory. Some whites described the Five Tribes as civilized because they had adopted plow agriculture and animal husbandry or lived in European-style homes. They dressed like white Americans, and some even owned black slaves.

Each of the Five Tribes established autonomous states or nations with their own laws, courts, schools, and Christian churches. Some developed a writing system patterned after one devised earlier by the Cherokee Sequoyah. When the American Civil War came, the Five Tribes were divided as to which side to support. The Choctaws and Chickasaws fought predominantly on the Confederate side. The Creeks, Seminoles, and Cherokees were split between supporting the Union and the Confederacy. The Cherokees actually fought their own civil war over supporting the opposing sides.

When the U.S. Civil War ended, the federal government adopted a policy to detribalize the Indians and curtail their control of tribal lands given to them in perpetuity by government treaties. The U.S. Supreme Court in 1870 effectively affirmed that Congress had the power to overturn government treaties. Beginning in the 1870s, the federal government stopped using treaties as instruments of negotiation and simply made "agreements" with the Indians.

During the years following the Civil War, Indian Territory became a haven for outlaws because Indian courts had no jurisdiction over non-Indians and U.S. jurisdiction was administered from Fort Smith, Arkansas. By the late 1860s and early 1870s, whites in neighboring states increasingly craved settlement on Indian lands. At first the federal government said no to non-Indian settlement. The railroads, however, soon obtained the rights to go through Indian Territory and, once tracks were laid, sought to open the land for settlement. The white man's courts next determined that some land in central Indian Territory did not belong to Indians. These "unassigned lands" were opened to settlement using a land run in 1889.

The land run attracted many honest and upstanding settlers, but others did not respect the rule of law. For more than a year, the settlers were a law unto themselves, save for the efforts of a few U.S. marshals working out of the federal courthouse in Fort Smith. Even after Oklahoma Territory was formed in June 1890, federal legislation provided for no form of government or civil law.

The Sauk and Fox, Iowa, and Pottawatomie reservations in eastern Oklahoma were next opened to settlement. Later Cheyenne and Arapaho land, the Cherokee Outlet, and the Kickapoo Indian reservation were opened to settlers. Greer County, previously part of Texas, was given to Oklahoma Territory in an 1896 decision by the U.S. Supreme Court. A lottery system, begun in 1901, distributed land to settlers, but later, auctions were used to allocate open land for settlement. Oklahoma Territory and Indian Territory were combined to make Oklahoma a state in 1907, and later that year a state constitution was adopted that is the longest governing document of any government in the world.

Oklahoma's territorial period provided insufficient time for settlers to establish order, direction, and the infrastructure needed for a stable society and economy. Thus the early years of statehood were turbulent, beset by much civil unrest and problems with vigilantes, bootleggers, and racists. The state's first legislature imposed segregation, and in 1921 Tulsa was the scene of one of the worst race riots in American history. Prohibition, enacted at statehood, was the law, but nearly everyone except the drys ignored it before it ended in 1959. Then came the oil boom and sudden growth of boomtowns. The name "Oklahoma" became synonymous with "oil." By the 1920s, Oklahoma had also gained the reputation as one of the nation's great granaries and cattle kingdoms, but then came the Depression of the 1930s, the Dust Bowl, and World War I.

Because Oklahoma became a state much later than most other neighboring states, many Oklahomans sought to overcompensate in their efforts to quickly build their state and erase a feeling of inferiority. Their actions did result in many spectacular achievements, but other Oklahomans chose social isolation and unconventional beliefs, perhaps because they lacked education. For instance, they supported schools but favored athletic achievement over intellectual accomplishment, including critical thinking, and they condoned corruption.

Oklahoma's resulting culture is not moralistic. It does not reject corruption and often lacks a real sense of what is right and wrong. It is characterized by a traditionalism stressing social and family ties that have created a political culture in which some families run the government and others have little to say about it. Political leaders are largely conservative and view their role as custodial rather than promoting innovation. Oklahoma's government has a practical orientation emphasizing limited government intervention in the private activities of its citizens. At the same time, it has corrupt politics with politicians often profiting from their political activity. Such things are accepted by many Oklahomans as fact and are often viewed as the way things are and should be. They seek to maintain the status quo. At the same time, many Oklahomans seek to project an image of their state that often does not match reality.

Many of the stories in this book reflect this culture. Most of them were first published during the state's centennial in 2007 in a weekly newspaper column, "Oklahoma Reflections," carried by twenty community newspapers. Other stories were written for Associated Press and published in member newspapers the same year throughout Oklahoma. For this book, many of the stories have been revised and expanded, and other stories have also been added.

The author wishes to thank David Stringer, former publisher of the *Norman Transcript* and Community Newspaper Holdings, Inc., and Lindell Hutson, retired Oklahoma City bureau chief of the Associated Press, for permission to use many of the stories on the pages that follow.

I hope these stories remind readers that Oklahoma's history is as rich and colorful as the land itself. The stories may help them understand the state's complex past and explain why Oklahoma is what it is today.

David Dary
On Imhoff Creek
Norman, Oklahoma

Part I

~

The Land, Rivers, Towns, and Wild Creatures

O lands! O all so dear to me—what you are,
I become part of that, whatever it is.

Walt Whitman

The Cross Timbers

THE FIRST OUTSIDER TO BRING Oklahoma's Cross Timbers to the world's attention was Washington Irving, the prominent nineteenth-century American writer best known for "The Legend of Sleepy Hollow" and "Rip Van Winkle." He made a tour through what is now Oklahoma in 1832. The full story of Irving's visit is told elsewhere between these two covers, but he found much of the Cross Timbers impassible. These upland forests have an abundance of post oaks, blackjacks, hickories, and elms plus a heavy undergrowth of grape vines and greenbriers. The Cross Timbers stretch from southeastern Kansas south across Oklahoma and deep into North Texas.

Washington Irving wrote that Indians on hunting expeditions west of the Cross Timbers frequently started fires that burned east, penetrating the forests and "sweeping in light transient flames along the dry grass, scorching and calcining the lower twigs and branches of the trees and leaving them black and hard." Irving added that he would "not easily forget the mortal toil and vexations of the flesh and spirits that we underwent occasionally, in our wanderings through the Cross Timber. It was like struggling through forests of cast iron."

Two years later, in the summer of 1834, Col. Henry Dodge traveled with his dragoons through the Cross Timbers in what is now southern Oklahoma. Dodge described them as a great thicket "composed of nettles and briars so thickly matted together as almost to forbid passage." Josiah Gregg, a Santa Fe trader who traveled through the area several times during the early 1840s, described the Cross Timbers as the "fringe" of the great prairies. "Most of the timber appears to be kept small by the continued inroads of the 'burning prairies'; for, being killed almost annually, it is constantly replaced by scions of undergrowth; so that it becomes more and more dense every reproduction."

Randolph B. Marcy, a career army officer, led an expedition in

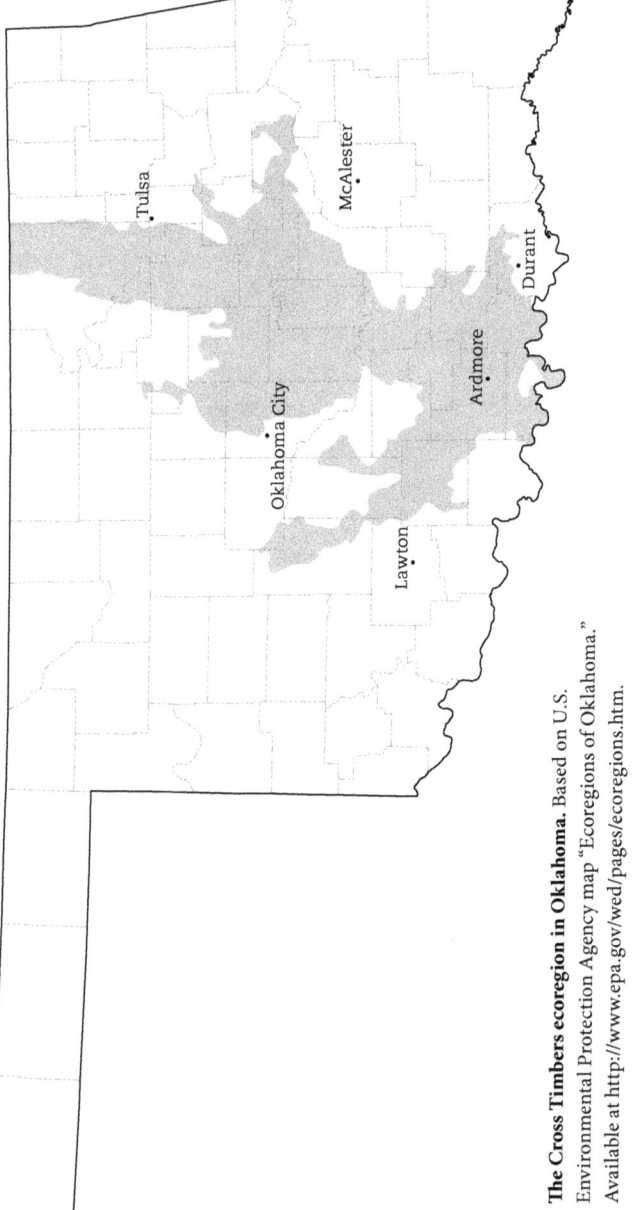

The Cross Timbers ecoregion in Oklahoma. Based on U.S. Environmental Protection Agency map "Ecoregions of Oklahoma." Available at http://www.epa.gov/wed/pages/ecoregions.htm.

1852 to search for the source of the Red River. He observed that "the Cross Timbers appear to have been designed as a natural barrier between civilized man and the savage, as upon the east side there are numerous springs, abundance of timber, exuberant vegetation, and an interspersion of glades and small prairies." In contrast, Marcy described the region west of the Cross Timbers as "barren and desolate wastes" with few streams and little woodland along water courses. Marcy's 1853 report to the Thirty-second Congress established the Cross Timbers in the public mind as a demarcating line between the civilized East and the frontier West. In fact, the expression "beyond the Cross Timbers" came to signify the West and its challenges and opportunities in the minds of many Americans. By 1835, one government map published in Washington, D.C., labeled the Cross Timbers as the "western boundary of habitable land."

Before the arrival of the white man, scientists believe, the Cross Timbers covered more than 30,000 square miles. The size began to shrink after Indian Territory was opened to settlement in 1889 and settlers began clearing trees on many level areas of the Cross Timbers to plant crops or provide grazing for their livestock. This continued well into the twentieth century.

Today the size of the Cross Timbers is considerably smaller than in the early nineteenth century. Some scientists believe that only about five hundred square miles of ancient Cross Timbers still survive in the rugged uplands of eastern Oklahoma. Growing in the soil under the trees is a wealth of plant species, some rare and native to Oklahoma. Natural conditions seem to have preserved the surviving Cross Timbers. The trees are not ideal for lumber production. Then too, these short, stout oaks grow on steep terrain and poor soil not suitable for agriculture.

In one area of northeastern Oklahoma near Sand Springs, the ancient trees are protected. At the Keystone Ancient Forest Preserve, scientists found a red cedar more than five hundred years old growing on a sandstone bluff. Not far away was another ancient post oak more than four hundred years old and standing only twenty feet tall. The Cross Timbers region in Oklahoma is one of the least disturbed forest areas left in the eastern half of the United States.

Eastern interest in the Cross Timbers gradually faded after the run of 1889, and the area itself gradually shrank as settlers cleared land to grow crops. That decline went generally unnoticed. Even today, although people notice their subtle beauty, the remaining Cross Timbers receive little attention from the public and are rarely associated with Oklahoma's colorful history. Even the fact that the Cross Timbers constitute the largest single type of ecosystem in Oklahoma is generally forgotten. Animals and plants depend on the system, which in turn depends on them.

The Cross Timbers are a big part of Oklahoma's cultural heritage. More than a century ago they provided wood for the Indians and pioneers, a home for wildlife that kept the human population fed and clothed, and hiding places—not only for wildlife but also for Anglo-Americans trying to avoid hostile Indians and Indians wanting to ambush their enemies. The surviving Cross Timbers provide oxygen and protect the soil from erosion and continue to be important to the state's ecology. But they must not be forgotten as a living monument to the history of Oklahoma, a treasure that should be preserved.

Some Wild Creatures

WILD BUFFALO, GRAY AND RED wolves, black bears, pumas, and pronghorns once freely roamed what is now Oklahoma. Most of the wild species are gone. Zoos, wildlife refuges, and a few private citizens, however, preserve living examples of some of these magnificent animals.

BUFFALO

The American buffalo or bison (*Bison bison*) was made the official animal of Oklahoma by a resolution in the state senate in 1972. Long before the first Europeans arrived, thousands upon thousands of buffalo roamed what is now Oklahoma.

The buffalo is the largest mammal native to the state. A full-grown bull might stand five or six feet tall at the shoulder or high part of the hump and weigh from 1,900 to 2,500 pounds. Some old-timers on the southern plains claimed to have seen bulls weighing 3,000 pounds.

The buffalo provided Indians with the essentials for life. Large groups of Indians on foot would surround or circle as many buffalo as they needed and then kill the animals with lances and bows and arrows. After the Spanish brought horses into North America and Indians acquired them, a few Indian hunters on horseback could kill what buffalo they needed for food. The buffalo, however, provided more than meat for the Indians.

Buffalo robes provided Indians warmth in winter. The hides scraped clean of hair provided material for garments and ropes. From sinew Indians made bowstrings and twine, and the animal provided tallow and grease. Buffalo bones were used as implements and weapons, and glue was produced from the animal's hoofs. Buffalo chips provided fuel for fires and were sometimes stacked like stones for markers.

Historical evidence suggests that Indians killed only as many buffalo as they needed until the arrival of white traders, with whom Indians began trading buffalo robes for goods. During one year in the 1860s, a Kansas trader obtained 23,600 robes from the Comanches and 3,500 robes from Apaches and Cheyennes in Indian Territory. The Osage and Kaw Indians traded 4,000 robes. The best robes were taken from buffalo killed in late fall and during the winter when the animal's hair was longest.

Following the Civil War, Texas cattlemen drove their herds of longhorns north to the Kansas cattle towns. George W. Saunders recalled that in 1870, "the plains were literally covered" with buffalo. Some of Saunders's cowboys raced toward a herd and tried in vain to kill some buffalo with their pistols. Another Texas cattleman, B. A. Barroum, recalled that as his herd of longhorns traveled midway between the Red Fork and the Salt Fork rivers in 1874, his cowboys had to stop their cattle until a very large herd of buffalo passed.

Killing buffalo for their robes changed in the early 1870s when the world's supply of cattle hides dwindled. Tanners looked for new sources and in 1872 found that buffalo hide could be used to make a strong leather. It was then that the white man's slaughter of the buffalo began in earnest on the southern plains. Although hunters were told not to hunt buffalo in Indian Territory, most ignored the warning and hunted them in what is now the Oklahoma Panhandle and the western half of the state. Neal Evans, a trader at Fort Sill, obtained hides from Indians and shipped about 10,000 a year to eastern tanneries. Many thousands of buffalo were slaughtered in what is now Oklahoma, but exactly how many were killed is not known.

By 1877, nearly all but a handful of wild buffalo on the southern plains had been slaughtered for their hides. When Oklahoma became a state in 1907, wild buffalo were only a memory. By then a small group of men in the East had begun trying to save the animal from extinction by organizing the American Bison Society in 1905. One society member, William T. Hornaday of the Smithsonian

Institution in Washington, D.C., offered to donate a few buffalo if the federal government would establish a refuge in what is now southwestern Oklahoma. Congress agreed and established the National Wichita Forest Reserve—now the Wichita Mountains Wildlife Refuge—north of Lawton. Just before Oklahoma officially became a state, fifteen buffalo were shipped by train to the preserve and turned loose.

Whites and Indians alike hailed the return of buffalo to Oklahoma. Several hundred wild buffalo roam the refuge today, and motorists can see them close up as they drive through the open range. Hundreds of live wild buffalo may also been seen on the Tallgrass Prairie Preserve near Pawhuska and on the farms and ranches of many private citizens who also are saving the buffalo for fun and profit.

Just before the state's centennial, the Spirit of the Buffalo project started by the Nature Conservancy introduced large fiberglass buffalo decorated by Oklahoma artists. These buffalo can be seen at different locations in the Oklahoma City metro area.

GRAY AND RED WOLVES

Gray wolves (*Canis lupus*) once roamed the forests and plains of Oklahoma. They formed packs of six to ten animals made up of one or more families. Wolves mate for life and have litters of five to seven pups. Extremely social animals, wolves have a highly organized dominance hierarchy. They kill large and small game for food. While they often hunt buffalo, pronghorn, and deer, they also eat fruits and berries.

Like gray wolves, red wolves (*Canis rufus*) also once roamed the timberlands and plains. They are carnivores, generally hunt at night, and are good swimmers. Unlike the gray wolf, the red wolf has small litters, usually four pups. One of the earliest recorded sightings of wolves in the state occurred when Jean-Baptiste Bénard de la Harpe and his party were traveling through what is now Muskogee County near the modern town of Haskell. The year was 1718, and de la Harpe wrote, "One buffalo herd was followed by a pack of wolves as large as those in France."

A similar report was made in 1765 when French soldier Jean Baptiste Brevel passed through the Wichita Mountains heading for Santa Fe. He reported that gray wolves frequently followed herds of buffalo and elk. Most authorities believe that gray wolves still existed in Oklahoma as late as 1900, and full-blooded red wolves lived in the area until about 1950. Officially, both gray and red wolves are considered extinct in Oklahoma although there have been unconfirmed reports of grays seen in southwestern and northwestern Oklahoma including the Panhandle. Similar unconfirmed reports of red wolves have occurred in southeastern, south-central, and southwestern Oklahoma.

BLACK BEARS

Black bears (*Ursus americanus*) were once plentiful in what is now Oklahoma, especially in the Cross Timbers of eastern and central Oklahoma. When Washington Irving toured Indian Territory in the 1830s, his party saw black bears at least five times. Josiah Gregg later reported observing them in the Cross Timbers where they lived chiefly on acorns and other fruits. Black bears were also common in the Wichita Mountains, and the skins of a female black bear and her cub killed there around 1900 are housed in the National Museum of Natural History at the Smithsonian. Both animals were killed in the Wichita Mountains.

Early accounts of black bears in Oklahoma are plentiful, but their number declined rapidly as the animals were killed by hunters. One report suggests the last four black bears in the Wichita Mountains were killed in 1934, but in 2007 there were confirmed sightings of black bears in eastern Oklahoma. In 2009 Oklahoma permitted the hunting of no more than twenty black bears by hunters using bows and arrows or muzzleloaders. Some authorities believe the animals have migrated from the Ouachita and Ozark National Forest in Arkansas into the woodlands of eastern Oklahoma and even north into southwestern Missouri. They also are believed to exist in small numbers in southwestern and northwestern Oklahoma, and also toward the western end of the Panhandle near Black Mesa.

Pumas

Pumas (*Puma concolor*), also called mountain lions and cougars, once were numerous in Oklahoma. One early account by explorer and scientist Lt. J. W. Albert in 1845 relates how his party flushed a puma from a deep ravine near the Canadian River about twenty to thirty miles from Antelope Buttes, now called Antelope Hills in modern Roger Mills County. In 1851, S. W. Woodhouse, a naturalist with the Sitgreaves expedition, sighted a puma near a swamp in Indian Territory. About a year later Capt. Randolph B. Marcy's party killed a puma measuring eight and one-half feet in length near the mouth of a branch of Cache Creek in modern Cotton County, and around 1900 another mountain lion was killed in the Wichita Mountains. Since then reports of cougar sightings have declined.

Mountain lions are usually solitary. The female can have three cubs per litter, and the young stay with their mother for nearly two years. They prefer living in woodlands, forests, mountains, and especially in high inaccessible areas. They are known for a "scream" call and mostly roam at night.

For years rumors have persisted that the Oklahoma state fish and game people released mountain lions into the state to keep the deer population down. There is no truth to these rumors that appear to have been concocted by deer hunters who liked to tell tall tales around their campfires.

Some authorities believe a few mountain lions wander into the Oklahoma Panhandle from New Mexico and into eastern Oklahoma from Arkansas following major waterways or traveling through thinly populated areas while others are probably native to Oklahoma.

During the last half of the twentieth century, mountain lions were reported in rural areas of the eastern, southwestern, and western portions of the state as well as in the western part of the Panhandle. Confirmed reports of mountain lions in Oklahoma have been documented in recent years. Remains of a dead mountain lion were found on a ranch in Dewey County, and another was struck and killed by a motorist near Purcell just off I-35. In 2004, a train struck and killed a mountain lion in north-central Oklahoma about forty miles south of Arkansas City, Kansas. The 114-pound animal was wearing a radio collar attached by wildlife scientists from South Dakota State University. The mountain lion was last tracked by its collar in the Black Hills of Wyoming hundreds of miles from Oklahoma. At the start of 2010, Ryan Ritter, an Atoka businessman, photographed a mountain lion on a trail camera crossing his property in southeastern Atoka County.

Pronghorns

Pronghorn antelope (*Antilocapra americana*) were numerous throughout most of modern Oklahoma before settlement. They existed everywhere but in the cypress-oak floodplains, the oak-hickory-pine Ouachita Highlands, and the oak-hickory Ozark Plateau. Seemingly preferring the open grasslands that provided excellent grazing, pronghorns were once almost as numerous as buffalo, some authorities believe. The animals can reportedly sprint up to seventy miles per hour and maintain speeds of up to forty miles per hour. Early explorers made note of this speed; Col. Randolph Marcy saw them in the Wichita Mountains in 1852 and observed that several greyhounds with his party could not catch the pronghorns.

Trader Josiah Gregg saw many in 1839 near where Richmond in Woodward County stands today. Gregg wrote, "Although we had encountered but very few buffalo since we left Spring Valley, they now begin to make their appearance again; though not in very large droves; together with the deer and the fleet antelope [pronghorns], which the latter struck me as being much more tame in the wild section of the prairies than I had seen elsewhere."

As late as 1890, pronghorns were numerous in Greer and Tillman counties. They rapidly disappeared, however, when homesteaders arrived and cut down and burned many trees and broke the sod to plant crops. Overgrazing of grasslands became commonplace after barbed wire fences were introduced.

Game laws did not exist to protect pronghorns and other wildlife. Over hunting occurred as ranchers sought to eliminate predators. To encourage their killing, bounties were placed on many wild animals. Mountain lions were shot, wolves poisoned, and bears hunted down. Settlers tended to kill all wild animals thought to harm livestock. There was little appreciation for wildlife other than as objects to slaughter for food, sport, or hides. Today, however, there is greater appreciation for conservation and for the lives of wild animals.

Oklahoma Rivers

~

COUNTING THE RECENTLY RENAMED Oklahoma River—the Oklahoma City portion of the North Canadian River—there are thirty named rivers in the state. The other twenty-nine are the Arkansas, Beaver, Blue, Canadian, Caney, Chikaskia, Cimarron, Deep Fork, Elm Fork of the Red, Elk, Glover, Grand River (the lower course of the Neosho), Illinois, James Fork, Little River (tributary of the Canadian), Little River (tributary of the Red), Kiamichi, Medicine Lodge, Mountain Fork, Neosho, North Canadian, Poteau, Prairie Dog Town Fork of the Red, the Red, Salt Fork of the Arkansas, Salt Fork of the Red, Spring, Verdigris, and Washita.

Are these all really rivers? Are not some of them creeks? What is the difference between a river and a creek? These questions are better answered by dictionaries than by science. The U.S. Geological Survey states that there are no official definitions for generic terms as applied to geographic features. Rivers and creeks are officially "linear flowing bodies of water" and are simply classified as "streams." The best dictionary definitions describe a creek as a natural stream of water that is smaller than a river, one that is often a tributary of a river, and identify a river as a large natural stream of water, larger and longer than a creek.

Each of the rivers mentioned above has a story behind its name. Some stories are more interesting than others, but each river in Oklahoma has played a role in the state's history.

The Arkansas River is a principal river in Oklahoma. All rivers in the state except those in the southern portion that are drained by the Red River flow into the Arkansas, which flows into the Mississippi River. From before the arrival of the first Europeans, the Arkansas River was used as a major avenue of commerce. Indians traversed the river and its tributaries in a variety of boats carrying trading goods or traveling to hunting grounds or other areas. Early French explorers gave it the name Arkansas from the Quapaw Indian word *Akansea* taken from the Siouan word *Ak-a-ko-ze*, which in English means "South Wind People."

The Cimarron River, a tributary of the Arkansas, begins in northeastern New Mexico and flows east into the Oklahoma Panhandle near Kenton, then crosses the southeastern corner of Colorado where it flows into Kansas. It reenters the Oklahoma Panhandle, flows again into Kansas, and finally continues back into Oklahoma, crossing the state to where it flows into the Arkansas River north of Tulsa. The Cimarron's name comes from the early Spanish name *Rio de los Carneros Cimarrón,* which in English means "River of the Wild Sheep." Early American explorers sometimes called the river the Red Fork of the Arkansas because of the water's color.

The Red River rises in two branches or forks in the Texas Panhandle and flows east between Oklahoma and Texas. The river got its name from the red-clay farmland along its course. From the 100th meridian, the western border of Oklahoma below the Panhandle, the south bank of the river is the boundary between Texas and Oklahoma until it flows into Arkansas. Spanish explorers were the first Europeans to discover the Red River in the sixteenth century, followed by French explorers.

Capt. Henry Miller Shreve, for whom Shreveport, Louisiana, is named, brought the first steamboat, the *Enterprise,* into the Red River in 1815. Steamboat pioneers Robert Fulton and his partner Robert R. Livingston claimed the sole right to navigate western waters, and they sued Shreve. A federal court in New Orleans turned down their claim, citing it as illegal. Congress then passed laws releasing every river, lake, and harbor in the United States from the interference of monopolies.

Travel by steamboat on the Red River began in 1838 and soon became commonplace. The most important boat landing on the Red River in Indian Territory was at Fort Towson in the Choctaw Nation about six miles from Doaksville. Floods, however, often created rafts—trees lodged together choking the channel—that sometimes closed river travel. Congress asked for money to remove what was then called the "Great River Raft" that obstructed the channel near the mouth of the river in northern Louisiana. Improving the channel stopped, however, when the Civil War began. At the time the Great River Raft extended for more than one hundred and fifty miles upstream. In 1878, more than a decade after the Civil War, the federal government removed the final remnants of the logjam.

In 1852, Randolph B. Marcy took an expedition and explored the headwaters of the Red River. He also explored the source of the Canadian River, another principal river in Oklahoma. Beginning in Colorado and traveling through New Mexico, the Texas Panhandle, and most of Oklahoma, the Canadian River sometimes is referred to as the South Canadian River to differentiate it from the North Canadian River that flows into it.

The origin of the Canadian's name is still debated. One Oklahoma historian wrote in 1929 that about 1820 the river was named by French traders who met a group of French Canadian trappers camped on its banks near where it flows into the Arkansas River in what is now eastern Oklahoma. Another authority says the river probably got its name from the Spanish word *cañada*, meaning canyon. The Canadian River does form a steeper canyon in northern New Mexico and a somewhat broad canyon in Texas, and this explanation of the name is contained in a few historical documents.

The portion of the North Canadian River recently renamed the Oklahoma River in Oklahoma County has been transformed into a series of river lakes with landscaped areas, trails, and recreational facilities on the banks. One state lawmaker who called for the name change said the river's name should promote Oklahoma, not Canada, and the Oklahoma River is the only river named for the state. So far, no one has suggested renaming the scenic Illinois River in northeastern Oklahoma or the Caney River—named for Caney, Kansas—which begins in southern Kansas and flows into Oklahoma.

The Poteau River that flows north for its entire course through the Ouachita Uplands of eastern Oklahoma and western Arkansas apparently got its name because early French explorers had to use posts or poles to navigate upstream. Poteau, Oklahoma, took its name from the river.

Here is how other Oklahoma rivers were named:

BEAVER RIVER—named for the beaver that once were plentiful in the flat-water stream.

BLUE RIVER—a tributary of the Red River. Apparently, it was given its name in 1977 by the United States Board of Geographic Names because its waters were not reddish in color.

CHIKASKIA RIVER—Osage Indian word meaning "white spotted deer."

DEEP FORK—named for its depth. The river is nearly as deep as it is wide. It is located in eastern Oklahoma County and flows into the North Canadian River.

ELM FORK RIVER—named for elm trees along its bank. It flows into the North Fork of the Red River.

GLOVER RIVER—origin uncertain. It may be named for a prominent Chickasaw, William Glover, one of the signers of the federal government's treaty with the Chickasaws in 1816.

GRAND RIVER—named for its impressive size and beauty. It is the lower continuation of the Neosho River in northeastern Oklahoma.

JAMES FORK RIVER—origin uncertain.

LITTLE RIVER—named for its width. The stream is a tributary of the Canadian River and flows ninety miles from northern Cleveland County to south of Holdenville, where it joins the Canadian.

LITTLE RIVER—not to be confused with the other stream by the same name, also named for its small size. It rises in southwestern Le Flore County in the Ouachita Mountains and flows into Arkansas, where it joins the Red River.

KIAMICHI RIVER—named after the French word *kamichi*, meaning "horned screamer," a wild bird found in the area. The bird is not to be confused with a South American bird often called by the same name.

MEDICINE LODGE RIVER—named by the U.S. Board of Geographic Names in 1968. It had historically been known as *A-ya-dalda-pa* or "Medicine River."

MOUNTAIN FORK RIVER—named for the mountainous country in Le Flore County and the Ouachita Mountains. It is a tributary of the Little River and joins that stream in McCurtain County southeast of Broken Bow.

NEOSHO RIVER—named for the Osage Indian word meaning "clear water." It is also known as the Grand River.

PRAIRIE DOG TOWN FORK RED RIVER—named by the Spanish for a Prairie Dog town in the Texas Panhandle. The stream rises northeast of Canyon, Texas, and it is the main tributary of the Red River. Beginning at the 100th meridian, it serves as the boundary between Texas and Oklahoma until the north and south forks join and become the Red River proper.

SALT FORK OF THE ARKANSAS RIVER—apparently named for the salt content of its waters. The stream rises in Comanche County, Kansas, and flows into Oklahoma to Alva, where it turns eastward until it flows into the Arkansas River south of Ponca City. Through history it has been known by at least seventeen other names including Kits Kait, Grand Saline, Ne Shudse Shunga, and Salt Fork River.

SALT FORK OF THE RED RIVER—also named for the salt content of its waters. It rises in Armstrong County, Texas, and flows into southwestern Oklahoma past Mangum and then south to join the Red River south of Altus.

SPRING RIVER—named for the springs that feed the stream. It rises in southwestern Missouri, flows into southeastern Kansas and then into northeastern Oklahoma.

VERDIGRIS RIVER—named with two French words, *vert*, meaning green, and *gris*, meaning grey. It rises west of Madison, Kansas, and flows into Oklahoma south of Coffeyville, Kansas. It joins the Arkansas River near Muskogee above the mouth of the Neosho River.

WASHITA RIVER—named from two Choctaw words, *owa* and *chito*, meaning "big hunt." The stream rises in the Texas Panhandle and ends when it flows into Lake Texoma in southern Oklahoma.

Stories about people and events along these Oklahoma streams would fill a large book. The streams were the lifeblood of early Oklahoma and remain important today.

Naming and Pronouncing Oklahoma Towns

~

NEWCOMERS TO OKLAHOMA ARE OFTEN corrected when they pronounce the names of some communities as they are spelled. For instance the city of MIAMI in northeastern Oklahoma is pronounced My-AM-uh. HOBART in southwestern Oklahoma is HOH-bert, and DURANT in the southeastern part of the state is pronounced Doo-RANT and sometimes DOO-RANT. The pronunciations of these and other Oklahoma towns are the result of how local residents have come to say them. Visitors unfamiliar with local pronunciations sometimes shake their heads when locals do not say a name as it is spelled. They understand more when they learn the origin of a town's name. Sometimes it is that of an early settler—white or Indian—an Indian tribe, or an event in Oklahoma history; or the community is named after a geographic feature or nearby landmark. Each town's name has its own story.

The forgotten town of Aaron in Jackson County starts a long list of Oklahoma names first compiled by Charles N. Gould about twenty-six years after statehood. Aaron was named for Calvin Aaron, an early settler. At the end of an alphabetical list is Zybra in southern Garfield County. Its name is a colloquial word from the 1890s meaning "a moving settler." Some Oklahoma towns have even had more than one name. Elk City in northwestern Beckham County started out as Crowe. As the town grew, residents changed the name to Busch, hoping that Adolphus Busch might be impressed and build a brewery there; however, apparently he was not because the brewery was never built. In 1907, residents renamed their town Elk City after Elk Creek, which runs through the community.

Stringtown in Atoka County was first called Sulphur Springs on July 9, 1877, by the U.S. Post Office Department. Before the month ended, citizens got the name changed to Springtown after the natural springs that flow out of the hills under the town. "Springtown" somehow became corrupted and became "Stringtown."

In eastern Oklahoma County the community of Harrah was first named Pennington but in 1896 was changed to Sweeny, the name of an early settler. In 1898, the post office changed the name to Harrah after a local resident. In northern Oklahoma County the town of Glaze was renamed Jones in 1898 for C. G. Jones, an Oklahoma City industrialist and railroad promoter. The nearby town of Luther was named after Jones's son.

President Benjamin Harrison established the United States Board of Geographic Names (USBGN) in 1890, and after its authority was extended by President Theodore Roosevelt in 1906, the board assumed the responsibility of establishing names for federal use that were based on the recommendations of authorities on geographic names in each state.

In 1926, Oklahoma governor Martin Trapp, at the request of the USBGN, commissioned the first Oklahoma Geographic Names Board (OGNB). He appointed board members already working for the state so he would not have to provide additional funds. The OGNB did not propose to initiate any reforms and soon ceased to exist. In 1965, however, the responsibilities of the almost-forgotten board were assigned to the Oklahoma Geological Survey.

When Gould was compiling his list of town names in 1932, he recalled visiting with a clerk in the U.S. Post Office Department in Washington, D.C., who told him that when names were not included in requests for post offices, he assigned the names of his family, neighborhood children, and friends. Many of the names were feminine. The evidence suggests that the USBGN delegated many name selections to the post office department and usually accepted names of Indian origin in Oklahoma. For instance, Tahlequah (TAL-uh-quah) in Cherokee County is derived from the Cherokee word *Talikwa* or *Tallico*, meaning an old Cherokee town. *Kee-Too-Wah*, a town no longer in existence in Cherokee County, took its name from a political society organized in 1859 by Northern sympathizers among the Cherokees.

Okmulgee (Oak-MUL-gee)—the city and county—was named after a Creek town in Russell County, Alabama. It comes from a Creek word meaning "boiling waters." *Tishomingo* (TISH-oh-MING-goh) in Johnston County is named after Chickasaw Chief Tishomingo. *Tuskahoma* (TUS-kuh-HOME-uh) in Pushmataha County is a Choctaw word meaning "red warrior." *Anadarko* (AN-uh-DAR-koh) in Caddo County got its name from a corruption of the Caddo word *Na-da-ko*, the name of one of the Caddoan tribes. Skullyville in Le Flore County got its name from a Choctaw word meaning "money town" because Indian annuities were paid out at the nearby Choctaw agency.

Many Oklahoma communities were forced to come up with their own names when they applied for post offices. Names were usually selected locally and were often the names of the postmaster, owner of the general store, or other local residents. Cavnar in Comanche County got its name from John Cavnar, a local merchant. Pirtle in Bryan County took its name from local resident Milton A. Pirtle. Dutton in Grady County was named for William R. Dutton, the postmaster at Anadarko. Plunkettville in northern McCurtain County took its name from Robert C. Plunkett, the first postmaster.

Why Oklahomans chose some names remains a mystery. Kingfisher County had the towns of Alpha and Omega, named after the first and last letters of the Greek alphabet, but only Omega survived. In Pottawatomie County, there were towns called Romulus and Remus, after ancient Rome's mythical founders. Romulus killed his twin brother Remus, and in Oklahoma Romulus also survived longer than Remus.

Many town names were created from other words. In northeastern Blain County, the town of Okeene (oh-KEEN) was coined by Elmer Bordrick from the words "Oklahoma," "Cherokee," and "Cheyenne." The town of Okarche (Oh-CAR-chee) that straddles

Kingfisher and Canadian counties was named by Charles Hunter in 1896. He combined OK (from Oklahoma), AR (from Arapaho), and CHE (from Cheyenne).

McAlester (Mack-AL-ester) was named for John J. McAlester, prominent merchant and coal producer in Pittsburg County. McAlester was a member of the first Corporation Commission and was the second lieutenant governor of Oklahoma. Tulsa got its name from Tulsey Town, an old Creek community in Alabama. Lawton in Comanche County received its name from Maj. Gen. Henry W. Lawton, killed during the Philippine insurrection. Woodward in Woodward County was name for Brinton W. Woodward, a director of the Santa Fe Railroad. Pine Ridge, located six miles south of Fort Cobb in Caddo County, was named by the owner of a local grocery store and adopted by local residents. He borrowed the name of the setting for the network radio comedy program *Lum and Abner,* which related the fictional adventures of two storekeepers and aired between 1934 and 1952.

There were two towns named Wouldbe, one in Creek County and another near Billings in Noble County. Both never amounted to much like so many other small communities that dot the Oklahoma landscape, including Douthat in Ottawa County, which had a post office from early 1917 until perhaps the 1930s. Named for Zahn A. Douthat, the townsite owner, the town died by the 1950s. Wolf, once a prosperous little town located twelve miles south of Bowlegs in Seminole County, has only a handful of residents today. Cookietown, close to the Red River in Cotton County, once had a general store whose owner handed out cookies to children, giving the community its name. Santa Fe east of Duncan in Stephens County had a post office from 1921 until 1943.

Beer City in modern Beaver County just south of Liberal, Kansas, was a wild and woolly town in the late 1880s. The town's White Elephant Saloon reportedly was a watering hole for outlaws who came to drink and see Pussey Cat Nell and her girls. By 1890s the tiny town dried up after the railroad arrived at Liberal, Kansas.

Norman got its name during the land run of 1889 after the Atchison, Topeka and Santa Fe Railway arrived in 1887. Several years earlier, the U.S. Land Office had hired a professional engineer named Abner E. Norman to survey a large area of Indian Territory. Near a watering hole the survey crew burned the words "Norman's Camp" into an elm tree. When the land run of 1889 occurred, arriving settlers decided to keep the name Norman.

Another community with an interesting story is El Reno. In 1889, a 160-acre town site was platted and called Reno. When the town's folk requested a post office, postal officials in Washington refused to accept Reno because Fort Reno and Reno City were nearby. There would be too much confusion. William C. McDonald, a visiting attorney and cattleman who later became the first governor of New Mexico, came up with the idea of adding the Spanish word *El*, meaning "the," before the word "Reno." The postal officials accepted the name, and El Reno got its post office.

An early settlement in Oklahoma Territory was Appalachia, located seventeen miles west of present-day Tulsa on the north bank of the Cimarron River (site is near the modern Keystone Dam). The settlement was established in 1893 by the Monarch Investment Company of Kansas after it purchased farmland near the junction of the Cimarron and Arkansas rivers and laid out town lots that sold for twenty dollars each. Appalachia got its name because old-timers in the area thought the region reminded them of the Appalachian Mountains in the East. Monarch thought their new town of Appalachia would boom because it was located in Oklahoma Territory. On the other side of the Cimarron River was dry Indian Territory. Soon at least seven saloons opened for business in Appalachia, and the saloons were frequented by many residents of Indian Territory, especially Red Fork and Sapulpa. To help the thirsty customers reach Appalachia, its residents constructed a swinging bridge across the Cimarron. Reportedly, the most prosperous saloon in Appalachia was owned by Lee McAfee, a former sheriff from Paris, Texas. When Joe Wierman, a deputy U.S. marshal, arrived to keep law and order, he decided to open a saloon on the south side of the Cimarron just across from Appalachia. He attracted many customers who did not like crossing the river on the shaky swinging bridge to Appalachia. The town soon lost business, and Appalachia became deserted before statehood in 1907.

Following is a list of other Oklahoma cities and towns and how they received their names:

ALTUS in Jackson County was first called Frazier. When high water destroyed the town, residents rebuilt on higher ground and renamed their community using a Latin word meaning "high."

ANTELOPE in southwestern Roger Mills County took its name from the nearby Antelope Hills.

ATOKA in Atoka County was named for Captain Atoka, a Choctaw ball player, for whom the county was later named.

BEAVER in Beaver County took its name from the Beaver River.

BLACKBURN in Pawnee County was named for Sen. Joseph C. S. Blackburn of Kentucky.

BOISE CITY in Cimarron County was named after Boise, Idaho.

BROKEN ARROW in Tulsa County is named for a Creek word meaning "broken arrow."

BURNEYVILLE in Love County is named for David C. Burney.

CALUMET in Canadian County comes from the French *chalumet*, meaning "shepherd's pipe."

CANUTE in Washita County is named after a King of Denmark.

CHICKASHA (CHICK-uh-shay) in Grady County comes from the word Chickasaw.

COWETA in Wagoner County is named for a Creek town in Alabama.

DAVIS in Murray County is named for Samuel H. Davis, an early merchant.

DOAKSVILLE in Choctaw County is named for Josiah Doak who established a general store in the late 1830s near Fort Towson.

DRUMM in Alfalfa County was named for Major Andrew Drumm, an area rancher.

EDEN in Payne County was named for the biblical Garden of Eden.

ELMORE CITY in Garvin County was named for J. O. Elmore, early resident.

FAIRVIEW in Major County took its name from its scenic location east of the Glass Mountains.

FOURMILE in Ottawa County got its name because of its location four miles from the Kansas state line.

FURRS (now Henryetta) in Okmulgee County was named for resident Albert C. Furr. It was renamed Henryetta for Henry G. Beard, a local resident.

GENE AUTRY (formerly Berwyn) was named in 1942 for the prominent singer and western movie star.

GOTEBO (GO-tuh-boh) in Kiowa County was first named Harrison. It was renamed for the chief of a minor band of Kiowa Indians.

HAMMON in Roger Mills County was named for J. H. Hammond, Indian agent.

HUGO in Choctaw County was named after Victor Hugo, French novelist.

IVANHOE (now Custer) was named for a character in a Sir Walter Scott novel. Custer was named for George A. Custer, who died at the Little Big Horn.

Kingfisher in Kingfisher County was named for King Fisher, operator of a stage station.

Langston in Logan County was named for John M. Langston of Virginia.

Leeper in McClain County was named for William P. Leeper, prominent Chickasaw.

Marlow in Stephens County took its name from the nearby Marlow Brothers Ranch.

Medford in Grant County borrowed its name from Medford, Massachusetts.

Mulhall in Logan County got its name from Zack Mulhall, rancher and showman.

Newman (now Stigler) in Haskell County was named for Dr. Martin W. Newman, an early physician. Stigler was named for Joseph S. Stigler, townsite developer.

Oologah (OO-lah-gah) in Rogers County is named for a Cherokee chief.

Orion in Major County is named for the constellation in the northern sky.

Pawhuska (Paw-HUSK-uh) in Osage County is named for an Osage chief and means "white hair."

Ponca City (formerly New Ponca) in Kay County was first named Whiteagle in 1896, renamed New Ponca in 1898, and changed to Ponca City in 1913.

Quapaw (QUA-PAW) in Ottawa County took the name from the Quapaw tribe.

Ringling in Jefferson County was named for John Ringling, circus owner.

Sapulpa (Suh-PUL-puh) in Creek County was named for James Sapulpa, son of a Creek leader.

Skiatook (SKY-uh-tuk) on the line between Tulsa and Osage counties was named for a prominent Osage Indian.

Slaughterville (SLAHT-er-vil) in Cleveland County took its name from James Slaughter, who operated a grocery store.

Stillwater in Payne County took its name from nearby Stillwater Creek.

Talihina (Tal-uh-HEE-nuh, sometimes pronounced Tal-uh-HEE-nee) in Le Flore County took a Choctaw word meaning "railroad" for its name.

Tonkawa (TONK-uh-wah) in Kay County took its name from the Tonkawa tribe.

Utica in Bryan County was named after Utica, New York.

Vinita in Craig County was named by E. C. Boudinot as a diminutive of Vinnie Ream, a well-known sculptor.

Watonga (Wah-TONG-uh) in Blaine County took its name from an Arapaho chief.

Weatherford in Custer County was named for William J. Weatherford, deputy U.S. marshal.

Zeb in Cherokee County was named for Zeb Keahea, a local resident.

When Oklahoma Got Electric Lights

MANY OLD-TIMERS REMEMBER WHEN candles, kerosene lamps, and the flickering flames of fireplaces were the only means of lighting their Oklahoma homes at night. Such methods of lighting were still in use in some rural areas half a century ago, but electric lights have since replaced most.

As the land run of 1889 was occurring, new inventions were being developed in the East that would bring electric lights to Oklahoma. Sir Joseph Swann in England and Thomas A. Edison on America's East Coast invented the first electric incandescent lamps during the 1870s. In 1887, two years before the Unassigned Lands were opened to settlement, Nikola Tesla, an associate of Edison, introduced a system for alternating current generators that allowed for improved transmission of electricity.

After Oklahoma City, Guthrie, and other towns were established, community leaders knew their towns should have electric lights to be progressive and attract residents. In Oklahoma City, the Oklahoma Ditch and Water Power Co. was formed and dug a six-mile-long ditch from the North Canadian River (now called the Oklahoma River). The ditch was thirty-two feet wide and ten feet deep and dropped thirty-two feet from the river. The idea was to let the water generate electric power at a power plant constructed at Robinson and Frisco streets. The gates were opened on Christmas Eve 1890 and the water flowed. Although a few light bulbs at the plant burned brightly, the sandy banks of the ditch absorbed the river water faster than the river could keep it filled, and the project was soon abandoned.

The company that tried waterpower joined with Oklahoma City Light and Power Company to build a steam-driven electric power plant, which was constructed in 1892. The steam system worked, but the companies lacked sufficient funds to expand the plant size. By 1900, Oklahoma City had a population of about 10,000. Oklahoma

City Light and Power provided service for 89 street arc lamps, 120 commercial arc lamps, 700 incandescent lamps in homes, and 200 horsepower of electric motors. Businesses had meters, but residents had a flat monthly rate. The company went into receivership, and in 1902 it changed hands and was incorporated as the Oklahoma Gas & Electric Co. It received its first franchise from the city council early in 1902. With additional funds, OG&E began to enlarge its power facilities and extend electric lines. Before the improvements were completed, the company cut all residential service on Saturday nights because of the heavy demand of businesses in downtown Oklahoma City.

In 1902, OG&E had 1,400 customers and over 76 miles of lines, but by 1905 there were 4,500 customers receiving service over 227 miles of lines. The company's efficiency resulted in a 15 percent reduction of rates. By 1910, when Oklahoma City's population exceeded 50,000, OG&E began expanding outside of the city.

In the meantime, other cities and towns in Oklahoma, including Perry, Ponca City, and Cherokee, had electric power plants. Some plants were privately owned, but others were owned by local municipalities. The one in Cherokee in Garfield County was built early in the 1900s by Mayor A. J. Titus, who laid out the town.

In Oklahoma City, some residents believed that if a flatiron was placed on top the electric meter box, the meter would run slower and the bill would be less. When meter readers visited homes where this was tried, they were delayed entry by homemakers who ran to their meters to remove the irons before letting the meter readers inside, so meter reading sometimes took longer than usual.

In northeastern Oklahoma, electric power plants were established in several communities before statehood, including the Vinita Electric Light, Ice, and Power Co., founded in 1889. In 1913, Frederick Insull, a nephew of Thomas Edison's secretary and aide Samuel Insull, reorganized these small companies into the Public Service Company of Oklahoma (PSO), which merged several electric companies from

Tulsa, Coalgate, Guthrie, Atoka, and Lehigh. The company's headquarters were established in Tulsa in 1916. PSO soon expanded its service throughout eastern and southwestern Oklahoma. By 1927, the company provided power to eighty-two towns.

In Oklahoma City, the headquarters of Oklahoma Gas & Electric, the company continued to expand its service areas. In 1917, OG&E acquired the electric power systems in Norman and El Reno and installed transmission lines from Oklahoma City. OG&E also acquired the Enid Electric and Gas Co., expanding service into northwestern Oklahoma. Between 1917 and 1930, OG&E purchased many other electric systems and soon served Chandler, Muskogee, Shawnee, Ardmore, Ada, Durant, Sapulpa, Holdenville, Seminole, and other areas in western Arkansas. Although OG&E sold all of its gas properties in 1928, because the company's name was so well known, it did not remove the word "gas" from its name.

By the early 1930s, Oklahoma power companies were expanding their service into rural areas even before President Franklin Roosevelt convinced Congress to establish the Rural Electrification Administration (REA) in 1935. OG&E acquired Western Light and Power Co. in 1936, adding service to Woodward, Wakita, and other communities in northwestern Oklahoma.

In 1971, OG&E and PSO swapped a few service territories to the benefit of both companies. Also in the 1970s, power plants began to shift from natural gas to low-sulphur Wyoming coal to fuel their operations. Today, Oklahoma, Gas & Electric, the Public Service Company of Oklahoma, thirty-five municipal-owned electric plants, and twenty-eight member-owned nonprofit rural electric cooperatives provide electric power across Oklahoma.

Oklahoma's Black Gold

INDIANS DISCOVERED OIL IN WHAT is now Oklahoma more than half a century before statehood. They discovered green oil (crude shale oil) along numerous springs and streams. One discovery was at New Springplace north of Tahlequah in the Cherokee Nation, and another at Boyd Springs northeast of modern Ardmore in the Chickasaw Nation. A Chickasaw agency report dated August 29, 1853, notes: "The oil springs in this [Chickasaw] nation are attracting considerable attention, as they are said to be a remedy for all chronic diseases. Rheumatism stands no chance at all, and the worst cases of dropsy yield to its effects. The fact is that it cures anything that has been tried."

In 1859, Lewis Ross, brother of Cherokee Chief John Ross, sank a deep well for water at his saltworks along the Grand River. Ross struck oil that flowed about ten barrels a day for one year before stopping for lack of pressure. Although found accidentally, it was the first oil well in Indian Territory.

There were few national markets for oil until after 1859, when Col. Edwin L. Drake drilled a successful oil well at Oil Creek—later Titusville—Pennsylvania. The find led to the distilling of oil to produce kerosene. Ten years earlier Abraham Gesner, a physician, had developed and patented the process. Until kerosene was developed, people relied on light from candles and lamps fueled by whale oil in their homes and businesses. Kerosene was sometimes called coal oil although true coal oil was cooked out of finely ground coal. As the petroleum industry developed during the latter half of the nineteenth century, stories of the discovery of oil in Indian Territory attracted whites in search of what became known as black gold.

Oklahoma's first oil company was the Chickasaw Oil Co., incorporated in 1872 under the laws of the State of Missouri. Because of the demand for coal by the railroads, the company concentrated on mining coal and did not develop oil resources. Next, the general council of the Choctaw Nation created the Choctaw Oil and Refining Company in 1884. Dr. H. W. Faucett, who had been involved in the pioneer oil industry in Pennsylvania, was involved, but delays and financial problems forced the company to close. After the Unassigned Lands were opened to settlement in 1889, the search for oil intensified. On April 15, 1897, the Cudahy Oil Co. brought in the Nellie Johnstone No. 1, the first commercial oil well in Oklahoma. It was located on the south bank of the Caney River near modern Bartlesville.

In 1896, the Osage Nation made a deal giving the Indian Territory Illuminating Oil Co. (ITIO) a ten-year lease to drill for oil over a vast area of Osage land. Slow to get started, ITIO president H. V. Foster decided in 1903, three years before the company's lease was to expire, to split up the Osage Nation lease and auction hundreds of small subleases. Under an elm tree, men came to bid on the leases. Journalists described the auction as taking place under "the million dollar tree" because of what the leases would eventually produce.

As the automobile with its combustion engine came on the scene, the oil strikes made on the Osage lands began the fortunes of the Fosters, L. E. and Waite Phillips, J. Paul Getty, Harry Sinclair, E. W. Marland, Bill Skelly, Josh Cosden, and Tulsa's Zarrow family. Even Kansan Alf Landon, along with many Osage Indians, became wealthy from Osage land oil.

In June 1901, a well struck oil at Red Fork across the Arkansas River southwest of Tulsa. Four years later (1905), Frank Chesley and Robert T. Galbreath were hunting on the property of Ida Glenn, a Creek Indian, several miles south of Tulsa. While chasing their dogs, Chesley discovered oil seeping from some rocks. With a lease in hand, Chesley, Galbreath, Charles F. Colcord, and J. O. Mitchell organized the Creek Oil Co. On November 22, 1905, their first well twelve miles south of Tulsa was a gusher. The Glenn Pool field was born. Almost overnight Tulsa boomed and became the "oil capital of the world."

An oil gusher. Courtesy of Western History Collections, University of Oklahoma Libraries (OGS, no. 475).

Seven years later, in 1912, Tom Slick and C. B. Shaffer discovered what became known as the Cushing-Drumright field, and in 1920 E. W. Marland brought in the North Burbank field that initially produced more than 2,500 barrels of oil a day. The next discovery was the Greater Seminole oil field in 1926 that attracted 20,000 oil field workers. Oil from this field, however, glutted the market, slowed production, and discouraged more oil discoveries until late 1928.

On December 4, 1928, six miles south of Oklahoma City, an exploratory well hit more black gold. The Oklahoma City field became one of the world's major oil-producing fields. Oil was even drilled from under the state capitol. One well was slant-drilled from across the street to oil sands beneath the capitol building. Technological advancements in oil drilling led to the passage of the state's first comprehensive legislation to conserve oil and gas. The legislation provided model statutes for other states to follow.

Oil revenue helped to stabilize the economy of Oklahoma City and the state and made it possible to develop cultural and industrial programs and improve the lives of many Oklahomans. When the Mary Sudik No. 1 blew wild in the Oklahoma City field on March 25, 1930, and was not capped for eleven days, it became the most publicized oil well in the world.

Part II

~

On Trails and Rails

*A wise man changes his mind,
a fool never will.*

Spanish proverb

Early Trails

LONG BEFORE THE FIRST Europeans arrived in Oklahoma, Indians in the area followed animal trails, especially those made by buffalo, which were the best because the animals chose the line of least resistance when traveling. Among other early travelers, Spanish explorers including Francisco Vásquez de Coronado are thought to have crossed portions of modern Oklahoma beginning in the 1500s. The earliest known Spanish trail ran from what is now eastern Texas through modern southwestern Oklahoma to Santa Fe. In many areas, deep ruts made by heavy-laden Spanish carts marked the trails. The absence of prominent landmarks meant that travelers relied on the ruts and the stars to guide them.

After Maj. Stephen H. Long took an expedition to the Rocky Mountains in 1820, he headed east following the Canadian River across modern Oklahoma. Long labeled the plains from modern Nebraska to Oklahoma as a "Great Desert . . . unfit for cultivation" and "uninhabitable by people depending upon agriculture." When Long returned to the East, Congress designated much of modern Oklahoma as Indian Territory and established Fort Gibson in present-day Muskogee County and Fort Towson in Choctaw County on Gates Creek near the confluence of the Kiamichi River with the Red River. Soldiers were stationed at these forts ostensibly to protect eastern Indian tribes that were removed to Indian Territory.

Government surveyors soon arrived in uncharted Indian Territory. They laid out a military road from Fort Gibson to Little Rock, Arkansas, in 1824 and soon built another road between Little Rock and Fort Towson. Later both forts were linked to Fort Coffee, built in 1834 on the Arkansas River in modern Le Flore County, Oklahoma. In 1831, the government hired Rev. Isaac McCoy, a missionary, to survey the boundaries of the Cherokee Nation to ensure the Cherokees had the seven million acres guaranteed them by the federal government. The following year, McCoy surveyed the boundaries of the Seneca, Ottawa, and Shawnee Indian reservations, and in 1833 Capt. Nathan Boone, son of Daniel Boone, surveyed a boundary between the Creek and Cherokee nations.

Gen. Henry Leavenworth took command of the military in Indian Territory in 1834 and ordered a road built from Fort Gibson to the Washita River. The route crossed the Canadian River, ran southwest past the sites of modern Holdenville and Allen, and ended at the Washita River. There, nine years later, Fort Washita was built fifteen miles northeast of modern Durant and fifteen miles east of present Madill. Josiah Gregg, a physician and Santa Fe trader, developed another trail from Fort Smith to Santa Fe in 1839 following a route first blazed in 1823 by two early Santa Fe traders. Gregg took about thirty men, several wagons, and two small cannon and followed the northern side of the Canadian River to the modern Texas Panhandle and on to Santa Fe.

By the time the Mexican War began in 1846, a north-south trail had developed across eastern Indian Territory carrying emigrants settling in Texas. This Texas Road, as it became known, stretched from Baxter Springs in modern southeastern Kansas, south through eastern Indian Territory, to Fort Gibson. Another trail, starting in St. Louis, Missouri, joined the Texas Road where Salina, Oklahoma, now stands. Six stagecoach stations were located between Baxter Springs and Fort Gibson, providing fresh horses, food, and lodging for travelers. From Fort Gibson, the Texas Road ran southwest past Honey Springs and crossed the Canadian River near modern Eufaula. It continued southwest to Boggy Depot in modern Atoka County, where the road split. Travelers could go directly south across the Red River into Texas or continue west to Fort Washita and then across the Red River north of modern Preston, Texas.

Following the discovery of gold in California in 1848, Gregg's route became the principal trail across Oklahoma for gold seekers. In the spring of 1849, Capt. R. B. Marcy and a body of troops escorted five hundred gold seekers over this route, which also later became a U.S. mail route. Shortly before Marcy's expedition, a group of 130 California-bound gold seekers led by Capt. L. Evans of Fayetteville, Arkansas, took forty wagons and set out from western Arkansas. They crossed the Grand River near modern Salina in what is now northeastern Oklahoma, and moved northwest where they crossed the Verdigris River north of where Claremore stands today. They continued northwest until they reached the Santa Fe Trail in what is now central Kansas. Because Cherokee Indians also traveled this route, it became known as the Cherokee Trail.

Soon another branch of the Cherokee Trail ran from Fort Smith across the Cherokee Nation crossing the Grand River at Fort Gibson. It followed and then crossed the Verdigris River, going northwest to the Arkansas River to the Santa Fe Trail near Fort Mann, Kansas. A third route ran from Fort Smith past the future Oklahoma communities of Perryville, McAlester, and Boggy Depot to Fort Washita. The trail then crossed the Red River into Texas and ran southwest across Texas to El Paso. Over these routes at least 25,000 gold seekers crossed modern Oklahoma bound for California between 1849 and the early 1850s.

The Oregon Trail, located farther north in present-day Kansas and Nebraska, carried many more gold seekers, but the southern routes through Oklahoma had an advantage. Spring came earlier and grasses greened up sooner for livestock to eat on the southern plains, meaning gold seekers taking the southern routes could start earlier than travelers to the north.

A lesser-known trail called Whiskey Road ran from Fort Smith up the northern side of the Arkansas River to what is now Webbers Falls. U.S. troops patrolled this route regularly to stop peddlers from bringing large shipments of whiskey into Indian Territory.

Many other trails crisscrossed Oklahoma during the first half of the nineteenth century. Many of them later became wagon roads, and today some of them are the routes of modern highways. In fact, in central and western Oklahoma, some of today's highways follow trails first made by buffalo.

Important Early Oklahoma Trails

1500s—Spanish explorer Coronado crosses the modern Panhandle.

1600s—Other Spaniards cross portions of the area. (The earliest-known Spanish trail ran from eastern Texas through southwestern Oklahoma and westward to Santa Fe.)

1820—Major Long leads the first government expedition to the Rocky Mountains, crossing present-day Oklahoma on his return.

1824—After Forts Gibson and Towson are built in eastern Indian Territory, roads are built linking the posts to Little Rock, Arkansas.

1834—A military road is constructed from Fort Gibson to the Washita River where Fort Washita is later constructed.

1839—Josiah Gregg develops a road across Indian Territory.

1846—Settlers travel the Texas Road—running north and south across eastern Indian Territory.

1848—Gregg's route across modern Oklahoma becomes the principal southern route for California gold seekers.

1849-1850s—Other trails are developed by soldiers and emigrants traveling through the area because whites were not permitted to settle in Indian Territory. Many gold seekers headed to California also cross what is now Oklahoma from 1849 into the 1850s.

Military Forts

AT ONE TIME OR ANOTHER during the nineteenth century, nearly fifty military forts and camps dotted the landscape of what is now Oklahoma. Many were short-lived; most are no longer active. The earliest forts are Fort Gibson, located northeast of modern Muskogee, and Fort Towson, east of present-day Hugo in southeastern Oklahoma. About 130 miles apart, the forts were founded in 1824 to guard against intertribal warfare as eastern tribes were moved into Indian Territory.

Fort Gibson remained an active post until 1890. Although Confederates occupied the fort from 1861 to 1863, it was the most important federal post in Indian Territory. Soldiers stationed there, however, considered it dull, and for excitement they visited nearby "hog ranches," where they found girls, gambling, and whiskey.

In 1833, Gen. Matthew Arbuckle, who founded Fort Gibson, ordered the digging of a well. Two prisoners in the Fort Gibson guardhouse got the job, and at the end of each day they reported their progress to the officer on duty. After eighteen months, the prisoners reported that the well was 465 feet deep but that they had not struck water. A new officer at the post thought this strange, investigated, and found that the well was only fifteen feet deep. The prisoners had struck bedrock. Off to the side the officer found a large underground room, which explained why the men kept removing dirt from the well. The officer found the prisoners calmly playing cards in the room, which stayed cool in the summer and warm in the winter. The prisoners were sent to the guardhouse.

Fort Towson remained an active military post between 1824 and 1829 and again from 1854 to about 1855. When the military abandoned the post, it became the seat of government for the Choctaw Nation. Confederate forces occupied Fort Towson from 1863 to 1865 and directed all military operations in Indian Territory, including psychological warfare. They used a printing press to produce propaganda aimed at keeping the Indians on the Confederate side. It was at Fort Towson that Gen. Stand Watie, a Cherokee leader, surrendered the Confederate Indian cavalry, the last Confederate force to surrender, at the end of the Civil War.

A short-lived post in east-central Indian Territory was Fort Coffee, established in 1834 and located on a bluff about ten miles southwest of Fort Smith, Arkansas. Soldiers from Fort Coffee tried to stop whiskey from being smuggled into Indian Territory. The post was abandoned in 1838 but was occupied by Confederate forces from 1861 to 1863 during the Civil War.

There were four camps or forts in Oklahoma named for Gen. Matthew Arbuckle. He reportedly served on the staff of Andrew Jackson at the Battle of New Orleans. The first Camp Arbuckle was located near Fort Gibson from 1832 into early 1833. The second Camp Arbuckle, existing for five months in 1833, was located seventeen miles northwest of modern Tulsa. A third post called Fort Arbuckle was located was just north of modern Byars, Oklahoma, near the Canadian River between 1850 and 1851. The last and most important Fort Arbuckle was seven miles west of modern Davis in south-central Oklahoma. Established in 1851 at a crossing on the Washita River, the post was founded to protect Chickasaw Indians from Comanche Indians, who lived farther west in Indian Territory. Confederate forces occupied the post during the Civil War, but Union forces returned and operated it until it closed in 1870.

Fort Wayne was first established in 1838 about two miles south of modern Watts, Oklahoma. The post was named for Revolutionary War hero Brig. Gen. "Mad" Anthony Wayne. It was intended to be a link in a great line of forts protecting the American West. Because troops found the location unhealthy, the post was moved to about four miles north of modern Colcord near Spavinaw Creek, where it remained active until 1842 when it was turned over to the Cherokee Nation. When the Civil War began, Stand Watie took over the fort and organized the First Regiment of Cherokee Mounted Rifles. Later, Confederates occupied the site for several months before the war ended.

More important than Fort Wayne was Fort Washita, established in 1842 near modern Durant. Gen. Zachary Taylor selected its location and name. It became a supply center and a stop for gold seekers bound for California between 1849 and the 1850s. Confederates occupied the post from 1861 to 1865.

Another post with a short life was Fort Cobb, established in 1859 about thirty-five miles west of modern Chickasha. Soldiers at the post oversaw Indians on the southern plains. Fort Cobb was briefly occupied by Confederate forces at the start of the Civil War, but Union forces then reoccupied the post. It was at Fort Cobb that Phillip Sheridan and Lt. Col. George Armstrong Custer's troops camped following the Battle of the Washita in 1868. Soon the post was abandoned and its troops ordered thirty miles south to establish a camp on Medicine Bluff Creek in the Wichita Mountains. Rations were scarce, and the soldiers called it Camp Starvation. Other names for the new fort were suggested, but General Sheridan stepped in and named the post for Joshua W. Sill, a friend and classmate killed in the Battle of Stone River. The soldiers at Fort Sill watched over the nearby Comanche and Kiowa Indians. Today, Fort Sill remains an active military post and is the U.S. Army Field Artillery Center.

One year before Fort Sill was established, the army set up a storage depot in what is now northwestern Oklahoma called the Depot on the North Canadian. First called a camp, it became Fort Supply in 1878 and remained an active post until 1893. The last major post established during the nineteenth century was Fort Reno, west of modern El Reno. After the fort's founding in 1874 to supervise Indians at the nearby Cheyenne agency, its soldiers supervised the land run in 1889. Fort Reno remained an active post until 1948.

The remains of many early Oklahoma forts may be seen today. In other instances, however, little endures but historical markers. Today, those camps and forts reflect a colorful period of Oklahoma history.

Military Forts and Camps of Oklahoma

Camp Arbuckle no. 1 (1832–1833): located near Fort Gibson

Camp Arbuckle no. 2 (1833): located seventeen miles northwest of Tulsa

Fort Arbuckle no. 1 (1850–1851): located just north of Byars

Fort Arbuckle no. 2 (1851–1870): located seven miles west of Davis

Camp Armstrong (1852–1865): Confederate camp near Bokchito

Camp Augur (1873–1874): subpost of Fort Sill southwest of Grandfield

Fort Beach (1874): located on Otter Creek near Tipton

Fort Blunt (1863–1865): Civil War earthwork located on a hill above Fort Gibson

Camp at Boggy Depot (1862–1865): Confederate camp located near Tushka

Cantonment (1879–1882): located on the Canadian River near Canton

Camp Cass (1834): located four miles south of Stidham

Camp Chilocco (1885): subpost of Fort Reno located near Chilocco

Camp Choctaw (1834): located in Stephens County

Fort Cobb (1859–1861): located thirty-five miles west of Chickasha

Fort Coffee (1834–1838, 1862–1863): located ten miles southwest of Fort Smith in Indian Territory

Fort near the Crossing of the Washita: early name for Fort Arbuckle #2 located near Davis

Camp Comanche (1834): located on the Fort Sill reservation

Camp Davidson (1878–1882): located southwest of Altus

CANTONMENT DAVIS (1861–1862): located north of Muskogee near Bacone College

CAMP FRANK (1898): located south of Ardmore

FORT GIBSON (1834–1890): located northeast of Muskogee

CAMP GUTHRIE (1889–1891): located in Guthrie

CAMP HOLMES (1834–1835): also called Camp Canadian and Fort Edwards; located on the Little River near Holdenville

CAMP LEAVENWORTH (1834): located near Kingston

CAMP MCINTOSH (1862): Confederate camp located east of Anadarko

CAMP MASON (1835): sometimes called Camp Holmes; located east across the Canadian River from Purcell in southern Cleveland County

FORT MCCULLOCH (1862–1865): Confederate post located on the Blue River near Kenefic

CAMP NAPOLEON (1865): Confederate camp located on the site of Verden

CAMP NEOSHO (1850): located near Okay

CAMP OKLAHOMA (1889): subpost of Fort Reno located in Oklahoma City (then called Oklahoma Station)

CAMP OSAGE (1834): located south of Jesse

PERRYVILLE DEPOT (1862–1863): Confederate post located near Savanna

CAMP AT PURCELL (1889): subpost of Fort Reno near Purcell

CAMP RADZIMINSKI (1858–1860): located on Otter Creek south of Tipton

CAMP RECOVERY (1834): located north of Fort Gibson on the Arkansas River

Fort Reno (1874–1948): early names were Post at the Cheyenne Agency and Camp near Cheyenne Agency; located west of El Reno

Camp Ross (1863): Confederate camp near the home of Cherokee Chief John Ross near Park Hill

Camp Russell (1883–1886): subpost of Fort Reno located on the northern bank of the Cimarron River north of Guthrie

Camp Schofield (1889): located three miles east of Chilocco north of Ponca City

Sheridan's Roost (1870): located near Orion

Fort Sill (1869 to present): early names include Camp at Medicine Bluff Creek, Fort Elliott, Camp Starvation, and Camp Wichita; located north of Lawton.

Fort Smith (1817–1824 and 1833): first located in Indian Territory until the site was declared to be in Arkansas

Camp Steele (1862): Confederate winter camp located in Indian Territory twenty miles west of Fort Smith, Arkansas

Camp Supply (1868–1878): located east of the town of Fort Supply in northwestern Oklahoma

Fort Supply (1878–1893): originally Camp Supply; became a fort in 1878

Fort Towson (1824–1829, 1831–1854, 1863–1865): located east of Hugo

Camp Washita (1834): located about three miles north of the Red River and a short distance from the Washita River; now under Lake Texoma

Fort Wayne (1838–1852; 1861): first located two miles north of Watts on the Illinois River; moved in spring of 1839 to north of present-day Colcord

Trading Posts and Early Businesses

LONG BEFORE PRESENT-DAY OKLAHOMA became part of the United States in 1803 in the Louisiana Purchase, Frenchmen came to trade with the Indians. These traders arrived after French explorer Jean-Baptiste Bénard de la Harpe visited the Three Forks area near modern Muskogee about 1719. At the junction of the Arkansas, Verdigris, and Grand rivers, French trappers and traders and Indians gathered to barter, making it an early trading center.

The prominent St. Louis Chouteau family established the earliest documented trading post in the Three Forks area in 1802. It was constructed on the site of modern Salina, the oldest permanent white settlement in Oklahoma. Joseph Revoir operated the post until he was murdered in 1821 by a Cherokee war party for supposedly supplying the Osages with guns and ammunition. Five years after the Chouteaus built the first trading post, Joseph Bogy, a French trader from Arkansas Post, constructed another trading post on the Verdigris River near modern Okay, Oklahoma. From Fort Smith keel boats loaded with goods and supplies traveled up the Arkansas River to the Three Forks to the trading posts. The boats returned with pelts and other items that the traders obtained from Indians.

In 1819, Arkansas Territory was carved out of Missouri Territory. Much of what is now Oklahoma then became part of Arkansas Territory, which was reduced in size in 1824 and again in 1828. In that year the boundaries of what is now Oklahoma, excluding the Panhandle and Greer County, were established, but Congress never passed an organic act for what became known as Indian Territory—it was never an official territory. When Congress sought to regulate trade with the Indian tribes in 1834, they called the region "Indian country" and annexed it to the judicial district of Missouri. Meantime, the federal government moved eastern tribes, including the Five Tribes, into the region, and eastern mapmakers began labeling it "Indian Territory."

Whites were already trading with Indians in the area. Nathaniel Pryor, who had been on Lewis and Clark's exploration, obtained a license to trade with the Osage Indians living in what is now northeastern Oklahoma. He built a trading post in 1819 on the Verdigris River about two miles north of where it runs into the Arkansas River. Col. Hugh Glenn, a businessman from Cincinnati, Ohio; the Chouteau family; and perhaps other traders may have invested in Pryor's trading post. It was there that Pryor, Glenn, and Jacob Fowler planned an 1821 trading expedition into the West. They followed the Arkansas River to the Rocky Mountains and returned east after making a profit.

The government acquired Pryor's trading post around 1825 to use as the Western Creek Indian agency. Another trading post called Neosho Post was built in 1825 by Pierre M. Papin, a cousin to A. P. Chouteau. It was located forty miles north of modern Salina on the Neosho River southeast of modern Miami and operated for several years. Sam Houston, a former governor of Tennessee and later president of the Republic of Texas, built a trading post about three miles from Fort Gibson in 1829. His post was often called Wigwam Neosho, and it remained in operation until 1833.

When the government built Fort Holmes near modern Holdenville in 1834, trapper James Edwards built a trading post across the Canadian River from the military fort. Fort Holmes was soon abandoned because conditions in the area were unhealthy for the soldiers. Edward's trading post, however, remained in operation for some time.

On the Red River in what is now south-central Oklahoma, Holland Coffee operated a trading post called Coffee's Station at different locations between 1834 and 1845. Coffee, a trapper, first led an expedition into the area of the forks of the Red River around 1834. His first post was located near an old Pawnee Indian village in the Choctaw Nation. Coffee employed thirty men at the post, which was surrounded by a tall stockade fence.

Coffee and his men made contact with Plains Indians and helped arrange treaty negotiations held in 1835 in what is now southern Cleveland County, across the South Canadian River from modern Purcell—a story that is told later in this book. The Chouteau family also opened a trading post nearby on what is now Chouteau Creek northeast of modern Purcell and south of present-day Norman and operated it for several years.

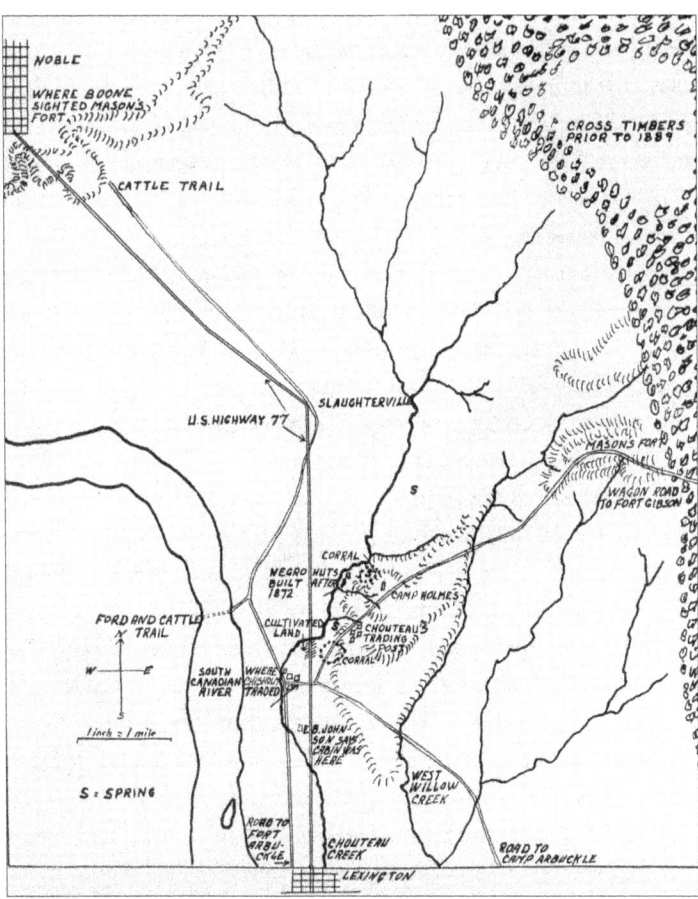

Camp Holmes and Chouteau's Trading Post. From Howard F. Van Zandt, "The History of Camp Holmes and Chouteau's Trading Post," *Chronicles of Oklahoma* 13, no. 3 (September 1935). Courtesy of Western History Collections, University of Oklahoma Libraries.

In 1836, Coffee moved his trading post up the Red River to the mouth of Cache Creek near modern Taylor. When Coffee learned that the post might be located on Texas soil, he moved it to Walnut Bayou near modern Burneyville. Abel Warren, a native of Massachusetts, ran Coffee's Station near Burneyville until about 1837 when the post was moved to Washita (Preston) Bend in Indian Territory across from modern Pottsboro, Texas. Coffee's Station served as a post office of the Republic of Texas in 1839, and it was there that Indians brought ransomed white captives taken in Texas to the trading post for exchange. In 1845, Coffee established the town of Preston, Texas, and operated his trading post there until his death in 1846. The location of that trading post is now under Lake Texoma north of Pottsboro, Texas.

For about eleven years, Abel Warren operated his own trading post, started about 1838 near the mouth of Walnut Creek in modern Love County, Oklahoma. Having success, Warren opened another post in 1847 or 1848 near the mouth of Cache Creek in modern Cotton County, Oklahoma, but it existed for only two years.

When Texans drove herds of longhorns across Indian Territory following the Civil War, a small trading post called Sewell's Stockade was established on the site of modern Jefferson in Grant County. It was located on the Chisholm Trail and served cowboys trailing longhorns north to the Kansas cattle towns.

During the 1860s, other trading posts were established in western Indian Territory. The most prominent was located just west of Camp Supply, now Fort Supply, in modern Woodward County, Oklahoma, established in 1868 by Albert E. Reynolds and William McDole Lee. They carried groceries and other items needed on the frontier. They also concentrated on buying buffalo hides and robes. During the 1870s, their business grew as hunters killed thousands of buffalo on the southern plains. Lee & Reynolds became the largest merchandiser in the region by 1878, the year Camp Supply became Fort Supply. The site of their trading post later became the town of

Fort Supply, but their business declined after nearly all of the buffalo on the southern plains were slaughtered for their hides.

Eleven years later a second surge of white merchants moved into what is now Oklahoma after the Unassigned Lands were opened to settlement in 1889.

Timeline of Commerce in Early Oklahoma (1700s–1880)

1719—Explorer de La Harpe visits Arkansas and Red rivers, followed by other traders in the area.

1802—Chouteau family establishes trading post where Salina stands today.

1807—Joseph Bogy establishes trading post near modern Okay.

1819—Nathaniel Pryor opens trading post on Verdigris River near juncture with Arkansas River.

1825—Pierre M. Papin establishes trading post on Neosho River, located southeast of modern Miami.

1829—Sam Houston opens trading post three miles from Fort Gibson.

1834—James Edwards builds trading post on Canadian River opposite short-lived Fort Holmes near modern Holdenville.

1834—Holland Coffee opens first of several posts called Coffee's Station on Red River in Choctaw Nation.

1838—Abel Warren operates a trading post near the mouth of Walnut Creek.

1869—Sewell's Stockade, on site of modern Jefferson in Grant County, caters to Texans driving longhorns north to Kansas.

1869—Albert E. Reynolds and William McDole Lee establish trading post near Camp Supply in modern Woodward County.

The Butterfield Overland Stage

THE BUTTERFIELD OVERLAND MAIL stage line first crossed what is now southeastern Oklahoma in 1858. It ran between St. Louis and San Francisco. The story of John Butterfield's line in Oklahoma began in 1857 when Congress voted to subsidize a semiweekly overland mail service to California. Butterfield, a former stage driver who went on to own stage lines in New York, organized a company and got the contract to carry mail and passengers from St. Louis to California.

It took Butterfield months of preparation before the stage line was ready to operate. He selected a southern route to avoid northern winter storms and difficult travel through the Rocky Mountains. He chose existing roads with hard surfaces and gentle grades. Butterfield hired eight hundred men to establish and operate his stage stations and bought about one thousand horses and five hundred mules

The first westbound coach (driven by John Butterfield, Jr.) to travel through Indian Territory. Engraving, by C. Edmonds, printed in *Frank Leslie's Illustrated Newspaper*, October 23, 1858. Courtesy of iStockphoto.com.

needed to pull one hundred Concord coaches purchased in New Hampshire. The brightly painted coaches were either red or dark green. All undercarriages were painted yellow with black or brown stripes. Two candle lamps were inside each coach, and two carriage lamps were mounted on the front of the coach behind the driver. Inside each coach were three wide seats—forward, middle, and rear. Each coach could carry five or six passengers plus a driver and a conductor who rode outside on the driver's box. Butterfield refused to carry gold, silver, or bullion to discourage holdups. Each passenger could take forty pounds of luggage and would pay two hundred dollars in gold to travel from Missouri to California. A fully loaded coach weighed four thousand pounds.

When Butterfield's service began in the fall of 1858, the stages only stopped to change horses. Sometimes passengers could buy a meal at the stops. The coaches made two trips weekly each way. Trying to sleep in a moving coach was difficult. When a comfort stop was requested, the stage would stop, and the men aboard would hurriedly find the nearest bush or tree. When there were women passengers, the driver stopped and assigned one side of the coach to men and the other to women. If any of the men happened to glance toward the women, the driver told them to turn their eyes.

Butterfield officials advised passengers that "the best seat inside is the one closest to the driver because there was less jolts and jostling." They added, "If you are asked to get out and walk, do so without grumbling. If a team runs away, sit still and take your chances. If you jump, nine shots out of ten you will get hurt." Passengers were also told not to complain about the food at the various meal stops. Men were told not to smoke strong tobacco in their pipes and to spit only on the leeward or downwind side. Drivers often told passengers to be good neighbors.

Westbound stages traveled west from St. Louis to Tipton, Missouri, and then turned southwest into western Arkansas and Fort Smith and into Indian Territory. The route across southeastern

Indian Territory covered nearly two hundred miles with twelve stage stations located thirteen to nineteen miles apart.

Stages crossed the Poteau River into Indian Territory on what one observer called "a shaky ferry." Seventeen miles to the southwest they came to Walker's stage station at the Choctaw agency, or Skullyville in what is now Le Flore County, run by Choctaw governor Tandy Walker. The station provided fresh horses to the stages, and Walker often helped to switch teams. Next came Trahern's Station at the Choctaw council house located in modern Le Flore County. It was operated by James N. Trahern, who also ran a small general store.

Holloway's Station, named for William Holloway, was next on the route. It was located at the entrance to a gentle pass called The Narrows, two miles northeast of Red Oak in modern Latimer County. A Choctaw Nation charter gave Holloway the right to charge anyone a toll to go over the pass. The next two stage stations were also located in modern Latimer County. First came Riddle's Station—named for trader John Riddle—located three miles east of modern Wilburton. Mountain Station, sometimes called Pusley's Station, named for stage agent Silas Pusley, was next. It was located two miles southwest of modern Higgins. From there the stage entered Pittsburg County and came to Blackburn's Station, located in a small community called Brush Settlement. Trader Casper B. Blackburn was the stage agent.

Continuing into what is now Atoka County, Waddell's Station came next for westbound stages, followed by Geary's Station, run by A. G. Geary, who also operated a toll bridge over the North Boggy Creek. Nearby, the stage road crossed the north-south Texas Road running from Missouri into Texas. Because of its location, Geary's Station was one of the more important stops on the Butterfield line in Indian Territory.

The next stop was Boggy Depot, located on Boggy Creek in modern Atoka County. The station was named for the creek and was located about four miles west of present-day Atoka. After entering what is now Bryan County, the stage came to Nail's Station, operated by Joel H. Nail, who had a mill and a general store at a crossing on the Blue River. Next was Fisher's Station, located about four miles west of modern Durant. The last stop in Indian Territory was in modern Bryan County at the Red River. There Benjamin F. Colbert, a Chickasaw tribal leader, operated a ferry and carried the coaches across the river into Texas.

Crossing Indian Territory on level ground, a stage might make fifteen miles an hour. The average speed between St. Louis and San Francisco, a distance of 2,800 miles, was five miles an hour. It took about twenty-five days to make the journey.

The Butterfield line operated from the fall of 1858 until June 10, 1861, when the Civil War abruptly ended its operation. The U.S. mail could no longer be carried through the Confederate states of Arkansas and Texas. The life of the Butterfield Overland Mail line was short, but it is part of the rich history of Oklahoma.

Early Cattle Trails and Ranching

IN ABOUT 1841, A FEW Texas cattle raisers began driving herds of longhorns north across Indian Territory to sell in Missouri and points east. The long drives were necessary because there were no good markets for cattle in Texas. The Texans did not realize they were doing work that legends would be made of. Their trail drives would later attract writers of dime novels and, even later, makers of modern Hollywood westerns. The early Texas trail drives entered Indian Territory at Rock Bluff on the Red River near modern Preston, Texas. The cattlemen drove their herds northeast to Fort Gibson and then followed a military road north along the Grand River before crossing into southwestern Missouri. The Texans came to call the route the Shawnee Trail.

In the 1850s, another Texas cattle trail evolved, following the Shawnee Trail from the Red River to modern Eufaula, where it branched east to Fort Smith and then turned north to modern Maysville, Arkansas, before crossing into Missouri. After Sedalia, Missouri, was founded in 1857, this route was called the Sedalia Trail.

As the Texans crossed Indian Territory, some Choctaw Indians charged ten cents a head for Texas cattle to cross their land. Texans protested but usually paid the toll. The Choctaw Tribal Council then took over the toll business and raised the toll to fifty cents a head. Other tribes also charged tolls; the Cherokees demanded seventy-five cents a head but were willing to accept live cattle as payment. Later some tribes charged Texans grazing fees to stop their herds at night on Indian lands.

Several thousand Texas cattle were driven across Indian Territory in the 1840s and early 1850s. The flow of Texas cattle slowed after stock raisers in Missouri noticed that many of their domestic cattle got sick and died after having contact with longhorns. Missourians called the sickness Texas Fever. Years later, the sickness was traced to ticks carried by the Texas cattle. Angry Missouri farmers organized vigilance committees to stop Texans from driving cattle into their state. In 1855, the Missouri legislature made it illegal to drive cattle from any other state into Missouri. Some Texans, after crossing Indian Territory, drove their cattle up the eastern border of Kansas Territory—organized in 1854—and sold them in Kansas City, Missouri. It was not until 1859 that the Kansas Territorial legislature stopped longhorns at its border because of Texas Fever.

The Civil War halted all Texas cattle drives across Indian Territory. When Texas ranchers returned home after the war, they found nearly six million cattle roaming the open ranges. Many were wild and unbranded and worth only one or two dollars locally. Needing money, Texans sought better markets for their cattle. In the spring of 1866, Texans drove 250,000 head to markets in Louisiana and Colorado. But most of the cattle were driven north and northeast and were stopped at the Missouri and Kansas borders for fear of Texas Fever. It was a difficult time for Texas cattle raisers seeking northern markets.

In the meantime, the Eastern Division of the Union Pacific (later the Kansas Pacific), was laying tracks west across Kansas. When the railroad reached the tiny settlement of Abilene, Kansas, 150 miles west of Kansas City, Missouri, an Illinois stock raiser named Joseph McCoy decided Abilene would make a good railhead market for Texas cattle. A hotel and stockyards were built, cattle buyers were notified, and printed flyers were distributed in Texas telling of the Abilene market. In 1867, about 35,000 longhorns were driven across Indian Territory and sold in Abilene.

Texans blazed their own trail to Abilene, crossing the Red River north of modern Gainesville, Texas, and driving their longhorns north. The trail passed just west of modern Ardmore, east of Oklahoma City, and west of Ponca City, before entering Kansas southeast of Wichita and continuing north to Abilene. The route the Texas drovers followed across Indian Territory was east of present-day Interstate 35. Even more cattle were driven north over this unnamed trail and sold in Abilene in 1868.

That year McCoy hired men to mark a more direct route many miles west of modern Interstate 35. The route followed was a wagon trail across Indian Territory between the Red River and modern Wichita, Kansas. Blazed a few years earlier by trader Jesse Chisholm, the trail crossed the Red River in Montague County, Texas; ran north past the future Oklahoma towns of Duncan, El Reno, and Kingfisher; entered Kansas near Caldwell, located south and a little west of modern Wichita; and finally later ran north to Abilene. The route became known as the Chisholm Trail.

Between 1867 and 1871, about 1.5 million cattle were sold in Abilene. But increasing numbers of settlers opposed the town's cattle trade because of the saloons, gambling, and prostitution it attracted. The Kansas legislature moved the quarantine line many miles west of Abilene, thereby ending the town's cattle trade. Longhorns could not be driven overland east of the line. The cattle trade shifted west of the quarantine line to other Kansas towns including Newton, Ellsworth, Brookville, Great Bend, and Wichita. These railroad towns remained cattle towns until 1876, when the north-south quarantine line was moved much farther west. That year, Dodge City, Kansas, became a major cattle town. When that happened, a new trail was laid out across Indian Territory to Dodge City. From Doan's Crossing on the Red River near modern Vernon, Texas, the trail ran across modern western Oklahoma to Camp Supply, a military post established in 1868. (In 1878, it was renamed Fort Supply.) The trail entered Kansas along the northern border of Harper County, Oklahoma, about sixty miles south of Dodge City. While some Texans called it the Dodge City Trail, it was better known as the Western Trail.

For nine years, Dodge City remained a major market for Texas cattle. In 1885, Kansas lawmakers quarantined the whole state, making it illegal to drive Texas cattle overland anywhere in Kansas. It was then that the Western Trail, the last major cattle route across Indian

Territory, faded into history. Nearly seven million Texas cattle had crossed Indian Territory between 1866 and 1885.

By the time the cattle drives shifted west over the Western Trail, Texas cattlemen had discovered the vast grasslands of what is now western Oklahoma and those in the Cherokee Outlet, a strip of land running 226 miles from east to west and 58 miles north to south along what was then Indian Territory's northern border. The area includes the rolling Osage prairies in the east and the gypsum sand dunes and the rugged Glass Mountains in the west. In 1883, two years before Kansas made it illegal to drive any Texas cattle overland in the state, the Cherokee Strip Livestock Association was formed, and cattlemen leased six million acres in the strip from the Cherokees. Seven years later, President Benjamin Harrison ordered the ranchers to remove all of their cattle from the Cherokee Strip amid plans to open the rangeland to white settlement.

Because ranching was a chancy business, the early cattlemen, both Indian and white, had to be self-reliant in order to survive winter storms, droughts, and government regulations. Most cattlemen resented government interference and had little respect for laws that impeded their progress rather than protect their investments. Some cattlemen survived and prospered. Most of those who did started out with very little and stuck it out until they made good. Through good and bad times, these cattlemen learned the intrinsic value of a dollar, how to make money and keep it. For example, in 1890 Wilson Nathaniel Jones, a Choctaw, owned 5,000 cattle on more than 17,000 acres near Caddo. He became known as the territory's "Indian cattle king." Frederick B. Severs, a Creek Indian, grazed about 8,000 cattle near Okmulgee. After several years, he also owned much of the town.

Today, cattle ranching is still prominent in many areas of Oklahoma. The traditions of rugged individualism and independence that first arrived with the Texans driving cattle to the railhead Kansas cattle towns still lives in Oklahoma's range and ranching culture. The long cattle drives, however, only live in history books, novels, and Hollywood westerns.

Major Oklahoma Cattle Trails (1841–1885)

Shawnee Trail (1841–1867): Crossed the Red River into Indian Territory at Rock Bluff near Preston, Texas, and ran northeast to Fort Gibson, then following a military road north along the Grand River to near the northeastern border of Indian Territory, before entering southwestern Missouri.

Sedalia Trail (1850s–1867): Followed a portion of the Shawnee Trail from Rock Bluff to modern Eufaula, turning east to Fort Smith, where it curved north and ran to Maysville, Arkansas, before entering southwestern Missouri.

Unnamed Trail (1867–1868): Crossed the Red River north of Gainesville, Texas, and continued north, running east of modern Interstate 35 past modern Ardmore, Oklahoma City and Ponca City before crossing into Kansas.

Chisholm Trail (1869–1876): Followed a wagon trail blazed by Jesse Chisholm, crossing the Red River in Montague County, Texas, and running north past the modern Oklahoma towns of Duncan, El Reno, and Kingfisher to Wichita, Kansas, before continuing to various Kansas cattle towns on railroads.

Western Trail (1876–1885): Entered Indian Territory at Doan's Crossing on the Red River north of Vernon, Texas, running north to Camp Supply (later Fort Supply), entering Kansas along the northern border of Harper County, Oklahoma, and continuing sixty miles north to Dodge City.

When the Railroads Arrived

AFTER MUCH OF MODERN Oklahoma was set aside early in the nineteenth century as Indian Territory, the eastern portion became the home of the Cherokees, Choctaws, Creeks, Chickasaws, and Seminoles. Whites could not settle in the territory. The Five Tribes farmed, raised livestock, and established their own governments. Their children went to mission schools founded by white church groups from the East. The federal government built a few forts ostensibly to keep white settlers out and to protect the Indians.

When the Civil War began, many but not all of the Indians in Indian Territory sided with the Confederacy. Many Indians died in the fighting while others died of starvation. Their tribal governments were torn by dissention. After the war, the federal government imposed harsh punishment on the tribes in Indian Territory regardless of whether they fought with or against the Union. They were pressured to sign new treaties, and some ceded their land in what is now western Oklahoma to the government for tribes being removed from other areas of the West. Within a few years, representatives of fifty tribes lived in Indian Territory.

To make money, railroads, banks, and large businesses in neighboring states wanted to open Indian Territory to white settlement. Bills were introduced in Congress, but each one failed. Railroads then began a campaign to establish routes through Indian Territory. Gradually, these whites promoting settlement of Indian Territory became known as Boomers. Trying to recover from the effects of the Civil War and reconstruction, Indians knew what would happen if the railroad entered Indian Territory. The trains would bring more whites and what the Indians believed were the evils of the white man's world.

The Indians fought to keep the railroads out, but under government pressure they granted permission for railroads to cross Indian

Territory. The government refused the railroad's request for land grants and agreed with the Indians' demand to provide only a two-hundred-foot-wide right-of-way. This was included in the legislation passed by Congress opening Indian Territory to railroads in July 1866. The Cherokee Council also passed an act reserving for their people an area of one square mile around each railroad station in the Cherokee Nation.

Three small rail lines reorganized and became the Missouri, Kansas, and Texas Railroad in 1870 and built south from Kansas across Indian Territory, reaching Texas late in 1872. The Atlantic and Pacific railroad (later called the Frisco line) built its tracks from Missouri into northeastern Indian Territory, reaching Texas in 1880. Seven years later, the Atchison, Topeka, and Santa Fe Railroad pushed south from Wichita, Kansas, across Indian Territory into Texas and Fort Worth. Indian Territory, however, remained off limits to settlement except by Indians.

Railroad officials inspect a rock cut on the Missouri, Kansas, and Texas Railroad line in 1872 south of present-day McAlester, Oklahoma. Courtesy of Kansas State Historical Society.

The Indians made little use of the trains. Many Texas cattlemen even refused to ship their longhorns north by railroad. It was cheaper to drive their animals over long-established cattle trails that crossed Indian Territory. The supporters of the railroads crossing Indian Territory hoped the rails' presence would open the region to settlement. Bankers, farm equipment manufacturers, and others who crossed Indian Territory by train saw the beautiful country just waiting to be settled and farmed. The Indians, however, continued to fight white settlement.

T. C. Sears—an attorney for the Missouri, Kansas, and Texas railroad—and Elias C. Boudinot—a Cherokee of mixed blood and an attorney—became known as Boomers for promoting settlement on public lands in Indian Territory. The two men reviewed laws relating to Indian treaties and in 1879 announced they had found 14 million acres of land in the territory that had not been given to the Indians. The lawyers claimed the land belonged to the American people and therefore could be settled.

Sears and Boudinot organized groups of purported settlers in North Texas, in Topeka, Kansas, and in Kansas City, Missouri. They opened Boomer offices in towns along the southern border of Kansas that attracted people ready to settle in Indian Territory. The federal government and the courts rejected Sears and Boudinot's contentions. Fearing that squatters would not stay out, Cherokee leaders protested to federal authorities, and troops were stationed at strategic points along the northern border of Indian Territory to keep settlers out.

David Payne, an Indiana native, launched another Boomer campaign. Payne had known Boudinot in Washington, D.C. Payne called for settlement in Indian Territory and quoted the Bible, namely God's command to Moses to "Go forth and possess the Promised Land." Payne led several expeditions into the territory only to be turned back by federal troops. He was arrested and charged in U.S. District Court at Topeka, Kansas, with conspiracy against the United States. To Payne's surprise, the court dismissed the charge on grounds that title to the Indian lands was indeed vested in the United States. The court added that the lands were public domain and ruled that settlement by qualified U. S. citizens was not a crime. Reviewing Indian lands in the territory, government attorneys soon found that Creek and Seminole Indians had a "residual interest" in some Unassigned Lands in what is now west-central Oklahoma.

As more and more people called for Indian Territory to be settled, the government gave the tribes cash payments to relinquish their rights to the Unassigned Lands. Business interests in Kansas continued to exert influence in Washington. Just before Congress adjourned in early March 1889, lawmakers approved opening the Unassigned Lands to settlement. President Benjamin Harrison soon signed the measure and issued a proclamation declaring that the land would be open to settlement at noon on Monday, April 22, 1889. The government staged a land run to give all settlers an equal chance. At noon on April 22, thousands of people made the run in wagons, on horseback, by train, and even on foot. By nightfall, tent cities sprang up, creating the future towns of Oklahoma City, Kingfisher, El Reno, Norman, Guthrie, and Stillwater.

Some people ignored federal law and sneaked onto claims the night before the run. At the appointed hour of the run, they would come out of hiding and make their claims. This led to disputes, and the word "Sooner" had a negative connotation for years in Oklahoma. Eventually, however, the word lost its unfavorable association. The University of Oklahoma adopted the word "Sooners" as the nickname for their football team, and later, as it was settled, Oklahoma became known as the Sooner State.

"No Man's Land"

THE OUTLINE OF OKLAHOMA's boundaries includes its long and narrow Panhandle. The story behind the state's unusual shape involves national politics, controversy, and people's desire to settle in what is today the Oklahoma Panhandle.

The story begins with the Compromise of 1850. The United States acquired a vast amount of land that Texas had claimed since its days as a republic. When Texas joined the Union as a slave state, it agreed not to extend its sovereignty over any territory north of 36 degrees and 30 minutes parallel north. Thus the northern boundary of the Texas Panhandle only stretched that far north, even though as a republic Texas claimed a strip of land stretching northward into modern Wyoming.

When Kansas Territory was created in 1854, its southern boundary was set on the 37th parallel, an east-west line agreed to in the Missouri Compromise of 1820 that called for all territory north of the line to be free and everything south to be slave. This left a narrow strip of land about 34 1/2 miles wide and about 168 miles long between Kansas and the Texas Panhandle.

Between 1850 and 1890, most government maps identified this strip of land as "Public Land" or "Public Land Strip." Many people, however, called it "No Man's Land." During the warm months of the year, this land strip was home to nomadic Plains Indians, mostly Comanches. The Cimarron Cut-Off of the Santa Fe Trail crossed the western end of the strip, and countless traders with their caravans of freight wagons traveled over the trail between Missouri and Santa Fe. Military expeditions also used the route.

During the 1860s, sheep herders from New Mexico settled near the western end of the strip. In 1874, white buffalo hunters ignored the no hunting rule and began to kill countless buffalo for their hides on the southern plains including in No Man's Land. The hunting

A sod house. Courtesy of Western History Collections, University of Oklahoma Libraries (Forbes Collection, no. 73).

increased after the free-roaming Indians on the southern plains were moved to reservations. In 1878, cattlemen arrived looking for free open range for their animals. It was not until about 1880 that Jim Lane, a former wagon freighter, became the first permanent settler in No Man's Land. He constructed a large dugout on Beaver Creek, brought in several wagons loaded with supplies, and opened a store in his dugout.

In 1885, the U.S. land office in Washington, D.C., concluded that No Man's Land was not part of Indian Territory—it was public land, and squatters could settle there. The news spread and land-hungry settlers who had suffered drought and economic depression elsewhere began to move into the area. Unfortunately, settlers found no government land office and no government surveys to facilitate homesteading or squatting. The settlers surveyed the land into quarter sections using "zinc pot" markers left in two-mile intervals along six-mile-square congressional townships surveyed in 1881 by the government. The settlers then squatted on the land they wanted, hoping that they could eventually acquire legal titles.

The settlers did not attempt serious farming. They could not afford the necessary equipment. Most simply grew the crops they needed to survive. Life was hard—especially during the cold winter months and during periods of drought.

Beaver and a couple of other communities developed in the eastern portion of No Man's Land during the late 1880s, and several post offices opened before 1890. Since there was no territorial or state government, many squatter communities set up citizen committees to resolve land claim disputes. Citizens also formed their own vigilante committees to maintain law and order. A few even hired men to be town sheriffs. They were needed because No Man's Land attracted many criminals who made their living stealing horses or swindling people out of their land claims.

By early 1887, the citizens of No Man's Land were working to organize their own territory to bring law, order, and formal government. On February 27, 1887, they held an election and selected nine delegates. A month later a territorial council was organized in the settlement of Beaver, the projected capital. They divided No Man's Land into five counties, made laws, and decided to send a delegation to Washington, D.C., to seek congressional recognition of what they named Cimarron Territory.

The citizens elected Dr. Owen G. Chase as their official delegate to go to the nation's capital. Another political faction, however, decided to send J. E. Dale to Washington. Both representatives showed up, but the importance of this outcome is still debated. Even though the Oklahoma Panhandle was larger than the states of Rhode Island and Delaware, the motion to create Cimarron Territory died because No Man's Land did not have a large enough population or the resources needed to become a territory.

No Man's Land did not get government including law and order until May 1890 when it became part of the Territory of Oklahoma. By then, however, it had lost population. Perhaps two-thirds of its residents had left the previous year to participate in the run of the Unassigned Lands on April 22, 1889. When Oklahoma became a state a century ago, No Man's Land was organized into three counties—Beaver, Texas, and Cimarron—and it became the Oklahoma Panhandle.

Part III

~

From Tipis and Lodges

Seek wisdom, not knowledge.
Knowledge is of the past,
Wisdom is of the future.

American Indian proverb

Making Peace with the Plains Indians

MORE THAN 175 YEARS AGO, thousands of Plains Indians camped in what is now southern Cleveland County, Oklahoma. Their chiefs signed their first treaty ever with the United States government and representatives of the Five Tribes. The date was August 24, 1835—an important moment in American and Oklahoma history, but one that has been forgotten by many people.

At the time, the U.S. Army considered the Plains Indians—the Comanches, Wichitas, Kiowas, Apaches, and a few other tribes—as "wild Indians" unlike the Indians in eastern Indian Territory. The Plains Indians roamed freely, following their commissary, the wild buffalo, on the southern plains west of the Cross Timbers.

About 1829 Sam Houston, the future president of Texas but at the time an Indian trader near Fort Gibson, urged the military to send a delegation and establish peace with the Plains Indians. The military did little until 1833, when some Osage Indians destroyed a Kiowa village in the Wichita Mountains and took a few prisoners.

The military was waiting for such an opportunity. In 1834, Gen. Henry Leavenworth and Col. Henry Dodge organized an expedition and returned the Kiowa prisoners to their home in what is now southwestern Oklahoma. The military then opened dialogue with the chiefs of the Plains Indians, who accepted an invitation to visit Fort Gibson to talk peace.

A party of Plains Indians that traveled east through the Cross Timbers to Fort Gibson said they would negotiate a treaty but not at Fort Gibson. They would do so only in buffalo country when the grass next grew after the snows had melted. When the new year arrived, the War Department in Washington, D.C., ordered Maj. R. B. Mason and a detachment of dragoons to travel west to the mouth of the Little River, south of modern Holdenville, and establish a post and prepare a campground for the meeting. The post was named

Fort Holmes, but, because conditions in the area were unhealthy for the soldiers, it was soon abandoned.

It was just as well that the military gave up the post, because the Plains Indians opposed the Cross Timbers as the meeting place. The Indians feared their enemies would attack them if they traveled into the Cross Timbers, the dense thicket of trees and undergrowth providing too many hiding places.

Knowing that the Plains Indians would not travel east through the Cross Timbers to sign a treaty, Major Mason selected another location, just east of the Canadian River a few miles northeast of modern Purcell and just northwest of present-day Lexington. He sent word of the new location to the Plains Indians, who said it was acceptable. Whether the military knew it or not, the new location was a favorite camping ground of the Comanches for their buffalo hunts. Major Mason and about fifty soldiers went to the new location; established Camp Holmes, using the name of the abandoned fort on the Little River; and made preparations to receive the Indians (see the map on page 51).

In late July 1835, perhaps as many as seven thousand Plains Indians began arriving, setting up their camps a few miles from Camp Holmes. Soon Gen. Matthew Arbuckle and Montfort Stokes, a commissioner appointed to negotiate treaties, arrived at Camp Holmes with two companies from the Seventh Infantry. With their arrival, there was a force of 250 U.S. soldiers at Camp Holmes. With them to sign the treaty came a delegation from the Creek, Choctaw, Muscogee, Osage, Seneca, and Quapaw tribes.

The meeting lasted six weeks. On August 24, 1835, representatives of the Five Tribes, U.S. representatives, and the chiefs of the Plains Indians signed the treaty. The Kiowas and Apaches missed the meeting but later signed the treaty, which contained the usual clauses of amity and friendship granting passage through Indian country for U.S. citizens heading for Santa Fe and Mexico. The accord also permitted the Indians to hunt and trap beyond the Cross

Timbers to the western limits of the United States. By the time the meeting ended, Col. A. P. Chouteau had constructed a small stockade and trading post west of the Canadian River on what is now Chouteau Creek. During the next few years, Chouteau carried on a considerable trade with the Comanches and other Plains Indians. Experienced in peacemaking, Chouteau gained the confidence of the Plains Indians. About 1837 a Comanche war party came to Chouteau's trading post and released three white women and children the Comanches had taken captive.

While Chouteau's post reportedly operated for many years, Camp Holmes, sometimes called Fort Mason, was occupied for only a short time. The government kept the post on its books and occasionally stationed a few soldiers there until just before the Unassigned Lands were opened to settlement in 1889. Camp Holmes was then abandoned.

Today nothing remains of Camp Holmes or of Chouteau's stockade and trading post, but in a roadside park on U.S. Highway 77 just north of Lexington, the modern traveler will see a large brown stone historical marker erected by the National Society of The Colonial Dames in Oklahoma. It serves as a reminder to passersby of the rich history that occurred in the area in 1835.

Mountains Named for the Wichita Indians

When Capt. Randolph Marcy took a military expedition in 1852 to locate the source of the Red River, he traversed a small mountain range in what is now southwestern Oklahoma. West of the mountains Marcy and his men camped near the site of an old Wichita Indian village located on a branch of Cache Creek. The Wichitas had since moved to east of the mountains, but Marcy found evidence that the Indians had grown corn near the site of the village. He observed that the site was "upon an elevated plateau, directly along the south bank of the creek." The site, he wrote, "commands an extended view of the country to the north, south, and east. From its commanding position it is well secured against surprise, and is, by nature, one of the most defensible places I have seen."

Marcy was impressed with the country. "The landscape here presented to the eye has a most charming diversity of scenery, consisting of mountains, woodlands, glades, watercourses, and prairies, all laid out and arranged in such peculiar order as to produce a most delightful effect upon the senses," wrote Marcy, adding, "This must have been a favorite spot for the Indians, and why they have abandoned it I cannot imagine, unless it was through fear of the Comanches."

The Wichitas called themselves *Kitikiti'sh*, meaning "raccoon eyes," because of tattoo designs around their eyes resembling the masks of raccoons. Whites called them the "Wichita," a word that comes from two words in their language—*neels*, which means "man," and *ee-tew*, which means "of the north." Spanish explorer Coronado was the first European to have contact with Wichita Indians in 1541 while searching for the fabled Quivira in what is now Kansas. Most of the tribe's early history is clouded in mystery, but it is known that they lived in modern Arkansas and Louisiana before moving west into what is now Oklahoma, Texas, and Kansas. For a time, many of them lived in south-central Kansas near the modern city of Wichita named for them. More than a decade after Marcy's Red River expedition, the Wichita Indians could be found living in the shadows of the Wichita Mountains near modern Fort Sill.

To understand the Wichitas' early history as recorded by whites, it is important to note that the vast region that is now Oklahoma was mostly unsettled country in 1837 except for the Osages, Cherokees, and other tribes moved by the government to Indian Territory. That year Martin Van Buren succeeded Andrew Jackson as president of the twenty-six states that constituted the Union. It was the year Samuel Morse patented the telegraph and the young community of Chicago was incorporated as a city while the city of Houston was incorporated as a city by the Republic of Texas.

Two years earlier in 1835, the Wichita Indians made their first treaty with the government, agreeing to live in peace with the United States and other tribes including the Osages. The Wichitas established a major village on Cache Creek but by 1837 had moved eastward and located near modern Fort Sill on the eastern side of what by then was being called the Wichita Mountains, one of the oldest mountain ranges in the world. The geologic history of the Wichita Mountains goes back about 300 million years when stratified layers of eroded silt were deposited on the area where the mountains are located today. Two hundred million years later the mountains were created by a tremendous uplift of the earth. The mountains were much higher than today, but 50 million years later erosion began and through the ages they were sculptured and chiseled by the elements. The once-lofty Wichita Mountains are now only a fraction of their original size.

Today the Wichita Mountains consist of two rugged ranges of red granite reaching nearly 2,500 feet at the highest point. They run several miles east and west and enclose a natural prairie. The rugged landscape is rich in lore that includes legends of Indian battles and Spanish treasure. Spanish miners reportedly searched for gold and silver, but found little in large quantities. The Spanish penetrated the region in the 1600s, and French traders first crossed the area during the 1770s.

Plains Indians found protection from their enemies in the Wichita Mountains long before the first Europeans arrived. The Indians also found solace at what is called Medicine Bluff, located near the eastern base of the mountains. The bluff is three hundred feet above a creek, whose waters are thought by Indians to have special powers. Wichita Indians may have given the bluff a name in their native language, identifying it as a place of mystery with special spiritual power, and the first whites in the area probably named it Medicine Bluff after learning that of the Indians' belief. Before whites arrived, however, Indians never called it by that name, apparently having no word for "medicine" until the first Europeans arrived.

The first American military officer to visit the Wichita Mountains was Col. Henry Dodge in 1834. He sought to make contact with Comanche Indians to get them to stop raiding Santa Fe traders on the Santa Fe Trail. The Comanches used the mountains as their base and raided deep into Texas and even into Mexico. In 1843, however, Texans visited the Comanches in the Wichita Mountains and made a treaty to stop them from raiding.

When Captain Marcy visited the Wichita Mountains, there was no military post in the immediate area. It was not until 1868 that the U.S. military established Camp Wichita on Medicine Bluff Creek at the eastern end of the Wichita Mountains. That camp became Fort Sill in 1869. Gen. Phillip Sheridan, who had a hand in establishing the post, visited the area and reportedly shot an elk.

Today the area is preserved as part of the 60,000-acre Wichita Mountains Wildlife Refuge. First set aside from the Comanche-Kiowa-Apache Indian Reservation in 1901 as a National Forest, it came under the Bureau of Biological Survey in 1935. Today, the U.S. Fish and Wildlife Service administers the refuge.

Much of the large wild game in the Wichita Mountains was gone by 1901. However, that year—as a gift of the city of Wichita, Kansas—

one bull elk was released; later a small herd of buffalo provided by the American Bison Society was released. In 1912, five Rocky Mountain elk were moved to the preserve from the National Elk Refuge near Jackson, Wyoming, and the following year the Wyoming refuge provided fifteen more elk.

Today, in addition to elk, the refuge maintains buffalo and longhorn cattle. Aside from wildlife viewing, visitors can fish in any one of several lakes, rock climb and rappel, follow hiking trails, and use shady picnic and campgrounds. Visitors also can follow a three-mile paved road to the 2,464-foot summit of Mount Scott located on the eastern edge of the refuge. Nearby—located in a special use area not open to the public—is Mount Pinchot, three feet shorter than Mount Scott.

The Wichita Mountains Wildlife Refuge is the second most visited federal wildlife refuge in the nation. Located near the center of the refuge is a visitor's center. Exhibits depict the colorful human and geological history of Oklahoma's oldest mountains, including Marcy's visit. Northwest of the center visitors can see Mount Marcy (2,425 feet), a visual reminder of Capt. Randolph Marcy's visit in the mid-nineteenth century. As for the descendants of the Wichita Indians, most now live on the north side of the Washita River around Anadarko, Oklahoma, in what is now Caddo County, northeast of the Wichita Mountains.

"Gopher John," Black Seminole

"Gopher John" was the nickname of John Horse, a black Seminole slave, who was also known as Juan Caballo and John Cowaya. Some people steeped in Seminole history consider him the father of Wewoka, Oklahoma, where he helped black Seminoles to settle in 1849.

The story of Gopher John is a mixture of fact and Seminole oral traditions. He was born about 1812 in eastern Florida. His father was Indian and his mother was black. Legend has it that as a boy he got his nickname after selling a U.S. Army officer some turtles. Pleased with the turtles, the officer asked John to bring him more turtles and put them in a pen, so John did and the officer paid him. The officer planned to hold a banquet featuring turtle meat, but the cook found only two turtles in the pen. Only then did the officer realize that John had repeatedly sold him the same turtles. Angry, but impressed by John's ingenuity, he made the boy find fresh turtles he had paid for and nicknamed him Gopher John.

Most black Seminoles were originally slaves in the United States who fled south to Spanish Florida and found refuge in Seminole-controlled areas. Most became slaves to the Seminoles, who treated them better than whites had.

The details of Gopher John's early years are hazy. He was born into slavery and grew to become a tall, fine-looking man admired for his coolness and courage. He had a flair for diplomacy, but he also was an expert shooter with a rifle. Gopher John married Susan July. They had one son, Joe Coon.

In Florida, he owned livestock and land that he cultivated. His life was peaceful until the early 1830s when white slaving parties began raiding Seminole villages looking for runaway slaves. All black men and their families were fair game.

At about the same time, President Andrew Jackson was trying to move the Five Tribes living in the southeastern United States to

"Gopher John." Engraving, attributed to N. Orr & S. C. Richardson, New York, printed in Joshua Giddings, *The Exiles of Florida; or, The Crimes of Our Government against the Maroons* (Columbus: Follett, Foster & Co., 1858). Courtesy of Western History Collections, University of Oklahoma Libraries.

Indian Territory. At first, the Seminoles were willing to move, but their attitude changed when U.S. soldiers tried to force them to do so and when whites began kidnapping their slaves. Seminole concerns for their slaves started the Second Seminole War.

During the war, Gopher John became well known as a Seminole military leader and negotiator. Even though he was a slave, he convinced more than five hundred black Seminoles to stop fighting on the assurance that the U. S. government would allow them to settle in Indian Territory.

Between 1838 and 1842, when the Second Seminole War ended, Gopher John traveled several times between Florida and Indian Territory helping groups of Seminoles to locate in Indian Territory. For his help, the Seminoles granted Gopher John his freedom in 1843.

When he escorted his black Seminoles to Indian Territory in 1849, he helped them establish their own community on a small creek in what is now central Oklahoma. They called their settlement Wewoka, meaning the "Village of Refuge"; the small stream today is Wewoka Creek.

For the Seminoles and their maroons (black slaves), life in Indian Territory became difficult. The government settled them on Creek land although the Creeks had fought against the Seminoles in Florida. The Creeks resented that Seminole slaves could own weapons and control their own labor; such practices were prohibited in the Creek slave codes.

After U.S. troops stopped fighting between the Seminoles and Creeks in 1849, Gopher John and another Seminole leader organized a group of unhappy Seminoles and maroons and moved to Mexico where slavery was illegal. In 1850, Mexican officials provided the black Seminoles with supplies and land grants at Nacimiento in the state of Coahuila bordering on Texas. In return, the black Seminoles patrolled the region for the Mexican government and subdued renegade Apache and Comanche Indians. The Mexicans considered Gopher John chief of the black Seminoles or *Moscogoes,* as they called them. Gopher John was given the rank of captain in the Mexican army. For nearly twenty years, Gopher John and the maroons lived peacefully in Mexico.

After the United States banned slavery during the Civil War, Gopher John apparently began to consider returning north of the Rio Grande. It was not until about 1870, however, when internal political problems occurred in Mexico, that Gopher John and a group of black Seminoles crossed the Rio Grande and settled at Fort Duncan near Eagle Pass, Texas. Several black Seminoles became scouts for the U.S. Army after the government promised that they and their families would eventually be allowed to own their own land in Indian Territory. Gopher John refused to become a scout, however, but at times did serve as an unofficial interpreter.

By 1876, Gopher John and many black Seminoles became dissatisfied with the government's delay in giving them land in Indian Territory. Gopher John led a group of maroons back into Mexico. In 1882, he went to Mexico City and met with President Porfirio Díaz in an effort to obtain previously issued Mexican land grants for his black Seminoles. Gopher John was successful. Five years later President Díaz issued an official statement protecting their land grants, but Gopher John did not live to see it. He died soon after his meeting with President Díaz. Some accounts suggest he died of pneumonia in a Mexico City hospital, but others say he was murdered by outlaws. The circumstances of his death are still a mystery. During his lifetime, Gopher John survived four assassination attempts—three by maroons who were unhappy with his ability to gain positive results for them, and one by Texans near Eagle Pass.

Gopher John was never able to return to Wewoka, Oklahoma. The city became the Seminole capital about 1855, and a capitol building and council house were built. However, today, aside from local museum exhibits, the only physical evidence of the Seminole capital is a pecan tree on the courthouse lawn, which served as the tribal whipping post.

Satanta, Kiowa Chief

SATANTA, A KIOWA WAR CHIEF, was perhaps the best-known Indian on the southern plains during the late nineteenth century. Settlers on the frontier feared him as a murderer, but easterners viewed him as an orator and diplomat for his people.

The story of Satanta begins about 1820 when he was born somewhere on the plains of modern Kansas or Oklahoma. His mother was apparently an Arapaho, and his father, Red Tipi, was a medicine man and keeper of the Kiowa medicine bundles. Like other Indian boys, Satanta trained to be a warrior as he grew into manhood. He was given the permanent name *Set-t'ainte,* meaning "White Bear." In time, whites anglicized *Set-t'ainte* and called him Satanta.

From the 1830s to the 1850s, Satanta fought as a warrior in campaigns against the Cheyennes and Utes. He also participated in raids

Satanta. Courtesy of Western History Collections, University of Oklahoma Libraries (Babcock Collection, no. 28)

in Texas and as far south as Mexico. While other young Kiowa males usually married by age twenty, Satanta's father put his son's marriage on hold to school him as a future Kiowa leader. Satanta married at about thirty when he became a subchief.

Little else is known about Satanta until the 1850s when U.S. Army records mention him. Soldiers recorded that Satanta stood more than six feet tall and had a magnificent physique. They noted that he had great intelligence and arrogance and a strong personality.

Satanta began taking part in Kiowa raids against the Cheyenne and Utes. He became principal war chief of the Kiowas about 1866. By then he was raiding white settlements in Texas.

Under pressure to stop the hostile Plains Indians, Congress established a commission to make peace and to move the Indians onto reservations. Near what is now Medicine Lodge, Kansas, the commissioners gathered in October 1867 to sign a treaty with Kiowa-Apache, Comanche, Cheyenne, and Arapaho Indians. The commissioners told the Indians they must stop raiding, allow the railroads to build across the plains, and move onto assigned reservations. In exchange, the commissioners promised to provide the Indians rations; to protect them from white buffalo hunters; to furnish them with schools, churches, and farming tools; and to teach them how to live like whites. When the Indian chiefs spoke, Satanta outshined the rest. In a strong and sincere voice, he said that his people neither wanted to give up their lands nor wanted any of the white man's churches. He said that they wished to live as they had, following the buffalo, and that his people simply wanted to be left alone. While his remarks on Indian and white relations were widely quoted in eastern newspapers, they did not sway the commissioners. When the treaty was drawn up, it contained things the Indians did not want. Still, Satanta and the other chiefs reluctantly signed the treaty.

When Satanta was slow in moving his people to their assigned reservation in what is now southwestern Oklahoma, Lt. Col. George Custer took him prisoner and held him hostage until the Kiowas moved to their reservation. There Satanta remained with his people for about two years; however, by early 1871, he became restless. When inadequate government provisions were delivered, Satanta and his followers quietly left the reservation and raided white settlements in Texas. More than a dozen Texans were killed. Satanta and about one hundred Kiowas attacked a wagon train owned by a Henry Warren near what is today Graham, Texas. Seven of twelve teamsters were killed.

When soldiers began searching for the Indians, Satanta, a young warrior named Big Tree, and an old warrior and medicine man named Satank returned to Fort Sill to claim their rations. An Indian agent at Fort Sill was shocked when Satanta freely admitted that he had led the attacks in Texas. He said he was assisted by Big Tree and Satank. The Indian agent turned over Satanta and the two other Indians to military authorities, who decided the three should stand trial for murder in Texas. They were handcuffed and shackled and loaded into a wagon; with a military escort, the party started for Jacksboro, Texas. On the journey, Satank became depressed and started singing a Kiowa death song. He then pulled a knife he had hidden under his clothing and tried to escape. A guard killed him.

When Satanta and Big Tree reached Jacksboro, Texas, a jury found them guilty of murder. They were sentenced to hang. It was the first time Indian chiefs were ever tried in civil court. For two years, they remained in prison at Huntsville, Texas. Humanitarians in the East called for their release, but Texans wanted them to die. Indian agents feared that if they were put to death, there would be an Indian uprising. The governor of Texas finally paroled Satanta and Big Tree. They were returned to Fort Sill in August 1873 and set free.

When summer came in 1874, Satanta and his followers were once again raiding settlements in modern western Oklahoma and the Texas Panhandle, attempting to stop the slaughter of buffalo for their hides by white hunters. Satanta was captured and returned to prison at Huntsville, Texas, in the fall of 1874. He soon became depressed over the prospect of spending the rest of his life in prison. On October 11, 1878, Satanta fell to the ground from a window atop the prison hospital.

Whether Satanta's death was suicide or murder is still debated. He was buried in the prison cemetery, but in 1963 a grandson received permission to rebury Satanta in the cemetery at Fort Sill where his grave can be seen today.

Cherokee William P. Ross, Father of Oklahoma Journalism
~

IT WAS IN 1844 THAT the first true newspaper was printed in what is now Oklahoma. The *Cherokee Advocate*, the official paper of the Cherokee Nation, was first published in Tahlequah on September 26, 1844. The editor of the *Cherokee Advocate* was William Potter Ross, a graduate of Princeton University. Ross is remembered as a man of medium height, weighing perhaps 165 pounds, having a pleasing manner, and possessing a gentle voice. Although an intellectual, he was not aloof and was easy to approach.

Ross was born August 20, 1820, at the base of Lookout Mountain on the Tennessee River a few miles south of Chattanooga. He was the oldest son of John Golden and Eliza Ross, who taught him to read and write. He attended a Presbyterian Mission School in Alabama operated by Rev. William Potter, after whom he was named. Ross later attended an academy at Greenville, Tennessee.

When young Ross was seventeen, his uncle, John Ross—Cherokee chief—paid his way to attend preparatory school at Lawrenceville, New Jersey, and then to attend Princeton. Ross was twenty-two when he was graduated at Princeton in 1842 first in his class of forty-four. While he was attending Princeton, many Cherokees were removed from the southeastern United States to Indian Territory. After graduation, Ross returned to his parents living at Park Hill, Indian Territory, the new cultural center of the Cherokee Nation. During the fall and winter of 1842, Ross taught school in a Methodist log church where Hulbert, Oklahoma, stands today.

In July 1843, Ross also attended an intertribal peace conference at Tahlequah, which several thousand representatives from about eighteen tribes attended. Ross was elected clerk of the senate of the national council early in October 1843 and helped to frame the Cherokee Constitution. When the national council voted to establish the *Cherokee Advocate,* a weekly newspaper, Ross was appointed editor. The paper was designed to inform and encourage the Cherokees in matters of agriculture and education and to provide them current news affecting Indians. As editor, Ross became the father of Oklahoma journalism.

Ross's editorials impressed the Cherokees. His work reflected his education in composition and proper use of the English language. He edited the *Cherokee Advocate* for four years, left the position in 1846 and 1847 to travel, and returned as editor in 1848 and 1849. Other Cherokees edited the paper until it was discontinued in 1851 for lack of funds. It was not until 1870 that the paper was revived and continued until the day after Christmas in 1874, when its office and equipment were destroyed by fire. Rebuilt, the paper continued to operate until March 3, 1906, when it ceased publication.

As the first editor of the *Cherokee Advocate,* Ross became well known as a writer and public speaker. When he stepped down as editor, he became a merchant and later practiced law. Between 1849 and the late 1850s, he served as a senator from the Tahlequah District in the Cherokee National Council. In 1860, he became secretary to Lewis Ross, an uncle, who was the Cherokee Nation's national treasurer.

When the Civil War began, many Cherokees including Ross sought to maintain a neutral position, but when the North abandoned its military forts in Indian Territory, the Cherokees had no choice but to make an alliance with the South. Many mixed-blood Cherokees and those who had intermarried with whites were slaveholders.

Although William P. Ross did not favor the alliance, he enlisted in the Confederacy in October 1861 and became a lieutenant colonel in the First Regiment of Cherokee Mounted Rifles and participated in the Battle of Pea Ridge in Arkansas in 1862. However, a majority of Ross's regiment changed their allegiance to the Union early in 1863 and went north with friends. When Union forces reoccupied Cherokee country later in the year, Ross returned and was associated with the sutler's store at Fort Gibson as part of the Union's Third

Regiment of the Indian Home Guard. Seeking to reunite his people, Ross encouraged Cherokees who had left their homes to return and lead peaceful lives.

When the war ended, Ross was a member of the Cherokee delegation attending a peace conference at Fort Smith, Arkansas, in September 1865. After Cherokee chief John Ross died in October 1866, the national council elected William P. Ross to complete the term. Ross continued to work for tribal unity. When Ross's term was up, Rev. Lewis Downing became chief, only to die in 1872. Again Ross was asked to complete the chief's term through 1875; he did and then stepped down.

Ross returned to journalism and became editor of the *Indian Journal* at Muskogee through 1876. He later edited the *Indian Chieftain* at Vinita and the *Broken Arrow* at Fort Gibson and later at Tahlequah.

William P. Ross died in 1891 at Fort Gibson and is buried in Citizen's Cemetery. While he is remembered as the father of Oklahoma journalism, Ross also is remembered as a fine writer, orator, and servant to the Cherokee people. Ross's influence on the Cherokee people still stands unchallenged.

William Porter Ross.
Courtesy of Research Division, Oklahoma Historical Society (no. 6373).

Jane Austin McCurtain

JANE AUSTIN MCCURTAIN was an Oklahoma pioneer and a woman ahead of her time. She became a leader of the Choctaw Nation and helped to shape its educational and political affairs. Jane Austin's story begins when she was born in 1842 near Fort Towson in what is now southeastern Oklahoma. Her father, Lewis Austin, was a full-blood Choctaw. He was mechanically inclined and owned mills, gins, and a tannery. Her mother, Mollie Webster, was one-quarter white. Together they sought to give their children the best education possible.

At age eleven, Jane Austin attended the Wheelock Female Academy located northeast of modern Millerton. The academy was established in 1832 by Rev. Allen Wright to educate Choctaw girls to become Christian women. When she graduated, Austin was selected as one of the most promising girls of the Choctaw Nation, and she received a scholarship and attended Edgeworth's Seminary at Pittsburgh, Pennsylvania. When the Civil War became imminent, she left school and headed back to Indian Territory. It took her two months to reach what is now Oklahoma, where she began teaching in a Choctaw school near Doaksville in the fall of 1861. Her teaching was short-lived, however, because Choctaw schools closed during the war.

It was then that she met Jackson McCurtain, a captain in Company G of the First Regiment of the Choctaw and Chickasaw Mounted Rifles commanded by Col. Douglas H. Cooper of the Confederate army. McCurtain later became a lieutenant colonel in the First Choctaw Battalion. After the war ended, McCurtain became prominent in Choctaw politics. In November 1865, Jackson McCurtain married Jane Austin at her home near Doaksville. They would go on to have five children.

For two years, the couple made their home about one mile east of Red Oak. In 1868, they moved to near modern Antlers. There Jackson was elected a senator in the Choctaw Council, and in 1870

Jane Austin McCurtain. Courtesy of Research Division, Oklahoma Historical Society.

he became president of the Choctaw Senate. He held the position until the death of Chief Isaac Garvin, when McCurtain automatically became chief of the Choctaws. He was elected chief in 1880 and again in 1882. During this period, Jane was her husband's primary adviser because of her good judgment. She wrote many Choctaw position papers demonstrating her loyalty to the Choctaw people, both politically and financially.

In 1883, Tuskahoma in Pushmataha County was chosen as the permanent seat of the Choctaw government. The McCurtains moved to the new location as the capitol building was being built. Soon the Choctaw people were becoming progressive, but they had their problems with coal miners, cattle ranchers, and railroads. When the St. Louis and San Francisco Railway, also known as the Frisco, laid its tracks south across the Choctaw Nation, the Choctaw Council refused to pay the railroad to have its tracks run through its capital at Tuskahoma.

After Jackson McCurtain died in November 1885, Jane Austin McCurtain stepped forward to help fill the leadership void among the Choctaws. She was highly respected by her people, who continued to seek her advice and aid. From her home near the council house at Tuskahoma, she exerted a strong influence on the Choctaw Nation for the next thirty-nine years. Just about every piece of legislation passed by the Choctaw legislature was influenced by Jane McCurtain's thinking. She loved her people and knew their history. She worked for their education and their assimilation with the whites.

In 1891, the Choctaw National Council established two new boarding schools. One was the Tuskahoma Female Seminary established near Jane McCurtain's home, and the other was Jones Academy, a school for boys located near Hartshorne. Jane McCurtain was appointed superintendent of Jones Academy in 1894.

She remained as superintendent until the signing of the Atoka Agreement in 1897 when the U.S. government became responsible for appointing teachers to the Choctaw schools. Most of the Choctaw teachers and superintendents, including McCurtain, were dismissed. By 1895, McCurtain was fifty-three years old and had become known as Aunt Jane. She spent the remainder of her life in her home near the Tuskahoma Female Academy, where she regularly invited some of the girls to spend weekends. The girls deemed it a great honor. Jane's slogan was "educate the boys and girls for leadership. The time is coming when we shall need them."

When Oklahoma became a state in 1907, the Choctaw council house was no longer used by Choctaw lawmakers. McCurtain was made custodian of the building, a position she held until her death in 1924. She never lost her dedication to the Choctaw people. In a time when women, especially American Indian women, rarely involved themselves in politics, McCurtain was a true pioneer. Her daily actions reflected her intellect and leadership. Between 1860 and 1924, Jane McCurtain knew every Choctaw chief and the intimate history of her people. Her contributions to Choctaw politics and education are legend.

Quanah Parker, Last Comanche Chief

QUANAH PARKER WAS THE last chief of the Comanche Indians. He reportedly never lost a battle with the white man. His story is that of a remarkable leader who made the transition from Indian life to that of the white man but on his own terms.

Parker was the son of Comanche chief Pete Nocona and Cynthia Ann Parker. His mother was white and had been captured at the age of nine in 1836 when Comanches raided a settlement called Parker's Fort in east-central Texas. In time, she accepted the Indian way of life and became the wife of Chief Nocona as a teenager. Soon she gave birth to a boy named Quanah, meaning "the fragrance of flowers." He was the first of three children she bore.

Exactly when Quanah was born is unknown, but it was between 1845 and 1852. He grew into a strong and capable warrior. In the early 1860s, however, Texas Rangers rode into the Indians' camp on the Pease River in northwestern Texas while the Indian men were away. Cynthia Ann Parker and her daughter Prairie Flower were taken to Fort Cooper. Soon Cynthia's uncle, Col. Isaac Parker, arrived at the fort and talked with Cynthia. He informed her that her mother had died but that a sister and brother were living. Cynthia accompanied Parker to East Texas to see the sister and brother.

Women in the Parker family took Cynthia's Indian clothing away and dressed her as a white woman. Everything Cynthia experienced was a cultural shock. Having lived in the open with the Comanches for twenty-four years, she believed indoor living would kill her and her baby. Her baby, apparently not immune to childhood diseases, died. A little while later Cynthia, heartbroken, died at her sister's home in Anderson County, Texas. When Chief Nocona learned of his wife's and daughter's deaths, he was so grieved that he too soon died.

Quanah soon joined the more powerful band of Comanches that regularly raided white settlements in northwestern Texas and proved

Quanah Parker.
Courtesy of Western History Collections, University of Oklahoma Libraries (Phillips Collection, no. 3303).

to be a natural leader. Col. Ranald MacKenzie took six hundred troops to stop the raids, but they never captured Quanah. The Indians seemed to disappear by magic after each raid. At one point, several Indians were captured, and Quanah's band stopped raiding for fear their captured brothers would be killed by the soldiers. The military concluded that Quanah's Indians were ready for peace and released the captives. Then Quanah's raids resumed.

Again Colonel MacKenzie and his troops tried to locate and capture Quanah and his band without success. At one point, they nearly captured them, but the Indians escaped. The soldiers destroyed the Indians' village and captured about one thousand of their horses. A white doctor carried a note from MacKenzie to Quanah promising fair treatment if he and his four hundred Indians would surrender. Much to the surprise of the military, Quanah agreed, and on July 2, 1875, he and his followers entered the Comanche reservation near Fort Sill.

Following their surrender, Colonel Mackenzie appointed Quanah as the chief of the Comanche people. Older chiefs resented Quanah's youth, his mixed blood, and his desire to learn English. Members of the white Parker family then wanted to claim Quanah, Cynthia Parker's only son. Family members eventually persuaded Quanah to go to Texas to learn the whites' ways and to become a cattle rancher.

In Texas, Quanah soon became ill and was placed on a brass bed that belonged to Parker's grandmother. Quanah begged to be taken outside and to see an Indian medicine man. While someone went in search of an Indian medicine man, a brush arbor open to the north and south winds was constructed in the yard. Quanah lay on a pallet on the ground with his head to the east. While no Indian medicine man could be found, Quanah's grandmother located a Mexican *curandera* who used herbs and prayers to cure illness. As Quanah lay on the ground, the Mexican medicine woman treated him with a bitter tea and said prayers over him while smoking tobacco-filled cornhusks. Quanah soon recovered and announced that he wanted to return to his Comanche people in Indian Territory.

By the time he returned to the reservation near Lawton, Quanah had learned much about the white man's world from his Texas experiences. He adopted his mother's surname and asked to be called Quanah Parker. He claimed land allotments in the area that today includes the town of Cache, and he purchased a twelve-bedroom mansion for his seven or eight wives. He negotiated easements on Comanche land for Texas cattlemen, became a major shareholder in a railroad, and served as an Indian judge. He also lobbied for Comanche rights in Washington, D.C., becoming friends with President Theodore Roosevelt. Parker tried to do right for both his people and his "paleVfaced friends." He is remembered as the man who led his people into the whites' culture after he saw that there was little alternative.

Quanah Parker died on Feb. 23, 1911. He was buried in full Comanche regalia next to his mother, whose body had been reinterred at Fort Sill's military cemetery on Chief's Knoll only weeks earlier.

Oscar Jacobson and the Kiowa Five

OSCAR BROUSSE JACOBSON was thirty-two years old when he moved to Oklahoma to head the School of Fine Arts at the University of Oklahoma in Norman. There he spent the rest of his life focusing world attention on Indian art.

Jacobson's story began with his birth in Sweden on May 16, 1882. In 1890, when he was eight, he came to America with his parents who settled at Lindsborg, Kansas. He graduated from high school and entered Bethany College in Lindsborg, where he studied under internationally known artist Birger Sandzen. Jacobson was graduated in 1908. During the next five years, he taught at Minneapolis College of Art and Design and at the state college of Washington. During the first half of 1915, he studied at the Louvre in Paris. When he returned to the United States, he was hired as director of the School of Art and art museum at the University of Oklahoma in Norman. Years later he recalled, "There wasn't much to direct."

After a year at OU, he took leave and completed a master of fine arts degree at Yale in 1916 and then returned to Norman, where he built a home located at 609 Chautauqua Avenue. He also began to reshape the academic style of art study at OU with a fresh attitude and the palette of the French moderns.

In the late 1920s, something happened that forever changed Jacobson and the study of art. Fewer than sixty miles west of Norman at Anadarko, Sister Olivia Taylor, a Choctaw, began teaching art to Kiowa Indian students at a mission school operated by St. Patrick's Catholic Church. Susie Peters, a woman working for the Indian agency in Anadarko, saw their art and was impressed. Peters organized an art club, encouraging the students to memorialize the Kiowa culture in their drawings. She sent some of the drawings to Oscar Jacobson at OU in 1926.

Jacobson was fascinated with what he saw. The students' art was

The Kiowa Five with Oscar Jacobson at Jacobson's home in Norman about 1928. *Left to right*: Monroe Tsatoke, Jack Hokeah, Stephen Mopope, Jacobson, Spencer Asah, and James Auchiah. Courtesy of Western History Collections, University of Oklahoma Libraries.

flat with ground planes of color. He invited the Indians to become special students at OU. Six Kiowa students—five boys and one girl—came to study with Jacobson. They were James Auchiah (1906-1975), Spencer Asah (1905/1910-1954), Jack Hokeah (1902-1969), Stephen Mopope (1898-1974), Monroe Tsatoke, also known as Hunting Horse (1904-1937), and Lois Smoky (1907-1981).

Smoky's parents rented a large home in Norman where all of the Kiowa students lived while they studied at OU. There the five boys became known as the Kiowa Five. (While Lois Smoky's art was included in nearly all of the early exhibits, she has not received the credit she deserves in the story of what became known as the Kiowa Five.) Jacobson provided the students with art supplies and studio space. He also provided them with a monthly stipend for their living expenses. He ignored suggestions that the Kiowa artists draw in a European style.

During the 1920s and 1930s, Jacobson's home became a meeting place for artists from Norman, Taos, and Santa Fe who were shaking up the art world. At the same time, Jacobson developed a market for Indian art that became known as the Oklahoma School. In time, thirty-one Kiowa artists came to Norman to study under Jacobson. He circulated their watercolors widely throughout the United States. In 1928, their works were featured at the International Art Congress at Prague, Czechoslovakia. The exhibit resulted in another showing in Paris. Newspapers in Paris, London, and elsewhere praised the art. Their work received so much attention that it was next included in an exhibition of southwestern art in New York City. The Kiowa Five became celebrities in the art world.

Jacobson's classes for Indian artists and those developed at the Santa Fe Indian School marked the beginning of the institutionalization of Indian painting. Jacobson lectured widely for the U.S. Park Service. During the Depression, he acted as a technical advisor for President Franklin Roosevelt's Public Works of Art Project in Oklahoma.

Three of the Kiowa Five—Hokeah, Asah, and Mopope—participated in the Intertribal Indian Ceremonies in New Mexico in 1930. Mopope, Auchiah, and Asah painted sixteen murals on the upper walls of the Anadarko Post Office in 1936 and 1937. Today, the works of the Kiowa Five and other Indians are highly collectable. So are more than five hundred landscape paintings that capture with simplicity the grandeur and dignity of the American West.

In 1945, when he was sixty-three, Jacobson retired from OU, but from his home on the northwestern side of the campus he and his wife Jeanne d' Ucel continued to encourage the development of Indian art. In 1951, the University honored Jacobson by naming the building housing the art museum for him. Today, Jacobson Hall is the visitor's center.

Oscar B. Jacobson was eighty-four years old when he died on September 15, 1966. His home, now owned by the University, was placed on the National Register of Historic Places in 1986. Today, the Jacobson House Native Art Center is used to exhibit Native American art and stands as a symbol of this art as a medium that speaks to the spirit of every person.

Part IV

Oklahoma Treasure Legends

*Dreams are true while they last,
and do we not live in dreams?*

Alfred Lord Tennyson

A Few Words about Treasure Legends

THE FOLLOWING QUOTATION APPEARED in the *Omaha World Herald* more than a century ago on May 29, 1904: "Oklahoma, for so many years the home of the outlaw and desperado, has her stories of buried treasure that rival in magnitude the tales of mammoth wealth buried along the Atlantic coast by Captain Kidd and ravagers of the Spanish main." The Nebraska newspaper was quoting from an article printed earlier in the *St. Louis Post-Dispatch* and written by an unnamed correspondent in Guthrie, Oklahoma Territory.

Indeed, Oklahoma has more treasure legends than most states. Most scholars have ignored them, however, because there are few facts and little documentation to prove they are true. Many such legends are based on oral recollections of old-timers, and they are difficult to prove. Still, treasure legends are fascinating because nearly everyone dreams of easy wealth. While such tales often appear to have some basis in fact, most contain more dreaming than anything else. Of course, storytelling was a popular pastime during the late nineteenth and early twentieth centuries before radio and motion pictures. Most communities had their own storytellers to provide entertainment, and there was always the tendency to embellish the stories as they were told and retold.

Some place names given by early settlers undoubtedly enhance many legends. Two examples are Robbers' Roost in the Panhandle and Robbers Cave (now a state park) located north of Wilburton in the hilly woodlands of the Sans Bois Mountains of southeastern Oklahoma. Robbers Cave is indeed a cave, but if any robbers ever used it their names are shrouded in mystery. Near Robbers Cave is the modern Belle Starr View Lodge, but it is doubtful that the female outlaw ever visited the site. Attaching her name to the place, however, does enhance the romance of the area.

Oklahoma's countless treasure legends are part of the state's folklore. They are part of the fabric of the state's history, and they serve a purpose. Maj. J. Fairfax-Blakeborough (1881–1975), an English writer, wrote:

> When a land forgets its legends,
> See but falsehoods in its past,
> When a nation views its sires
> In the light of fools and liars—
> 'Tis a sign of its decline,
> And its glories cannot last.

While the treasure legends that follow are interesting, entertaining, and even colorful, the reader should simply enjoy them as stories and not try to use them as roadmaps for treasure hunting.

Spanish Legends

OKLAHOMA'S TREASURE LEGENDS DATE back to the arrival of the first Europeans. Perhaps the oldest legend is the wildest wild-goose chase in recorded history: Spanish explorer Coronado's search for Quivira, or the Seven Cities of Cíbola, with streets supposedly paved with gold. Coronado probably crossed a portion of modern Oklahoma during the sixteenth century as his expedition wandered over more than three thousand miles of land previously unexplored by Europeans. Coronado never found the seven cities where streets were paved with gold.

By the seventeenth century, other Spaniards penetrated what is now Oklahoma and found the Wichita Mountains near modern Lawton. Spanish miners searched for gold and silver, but there is little proof they found gold in large quantities. However, the Spanish searches for gold gave rise to numerous legends of lost Spanish mines and buried treasures.

In northwestern Oklahoma southwest of the city of Woodward is the site of another Spanish buried treasure legend. In a dry canyon west of the town of Vici, human bones were found about 1900. According to tradition, Indians harassed a Spanish party traveling with several burros carrying gold. The Spaniards supposedly made a stand against the Indians in the dry canyon but buried their gold before being killed by the Indians. The bones were believed to be those of the dead Spaniards. About 1912 a few gold coins reportedly were found in the canyon, but no one has ever reported finding all of the Spanish treasure if it exists.

Another legend involves a Mexican pack train consisting of twenty-six mules traveling from Santa Fe east toward St. Louis carrying profits from a trading expedition around 1849. The Mexicans' mules were reportedly carrying gold bars plus supplies. As the pack train approached a ridge a few miles north of the modern town of

Cheyenne in Roger Mills County, a band of Indians attacked the Mexicans. They managed to fight off the Indians and fled into a ravine that led them to White Shield Creek, which runs west to east toward the modern community of Hammond. In the vicinity of where the creek makes an almost complete circle west of Hammond, the Mexicans made their stand against the pursuing Indians. According to tradition, all of the Mexicans were killed. Since the gold was very heavy, the Indians are said to have buried it.

Nearly fifty years later in 1890, an Indian carrying one gold bar arrived at the Cheyenne-Arapahoe agency. The Indian told the story of the massacre of the Mexicans, saying his grandfathers had been members of the party that attacked the Mexicans. As a result of the Indian's visit and his story of the treasure legend, men in the community searched with him for the gold but apparently never found it. Assuming the gold bars are still buried in the area—and considering that the Mexicans needed twenty-six mules to carry it along with their supplies—there was considerable gold that today would be worth perhaps three million dollars. No one has admitted publicly to having found the gold.

A similar legend is set in southern Cleveland County between Noble and Lexington. At some point in the early 1840s, a party of Mexican traders carrying a great deal of money, much of it in gold, was attacked by Indians after they left Chouteau's trading post—established during the late 1830s—located along Chouteau Creek. During the fight, some of the Mexicans buried their gold, supposedly on the bank of Chouteau Creek under a large walnut tree. When the battle ended, all but one of the Mexicans had been killed, and he buried the bodies of his friends. One Mexican was placed in a grave near where the gold had been buried under the walnut tree. The surviving Mexican then fled on foot and supposedly made his way to Mexico.

According to the legend, around 1900 an old Mexican appeared in the area and searched for the treasure for several weeks before suddenly dying. Just after World War I, Chouteau Creek was diverted to flow into the South Canadian River about two miles north of the town of Lexington, changing the course of the creek and causing the water to carve out sections of land along the banks. About 1920 a hunter discovered a skeleton on the creek's edge located close to the stump of a large walnut tree. Whether the hunter unearthed the treasure is not known, but a farmer in the area later dug up a large iron pot about one-half mile north of the site of Camp Holmes. Inside the iron pot was a small kettle, and inside the kettle was gold dust. It is possible that the Indians or someone else found the treasure and ignored the gold dust. There is still the possibility that the treasure remains hidden for someone to find.

Why Pioneers Buried Their Treasures

BEFORE THERE WERE ANY BANKS in what became Oklahoma, most pioneers kept money in their cabins, houses, or businesses, and most knew they were in constant danger of being robbed by thieves and marauders who crisscrossed Oklahoma from the Kansas line south to the Red River. Because most settlers were poor, outlaws set their sights on those who had obtained some wealth.

One such pioneer was John Hawkins, whose wife was a sister to Gen. D. H. Rucker of the U.S. Army. Hawkins had money. He tilled the land well, and as a trader and a stockman he made money. Hawkins lived about two miles southeast of Tahlequah in a combination log and frame house with great, wide stone chimneys at either end. Earlier it had been the home of William P. Ross, editor of the *Cherokee Advocate* and later chief of the Cherokee Nation. At some point in the 1850s, Hawkins became afraid that robbers might steal his wealth. He took $10,000 in gold and placed it in a metal box that he then sealed. That night he secretly buried the gold somewhere near his home but did not tell his family what he had done. He continued to make money farming, selling stock, and trading. He had no need for the gold he had buried. A few years later, however, Hawkins became ill. His health declined rapidly, and he soon realized he was dying, so he called his family members together at his bedside. When all had arrived, he tried to describe how he had buried the gold in a metal box and where he had buried it. Hawkins's voice failed and he died. He had waited too long to tell his secret. Family members searched for the buried gold but reportedly never found it. Hawkins's house near Tahlequah was destroyed by fire during the early 1900s.

Another legend is also set in the Cherokee Nation near Tahlequah in the early 1830s. An outlaw calling himself Chief Blackface, who claimed to be a Seminole, gained the reputation of being a robber who stole anything he wanted. Facts are thin, but he may have been a slave somewhere in the South who fled to Florida and was taken in by the Seminole Indians. In time, Blackface came to Indian Territory, where he became an outlaw. At one point, he attacked and killed a party of Mexican traders carrying gold. The legend tells how Chief Blackface hid his plunder in a cave located in the hills around modern Tahlequah. If there was a treasure, no one has admitted to finding it. Some old-timers in the area privately believe the treasure is still hidden waiting to be found.

Another story involving a well-known Indian has more substance. It is set in the area northwest of Atoka about 140 miles south of Tulsa. Benjamin Franklin Smallwood owned a farm west of Lehigh in Coal County and a dry goods store in Lehigh and was a stock raiser. It was common knowledge among those from whom he bought cattle that when it came time to settle up, Smallwood would go into the back room of his store, take the lid off an apple barrel filled with cash, and pay the seller.

About 1888, Smallwood was elected chief of the Choctaw Nation. In 1891, during his term, the federal government paid the Choctaw Nation for lands and coal mines. Chief Smallwood called a special session of the tribal council and asked the council to authorize the distribution of the monies before an audit. Times were difficult and the council gave its approval. For his work Smallwood reportedly received $5,500 from the funds disbursed.

It was cold when Smallwood started for his home. He rode through heavy rain with his $5,500. When he arrived home, he was not feeling well, and he did not have the money. He told his wife he had buried it on his farm under a mulberry tree. By morning, Smallwood had pneumonia. He died on December 15, 1891, at the age of sixty-two.

According to tradition, as Smallwood was dying, he whispered to his wife, "Remember the mulberry tree." Although his widow and others searched for Smallwood's buried treasure on the farm, it apparently has never been found.

Bryan County Treasures

ABOUT 1803, THE YEAR THE United States purchased Louisiana Territory from France, the area that later became Oklahoma was an unsettled region without any organized government or law and order. Bandits from Mexico traveled back and forth from south of the Rio Grande northeast into modern Missouri, robbing and stealing. Legend has it that they had a favorite camping place along the Blue River in modern Bryan County, Oklahoma. One site in particular was located about ten miles northeast of modern Durant. There the Blue River has many rapids, waterfalls, and ledge drops.

The legend relates how, after a successful raid into Missouri, the bandits returned to their camp on the Blue River with an iron strongbox containing about $105,000 in gold coins. It is unclear if other bandits or Indians followed the gang from Missouri, but, soon after the outlaws returned to their camp, riders trailing the robbers surrounded them. At first the Mexican robbers held off the attacking men, but, realizing that they could not hold out long against the attackers and that the strongbox was too heavy to carry, the leader ordered his men to bury the box. This was done before the Mexicans managed to escape and flee south into modern Texas.

The legend was made known in a story written by Paul Stephens for *The Oklahoman* on March 21, 1909. Writing from Durant, Stephens reported that a new group of searchers calling themselves the Mexican Treasure Exploration Company were digging a shaft on the site near the banks of the Blue River ten miles northeast of Durant. The shaft caved in, and the group gave up their search. Earlier treasure hunters had dug similar shafts but failed to find the treasure. Whether treasure hunters made later attempts to locate the strongbox is not known.

The region along the Blue River in Bryan County is the home of other treasure legends. One involves Jesse James, who supposedly had a private cache of loot in or near a cave in Bryan County. Most accounts say the cave had a small opening that led to two large rooms that were connected to each other by a small tunnel. How the legend came to be is not recorded, but during the early 1930s treasure hunters dynamited the cave twice trying to find the treasure but never found it.

Still another Bryan County legend involves four kegs of gold coins that were supposedly hidden in a cave close to the Blue River about five miles northeast of Brown, Oklahoma, which is northwest of Durant. The legend relates how during the Civil War Confederates stole four kegs of coins from the Union army in southern Kansas. The Confederates then fled south only to be attacked by outlaws who killed the Confederates and went to a camp on the Blue River. There outlaws supposedly hid the kegs in a cave before leaving quickly. The legend says the outlaws never returned to recover the treasure.

Hidden Treasures

A COMMON THEME IN TREASURE legends involve outlaws who are forced to bury or otherwise hide their loot from robberies because they are being chased by other outlaws or lawmen. One such legend involves four outlaws who robbed a bank in Wichita, Kansas, around 1900 and escaped with about $40,000 in gold coins. They fled south into Oklahoma Territory as a posse was organized and soon gave chase. The outlaws managed to outride the posse as they headed southwest toward the Wichita Mountains. Each outlaw reportedly carried his share of the loot, about $10,000 in gold coins. In time, the weight of the gold slowed the men's travel as their horses became tired.

As the outlaws neared the Wichita Mountains, a band of Indians attacked them, forcing them to make a stand and fight on the prairie. Soon two of them were killed and a third was seriously wounded. The fourth man was slightly wounded but, according to the legend, managed to recover the gold carried by the other three and bury it under cover of darkness. The injured outlaw then fled south into Texas, where he soon recovered. However, he then became ill and ended up in a Dallas hospital, where his condition became serious. When he realized he was dying, he confided to a friendly nurse the story of the robbery, telling her where the treasure was buried near the Wichita Mountains.

One version of the legend relates how the gold was buried in the rocks southwest of Mount Scott, but what is believed to be a more accurate account says it was buried Comanche County about four miles west and two miles south of modern Geronimo, Oklahoma, which is located several miles south of Lawton and the Wichita Mountains. The nurse later organized a party of four men and came to search for the treasure. They never found it.

The legend was forgotten until early in the twentieth century when a hired man struck something suspicious while digging postholes. He called his employer, who unearthed a gallon bucket, which seemed very heavy. The employer took the bucket to a bank in Lawton. There, a few days later, a group of men including the banker opened the bucket. What it held was never made public, but it did not hold the gold coins. The discovery renewed the legend, however, which persists today.

Still another tale of buried loot is set in and around the Arbuckle Mountains in south-central Oklahoma. The story tells of an army paymaster with army pay and his military escort bound for Fort Arbuckle being killed by outlaws on Mill Creek near Davis. Most of the outlaws were also killed, but one, a Mexican, managed to bury the stolen money before escaping. The surviving Mexican fled the area, but years later in the 1930s a party of Mexicans, apparently using information provided by the surviving outlaw, arrived in the area and camped on Mill Creek. They allegedly recovered some of the plunder but not all of it. Whether or not the remaining loot has been located is not known.

Another yarn about buried treasure does not include any outlaws. When Lt. Col. George Armstrong Custer and his Seventh Cavalry marched down the Washita River in 1868, his soldiers stopped to rest on Panther Creek near modern Clinton. The soldiers began to gamble, and one soldier won most of the money and decided to bury his winnings. Legend says it was secretly buried next to an old oak tree. Before leaving, the soldier made a map showing where he buried the money; however, sometime later, when he returned to the area, he could not locate the buried money.

Early in the twentieth century, a man named Redman and a friend were riding in the area and recalled the legend of the treasure. Redman jokingly said, "If I thought there was a buried treasure buried by the oak tree, I'd take a rod and run it down there." Redman's friend later returned to the location alone and tried the experiment. Based on what happened next, he apparently found the treasure. Redman's friend, a poor man, soon bought a farm and paid for it with cash.

There are two other treasure tales set in northeastern Oklahoma. The first story goes back to about 1873 when an Indian rancher named Lindsay lived on what local residents called Scaley Back Mountain, sixteen miles southeast of Claremore, northwest of Chouteau. Lindsay owned a large herd of cattle and drove them south into Texas. He sold them at Denison, Texas, for about $20,000, much of it paid for in gold. Lindsay returned to the Scaley Back Mountain area and for safekeeping buried the gold in a ravine near modern Chouteau. A few days later Lindsay was found dead. His treasure has never been found.

The second tale of treasure in northeastern Oklahoma is set near the town of Jennings, west of Sand Springs. A prominent landmark in the area is the Twin Hills, two low hills or mounds strewn with rock. Tradition has it that a government paymaster with a cavalry escort heading for Fort Sill was attacked by a band of Indians in the area. When the soldiers realized they were outnumbered, the paymaster supposedly buried $11,000 in gold. Only five soldiers survived the battle. Some of them later returned to the area but never located the gold.

The Tres Piedras Legend

THE SITE OF THIS TREASURE LEGEND is near modern Boise City in the far western Oklahoma Panhandle. The legend begins with Pierre LaFarge, an excommunicated French priest, who about 1800 was released from a French prison after serving time for murder. LaFarge sailed to America. Although he had been kicked out of the Catholic Church, he posed as a priest to find lodgings and food as he traveled across America. In New Orleans, he met a group of twelve other Frenchmen who were shady characters in their own right. LaFarge joined them in sailing across the Gulf of Mexico to Matamoros, Mexico. The former priest fit in perfectly with the other Frenchmen. They were determined to fill their pockets with anything valuable in the New World.

In Mexico, they learned that someone had buried silver and gold near Chihuahua for safekeeping. Ten heavily armed Mexicans guarded the treasure. Deciding to steal only the gold, the Frenchmen, fully armed, surprised the Mexican guards and killed all but two. LaFarge and the other Frenchmen carried off more than one hundred pounds of the gold but left the less valuable silver. Meantime the surviving guards notified Spanish authorities, who went after the criminals. LaFarge and the others fled north with the gold into what is now New Mexico.

When they reached the sleepy village of Santa Fe, they learned that gold had been discovered in the mountains somewhere near Taos to the north. They headed there and soon set up a placer mining operation near several small streams. Not having much mining experience, they found only a little gold, but working as miners was perfect cover for disposing of some of the stolen gold. In time they learned that more experienced Mexican miners had much success. Months after LaFarge and the Frenchmen arrived near Taos, they decided the nearby Mexican miners had accumulated sufficient gold worth stealing.

As the story is told, LaFarge and the others began robbing and killed more than twenty Mexican miners in the region. After a few months, the Frenchmen had acquired a large amount of gold, but their plundering had been expensive. The Mexican miners did not give up their gold easily. Six of the Frenchmen were killed in the robberies, leaving only LaFarge and six others. Somewhere in the mountains near Taos the seven men discussed what to do with the gold. LaFarge believed it should be taken back to France, where they could enjoy life to its fullest, and the others agreed. The men decided that LaFarge should pose as a priest, go to Santa Fe, find someone with smelting experience, and bring that person back to turn the gold into ingots.

At some point during the summer of 1804, LaFarge found José Lopat, a native of Spain, about thirty-five years old, living in Santa Fe. Lopat had worked with metals in Mexico City before moving north to Santa Fe. He returned with LaFarge to the mountains near Taos and built a small furnace to construct a mold. It took him three months to convert the gold into seven hundred ingots, each weighing seven and a quarter pounds. Together all of the gold ingots weighed more than five thousand pounds.

Their plan was to take the gold to New Orleans, where they thought they could ship it to France with some ease. Preparing for the journey, LaFarge and the six other Frenchmen acquired oxen and six large oxcarts that they filled with fur pelts. Outwardly, the carts appeared to be filled with furs, but hidden underneath were the gold ingots equally divided among the carts. The Frenchmen then hired about fifteen Indian servants, obtained supplies, and started east from the mountains onto the plains of what is now northeastern New Mexico. José Lopat traveled with them because he said he knew the country.

Exactly what happened next is not clear, but the party apparently followed trails used by Spaniards, Mexicans, Indians, and other travelers. The one they followed went east into what is now the Oklahoma Panhandle and may have followed what later was known as the dry route of the Santa Fe Trail. While the journey was slow because of the weight carried in the oxcarts, it apparently was uneventful until they reached a watering hole called Flagg Springs near the modern town of Boise City, Oklahoma, and several miles east of Black Mesa—the highest point in Oklahoma at just under five thousand feet—in modern Cimarron County—the only county in the United States that borders on four states (Colorado, Kansas, New Mexico, and Texas).

At Flagg Springs, the party found four traders who were heading west. One of the Frenchmen supposedly mentioned to the traders that they were taking furs to New Orleans, because they believed they could get a better price from fellow Frenchmen than from the Spanish in New Spain, who resented the French. The outlaws were surprised when the traders told them that France had sold Louisiana Territory to the United States in 1803. LaFarge and the others did not outwardly show much concern about the news until the four traders broke camp and continued west. They then had a serious discussion and concluded that when they reached New Orleans, the American authorities probably would not permit them to ship their gold to France and would confiscate it. When José Lopat was asked his opinion, he said arrangements could be made for a boat to meet the party along the Gulf Coast to transport the gold. He suggested that two of the best-fit Frenchmen go ahead to New Orleans, see what kind of arrangements could be made, and then return to the party. Lopat said such a round-trip would probably take three and a half months. LaFarge and the others decided to take Lopat's advice.

Two of the Frenchmen set out for New Orleans while LaFarge and the other two began to make a temporary camp near Flagg Springs. When four months had passed and the two Frenchmen had not returned from New Orleans, LaFarge and the others decided they had better bury the gold for safety; they also agreed that it would be a good idea to send José Lopat and the Indian servants back to Santa Fe before they buried the gold. To make certain that they would not leave, stop, and then come back to watch where they buried the gold, at least one of the Frenchmen escorted Lopat and the Indians more than a hundred miles in the direction of Santa Fe.

Details on what happened next are hazy, but the gold was buried in the ground near Flag Springs, and apparently stone markers were set nearby in the ground. The legend tells us it was about a year before anything happened. LaFarge, whose health was failing, returned to Santa Fe, where José Lopat happened to see him on the street. LaFarge told Lopat that all of the Frenchmen were dead and that he alone knew where the gold was buried near the spring. LaFarge apparently claimed that Indians had killed the others, but Lopat suspected LaFarge had killed the remaining Frenchmen. Regardless, Lopat learned that LaFarge was suffering from tuberculosis. He had returned to Santa Fe in hopes the higher altitude would cure him. Once it did, he planned to return to Flagg Springs and recover the gold ingots.

LaFarge never returned. He was soon bedridden, and a relative of a miner killed earlier by LaFarge and others near Taos learned the Frenchman was in Santa Fe. The miner's relative organized a posse to lynch LaFarge, but the former priest learned of this plan and with the help of a friend was placed in an oxcart under hay and taken somewhere outside of Santa Fe, where he died two weeks later.

Later, when José Lopat learned of LaFarge's death, he decided to journey to Flagg Springs and locate the buried gold. He made an extensive search but found nothing, not even any signs of digging. He soon returned to Santa Fe, where he later died on June 4, 1856, at the age of about eighty-seven years.

If it had not been for Lopat, however, the legend of the buried gold might have faded into history. Before he died, the old man began to tell the story, knowing he would never be able to return to Flagg Springs. Born in 1819, Lopat's son, Emanuel heard the tale many times and wrote down more than fifty pages telling it in the back of the Lopat family Bible. After Emanuel died in Denver, Colorado, in

1906, his sister, Angelina, had possession of the Bible. After she died in 1925, the bible was inherited by her niece, Mrs. Frank Boyles, of Denver.

Efforts to locate the Lopat family Bible today have not been successful, but it is the basis for the legend. Since the early 1840s, the legend has spread by word of mouth across the plains. Many treasure seekers have tried to find the gold ingots, but no one has ever said they were successful. Today, they would be worth more than two million dollars.

The Treasure Belle Starr Sought

THE INFAMOUS BELLE STARR is a central figure in a treasure legend set in the area near Briartown in Muskogee County. The area is known as Youngers' Bend and is located on the South Canadian River. After her first husband, outlaw Jim Reed, was killed, she reportedly lived with Bruce Younger for a short time in Kansas, and then she married Sam Starr in the Cherokee Nation in June 1880. Sam was twenty-three and she was thirty-two. At the time this story takes place, Sam and Belle were looking for a place to hide, and Youngers' Bend was then in the midst of outlaw country where fugitives from the law sought refuge.

Sam Starr supposedly told Belle about a Cherokee outlaw called Big Head, who had taken possession of a cabin and nearby land after the owner had left for points unknown. Big Head had recently died, and Sam said he had heard that he had buried $10,000 in gold on his land near Briartown. The couple agreed that the area would be a good place to hide from the law and that they could search for the alleged buried treasure. They moved into Big Head's cabin and took over the ten acres of land around it. They then began looking for the treasure but had no success. Their part of the story ended when Sam Starr died following a gunfight at Whitefield in Haskell County in 1886. Three years later in 1889, Belle Starr was killed in an ambush.

If Big Head's treasure actually existed, the Starrs apparently never found it. Countless other people have since searched for the legendary $10,000 in gold coins. If anyone found the treasure, they did not brag about it in public.

Belle Starr. Courtesy of Western History Collections, University of Oklahoma Libraries (Payne Collection, no. 2).

The Legend of California Gold

SOME TREASURE LEGENDS HAVE only one source and are difficult to document and prove. One such story came from a man named William Marks, who lived in what is now Pottawatomie County south of modern Shawnee in the late nineteenth century.

About 1898 Marks was traveling between Wetumka and the Arbeka Trading Post when drizzle and sleet began to fall. Since it was near dark, Marks stopped at the Andrews farm and found lodging for the night. As he was unhitching his team from his wagon, Bob Deere, a neighbor of Marks, rode up in his wagon with another man, named Timpkins. They also were seeking lodging for the night.

After Timpkins went inside the farmhouse, Marks asked Deere what he was doing in the area some distance from his home. Deere, an Indian who stood six feet, three inches tall, told Marks that Timpkins was a "money hunter." Deere then told Marks that in 1852 he was scouting for the government and working out of Fort Gibson. One night a white man rode up to his house asking for help. The man had been wounded, and Deere's wife treated his wounds. Mrs. Deere nursed him for about two weeks, but he did not recover and died. Before his death, the unidentified man told Deere that he was from Tennessee and related that when gold was discovered in California he and two other men went west to strike it rich. They found gold and then set out to return to their homes in Tennessee using two packhorses to carry their gold nuggets and gold dust.

Their trip was uneventful until they got to what is now central Oklahoma. A gang of outlaws started chasing the three forty-niners through the Cayenne Mountains (which are actually hills). The three men kept ahead of the outlaws and crossed Dog Ford on the Canadian River and then hid in some thick brush. They decided to bury their gold, which was in four sacks made of buffalo hide.

Near where they were hiding was a large red oak tree, underneath which they buried their gold. One of the trio then climbed the tree and carved a picture of a man with one arm and a chopping knife in his hand pointing down and to the southwest where they had buried the treasure. The three men then set out for Fort Gibson. Near Bald Hill the outlaws spotted the trio and gave chase. Two of the men were killed, but the third—although wounded—escaped as darkness fell. He wandered for a time until he saw a light in Deere's house and stopped for help. Deere said he had told the story to Timpkins, who said he could find the gold. Deere told Marks they were heading for Dog Ford when they decided to stop for the night.

After spending the night at the Andrews farm, Marks recalled that Bob Deere, without saying anything to anyone, suddenly left the next morning, leaving Timpkins without transportation. What happened during the night is not known, and Marks never saw Deere again. He later learned that Deere died of lung fever within a few days of leaving the farm. Marks related that he told no one about Deere's story. Two years later Marks had moved to the Creek Nation, and one morning he went hunting not too far from Dog Ford and met Harve Malot, who worked at the bank in Okemah run by W. H. Dill. Marks and Malot were talking about hunting when Marks noticed a large hole in the ground nearby. When he called Malot's attention to the hole, Malot said he had dug it, and Marks asked him what he was digging for.

Malot then confided in Marks and said he was digging for California gold that supposedly was buried in the area. Malot told a story similar to that told to Marks by Bob Deere two years earlier. Malot told how he had found two skeletons on the western side of Bald Hill that had been there for a long time. He said one of them had a bullet hole through the skull. Marks did not tell Malot that he had heard a similar story from Bob Deere, and the two men soon parted company.

Two weeks later Marks returned to the area to conduct his own search. After some time, he found a tree with a carving of a man with one arm pointing downward. It was about ten feet off the ground in a post oak tree, not a red oak as Deere had related. Marks climbed the tree and found that the carving was partially covered by bark that had grown over it. He spent some time digging in the area but found no gold.

It was not until 1931 that Marks told his story to Hazel Ruby McMahan, who was collecting pioneer stories for the Oklahoma Society of the Daughters of the American Revolution. After Marks told the story, he took McMahan to the area where he found the carving on the tree. Unfortunately, someone had cut down the tree, but its stump was still there. It was located about a quarter of a mile from a church near Dog Ford. The woman described the site as being on the North Canadian River above Baley Bridge, not far from what was the Dill Ranch.

Whether the story of the California gold is true is anyone's guess. If it is, no one has reported finding the gold.

He Did Not Know the Treasure Was There

A STRANGE TREASURE TALE IS set on a farm near Delhi in western Oklahoma in 1917. Just how long C. T. O'Kelley and his wife had lived on their farm is not known. They made a living raising livestock including hogs.

One day in June two young men appeared at the farm. Mr. O'Kelley had gone to a nearby town on business, leaving his wife alone. Early in the afternoon two young men arrived at the O'Kelley farm and knocked on the door. They asked Mrs. O'Kelley if they might inspect some of the hogs that were for sale. She gave them permission and returned to her house chores. The two young men stayed in the hog lot until after dark and then left.

Mr. O'Kelley returned from his trip a little while after the two men left, and his wife told him of the visit. Although the hour was late, Mr. O'Kelley took a lantern and went to the hog lot. He noticed that a large round stone that had been buried deeply in the ground in the center of the lot had been removed and was overturned on the ground nearby. Next to the stone was a large lard bucket that had been dug out from under the stone. The hole in the ground where the bucket had been was still visible. Holding his lantern close, Mr. O'Kelley could make out impressions of twenty-dollar gold pieces at the bottom and on the sides of the bucket, which had been nearly filled with the coins. Later he determined that the bucket probably had contained about $30,000 in gold coins before it was dug out.

This story was related in the June 24, 1917, edition of *The Oklahoman*. Mr. O'Kelley apparently reported the matter to local lawmen. From his wife's description of the two men, he learned that one man probably was a recently released convict from the Oklahoma State Penitentiary at McAlester. The other one was thought to be related to the first. A few days later an uncle of one of the young men, who lived in Greer County, reportedly deposited five thousand dollars in gold in a bank.

How the gold coins came to be buried on the O'Kelley farm and where they came from remains a mystery. As for O'Kelley, he told friends that he knows how it feels to be almost rich.

Part V

Outlaws and Lawmen

*Where there is no law,
there is no freedom.*

John Locke

The Mystique of Oklahoma Outlaws

IN 1930, THE WELL-KNOWN WRITER J. Frank Dobie wrote that "the only genuinely interesting men that Oklahoma has produced have been Indians and outlaws." This was five years after Dobie, who became a nationally known writer, stepped down as head of the English Department at Oklahoma A&M University (now Oklahoma State University) in Stillwater and returned to his native Texas.

Oklahoma did have many interesting Indians, and some of their stories are told in this book. Oklahoma's outlaws were also interesting, as a few of their stories told between these covers suggest. Some outlaws were daring and colorful. Many were small-time criminals who never learned right from wrong, and most came from broken homes and lacked formal education. None was a mental giant.

Oklahomans have been fascinated by its outlaws, probably because many of the early settlers were poor and had little formal education. They found it difficult to make a decent living. The outlaws, by contrast, thanks to mostly sensational newspaper reports, appeared colorful, romantic, and courageous enough to take what they wanted. Poor Oklahomans admired them. Some even imagined the outlaws to be like Robin Hood, stealing from the rich and giving to the poor. A few outlaw tales bear out the truth of this championing of the poor, but most outlaws kept their spoils. The views of many early Oklahomans were similar to those held by poor Mexicans who were fascinated by bandits. In Mexico, banditos were the folklore heroes, and many Oklahomans viewed their outlaws in a similar light.

Such was not the case in most other areas of the American West, where outlaws were generally viewed as bad men (and a few bad women). Vigilantes frequently took care of the outlaws by hanging them. Outside of Oklahoma, hardworking cowboys became the heroes after eastern writers made them appear glamorous. Eastern writers marveled at the hired men on horseback armed with six-guns and often carrying large knives. Cowboys dressed in strange clothing and wore large hats, and they did much of their work from the back of cow ponies.

Early Oklahomans also viewed outlaws differently because of their state's history. Indian Territory was free of white man's courts. Following the Civil War, Indian Territory became a haven for cattle rustlers, horse thieves, whiskey peddlers, and bandits from neighboring states. The only court with jurisdiction over Indian Territory was the U.S. Court for the Western District of Arkansas located at Fort Smith. The judge was corrupt, however. In 1875, President Ulysses S Grant replaced the corrupt judge with thirty-eight-year-old Isaac Parker, who hired two hundred deputy U.S. marshals to bring law and order to Indian Territory.

Some of the marshals were black because Indians distrusted white deputies. Among Parker's black marshals were Rufus Cannon, Ike Rogers, Grant Johnson, and Bass Reeves, the first black deputy marshal west of the Mississippi, whose story is told in this book. During the next twenty-one years, Judge Parker tried more than 13,000 cases. One hundred and fifty-six men and four women were sentenced to death by hanging. Seventy-seven were actually hanged. More than sixty of Parker's U.S. marshals and deputies were killed in the line of duty. Indian Territory appeared to be exciting and dangerous, and it caught the fancy of newspapermen who reported on the exploits of outlaws.

The infamous Belle Starr was convicted of horse stealing in Parker's court in 1882. She was sent to federal prison. When released, she returned to her home near modern Eufaula, where she was murdered in 1889. Her killer was never brought to justice.

Crawford Goldsby, better known as Cherokee Bill, became well known for robbing and killing at least seven, possibly thirteen, people. His career was short. When he was captured in the 1890s and taken to Parker's court, Goldsby was found guilty and hanged. He was only twenty years old.

The notorious Buck Gang was led by Rufus Buck and consisted of Sam Sampson, Maoma July, and brothers Lewis and Lucky Davis. They robbed, murdered, and raped. All five were found guilty and hanged in 1896.

Parker also tried civil cases. The most important was against David Payne, a Boomer, for illegally settling on lands in Indian Territory. Payne did not live to see the Unassigned Lands opened to settlement in 1889 and the founding of Oklahoma Territory. When the territory was formed, so was a new federal court at Guthrie, the territorial capital, from where U.S. marshals sought to track down outlaws. The jurisdiction of Judge Parker's court in Indian Territory ended in the fall of 1896, but outlaws continued to plague Oklahoma through the depression 1930s. There were nearly two hundred outlaws in Oklahoma between the end of the Civil War and the late 1930s, and many were convicted of their crimes. The majority were white, a fourth were black, and about twenty were Indians.

Into the 1920s, however, convicted outlaws were often granted leaves of absence from prison. A few early governors were lenient toward convicted criminals, including some who had committed major crimes. Some governors even gave convicted criminals leaves of absence from prison in what can only be called scandalous circumstances. Respect for law and justice was not uniform. But this began to change by the late 1930s when the era of outlawry started to fade into history.

On the pages that follow are the stories of Bill Doolin, perhaps Oklahoma's worst outlaw; Al Jennings; Al Spencer; "Pretty Boy" Floyd; and some of the early lawmen who brought many outlaws to justice.

Bill Doolin, Oklahoma's Worst Outlaw

PERHAPS THE MOST NOTORIOUS outlaw in early Oklahoma was William M. "Bill" Doolin, the son of an Arkansas farmer. Born on August 25, 1858, in Johnson County, Arkansas, Bill's early years were hard. His father died when he was seven. Bill had little schooling. As the only son, Bill had to help his mother run the family farm.

In 1881, when he was twenty-three, Bill left home and found a job helping to freight goods from Caldwell, Kansas, into Indian Territory. Bill soon met Oscar D. Halsell, a Texas cattleman who operated a cattle ranch on the Cimarron River about thirteen miles east of Guthrie. Because Bill had learned much about construction on his mother's farm, Halsell hired Doolin to construct ranch buildings and corrals. When Halsell learned that Doolin could not read or write, he taught him. Soon Bill was keeping the ranch books for Halsell, who trusted him completely.

After most of Halsell's cattle died during the vicious winter of 1882 and 1883, Bill went to Texas with Halsell to buy more cattle. Doolin worked for Halsell until about 1888, when the federal government ordered all cattlemen to leave the Unassigned Lands. Halsell abandoned his ranch.

Out of work, Doolin found a job on a ranch near the Pawnee agency on the Cimarron. A few months later a restless Doolin drifted into southern Kansas and worked on a ranch near Arkansas City. By this time, Doolin's outlook on life was changing. Thousands of settlers were moving onto what had been the open range after the Unassigned Lands were opened in April 1889. Doolin apparently became angry at the invasion of the land he loved. He moved to what is now northeastern Oklahoma and found work with Texan Tom Waggoner, who had obtained grazing rights in the Osage Nation northwest of Tulsa and had started the 3-D ranch. Doolin worked for Waggoner until 1890, when Oscar Halsell convinced Bill to move to the new town of Guthrie, where he had opened a livery stable. Doolin worked for Halsell during the winter of 1890 and 1891, but he did not like town life and resented the businessmen and their money.

At some point, Doolin met some of the Dalton brothers, whose parents lived eight miles north of Coffeyville, Kansas. Several of the Dalton boys worked as cowboys in Indian Territory. In the summer of 1891, Doolin went to Coffeyville to celebrate the Fourth of July, and several of his cowboy friends joined him. Doolin got two half-barrels and filled them with ice and beer, ignoring the fact that Kansas was then a dry state. When Coffeyville lawmen arrived and started confiscating the beer, Doolin and the other cowboys got into a gunfight, and two lawmen were wounded. Bill Doolin became a wanted man and soon joined the Dalton Gang to rob trains. However, when the Daltons tried to rob two banks at Coffeyville in the fall of 1892, Doolin was not with them—a fact that probably saved his life because four of the five outlaws in the gang were killed.

Doolin soon organized his own gang and robbed a train at Caney, Kansas, escaping with $1,500. Some days later, they robbed the bank at Spearville, Kansas, of $4,500. The gang's reputation grew as did the rewards for their capture.

In March 1893, Doolin married a preacher's daughter, Edith Ellsworth, in a secret ceremony at Kingfisher, Oklahoma Territory. In time they had one child, Jay Doolin, who later took the name Samuel Meek. For a wedding present, the gang robbed a train at Cimarron, Kansas, stealing one thousand dollars, but as Doolin fled, he was shot in the left foot. He recovered but had a limp the rest of his life.

When lawmen learned that the gang was in Ingalls, a town east of Stillwater, two wagons filled with lawmen rushed there on September 1, 1893. The outlaws were playing cards in a saloon. When one of them stepped outside, lawmen saw him and started shooting. Three marshals, two citizens, and two outlaws were killed in the battle that followed. One outlaw was captured, but Bill Doolin escaped.

After reorganizing his gang, Doolin robbed a bank of $262 at

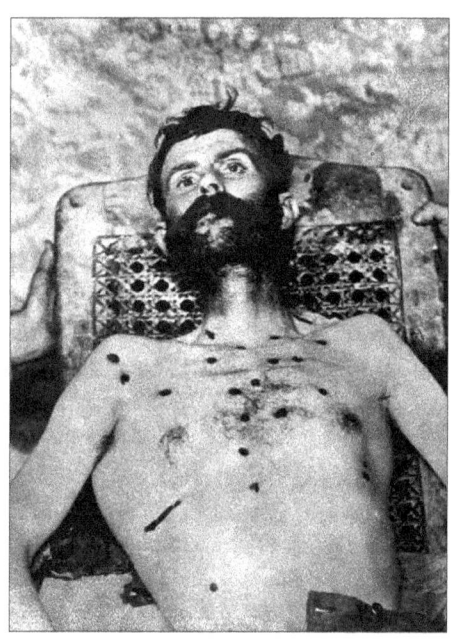

Bill Doolin in death. Courtesy of Western History Collections, University of Oklahoma Libraries (Rose Collection, no. 2040).

Pawnee, held up a railroad station in Woodward, and then took more than $3,000 from a bank at Southwest City, Missouri. By then the gang was getting too large, Dalton took some of the members and robbed a Rock Island train of nearly $1,500 at Dover, Oklahoma Territory. A posse chased them and killed one of member of Doolin's gang. It was the Doolin gang's last robbery.

Doolin fled to Eureka Springs, Arkansas, only to be captured and returned to Guthrie for trial, but he soon escaped and fled to New Mexico. Doolin was eventually located near Lawton, where he was visiting his wife and son. On August 25, 1896, lawmen found Doolin and ordered him to surrender. When he refused, Doolin was shot and killed. His body was buried in the Boot Hill section of Summit View Cemetery in Guthrie.

No one knows how many people were killed by Doolin and his gang. While he reportedly stole nearly $165,000 during his five years of crime, Bill Doolin's tragic end proved that crime does not pay.

William Coe, Oklahoma's Least-Known Outlaw

OLD-TIME NEWSPAPERS USUALLY CONTAINED information on the exploits of early Oklahoma outlaws. It was good copy and it sold papers, but present-day Oklahoma was not populated with newspapers until after Indian Territory was opened to white settlement in 1889. Because of this, William Coe may be Oklahoma's least-known outlaw. While Coe's career of crime lasted only a few years before territorial and statehood days, his story contains the adventure and excitement found in Hollywood westerns, and it deserves a page in the history of Oklahoma outlaws.

Coe's early life is mostly a mystery. By most accounts, he was a stocky man of about 175 pounds with whiskers and a moon-shaped faced. He supposedly was in his mid-thirties when he arrived in what is now the Oklahoma Panhandle at some point after the Civil War.

Where Coe came from is also unknown. One account describes him as a Texas farmer who became a captain in the Confederate army. When the Civil War ended and Coe returned to Texas, he found his home in ruin and his livestock stolen. It was then, according to this account, that he became an outlaw. Another account that rings truer claims that Coe was a stonemason and carpenter employed for a time during the Civil War at Fort Union on the plains of modern eastern New Mexico, and later at Fort Lyon on the banks of the Arkansas River in eastern Colorado. The facts are thin in both accounts.

Evidence is also lacking as to when Coe arrived in what is now Oklahoma, but it probably was about 1864. He found the region around Black Mesa to his liking. At the western end of today's Oklahoma Panhandle, Black Mesa—almost a mile high—is the highest point in the state. The location was perfect for Coe and his kind. The present-day Oklahoma Panhandle was then only a lawless and unsettled strip of land between Kansas and Texas called No Man's Land.

Four miles northeast of modern Kenton, Oklahoma, where Carrizo Creek meets the Cimarron River, Coe and his men are believed to have built a large stone building on a ridge that jutted out from a mesa. The location gave them a clear view of the Cimarron Valley and north up Carrizo Valley. The stone building had no windows, only four-inch square portholes that widened to eighteen inches or more on the outside. The portholes not only gave Coe's men good coverage when firing their weapons but also provided ventilation.

One account says the building was sixteen by thirty-six feet with walls thirty inches thick and a fireplace at each end and one door. Another account says there were two doors. The roof consisted of cottonwood ridge poles tightly laid next to each other and covered by a foot or more of dirt, which kept the building cool during hot

William Coe's "Robber's Roost" near Black Mesa in the Oklahoma Panhandle. Painting by Wayne Cooper, commissioned by the Oklahoma State Senate Historical Prevention Fund.

weather and warm in the winter. Coe reportedly brought in a piano, had a bar constructed, and even invited soiled doves—prostitutes—to live there. How many actually moved in is not known, but the hideout was so isolated and so far from other settlements that once they arrived they probably stayed a while. Coe apparently figured that having plenty of whiskey and girls was one way to keep his gang members together when they were not raiding and robbing.

In time, the stone building became known as Robbers' Roost, not to be confused with perhaps a half-dozen other "Robbers Roosts" scattered across the West, including one in southeastern Utah, another in southeastern Oregon, and still another in Wyoming.

It was to this area that Coe quietly gathered his gang. No one knows for sure how many men were in his gang. Estimates have ranged from thirty to fifty. They were not always together since Coe might send one group to rustle cattle and another to steal horses or other livestock.

In a small canyon about five miles from Robbers' Roost, Coe set up a blacksmith shop. It was equipped with tools stolen from Santa Fe traders. He even had a large anvil that may have been stolen in Kansas or Missouri. Here his men could shoe their horses and perform other ironwork. Near the canyon there was a pasture where the outlaws could keep horses, mules, and cattle. From Robbers' Roost, Coe and his gang roamed free far and wide, but they were not yet called the Coe Gang.

Perhaps the earliest documented account of Coe's adventures relate to a raid he led with his gang to the gold mining area around Elizabethtown, New Mexico Territory, and then a raid to steal mules from Fort Union. A detachment of the Third Cavalry captured Coe and three of the stolen mules. Other members in his gang apparently scattered with the other animals and loot before the soldiers arrived. Coe claimed he was innocent and demanded a chance to clear himself. Not knowing he was an outlaw, the soldiers turned him over to civil authorities. He was arraigned before a justice of the peace and bound over to the next term of court at Mora, New Mexico Territory. Coe paid his bond, however, and fled to Fort Lyon in Colorado Territory, where earlier he reportedly had or did work as a civilian.

In the meantime, a former New York City detective named Barrett was sent west to help the army put a stop to the robbing and rustling. He joined the Seventh Cavalry at Fort Lyon and was quickly promoted to the rank of sergeant. When he told General Penrose that he could catch the thieves, he was asked how many men he needed. Barrett said he needed only one good man who knew the country and two mules. General Penrose asked for volunteers, and the man who stepped forward to go with Barrett was none other than William Coe—known to both Penrose and the quartermasters at Fort Lyon where he had once worked. They agreed that Coe would be a good man to accompany Barrett. Both Coe and Barrett were given two cavalry horses, two pack mules, two Colt forty-five revolvers, and one Winchester rifle, along with ammunition, rations, and money.

It was a cool fall day when Barrett and Coe left Fort Lyon and headed south across the high plains. They rode twenty-five miles before stopping for the night at a ranch owned by two men named Higbee and Smith. The next morning Barrett and Coe, dressed in civilian clothes, resumed their journey south. Many days later a rancher discovered Barrett's body, buried with a rope still around his neck. When word reached Fort Lyon, Coe was labeled an outlaw and a wanted man.

After killing Barrett, Coe apparently fled to his hideout near Black Mesa. Days later, just after Christmas 1867, Coe and his gang rode into Trinidad in what is now southern Colorado, robbing, killing, and raping. They simply overwhelmed those they attacked, ignoring all civil and military authority. When Coe learned that a Mexican living in Trinidad had sent word to Texas rancher Charles Goodnight and his cowboys camped north of town asking for help, Coe and his gang fled south.

Old-timer accounts relate how Coe and his gang rustled and robbed throughout northeastern New Mexico and southern Colorado. They so intimidated ranchers and civil and military officials that they were a power unto themselves. Rarely did anyone oppose them. If they did, they knew they would be killed. From their hideout near Black Mesa, the outlaws occasionally raided freight caravans traveling the lower Cimarron Route of the Santa Fe Trail that crossed what is now the far western end of the Oklahoma Panhandle not far from Robbers' Roost.

In the spring of 1868, Coe and his gang stole more than three thousand sheep from the grazing camps of Juan and Vicente Baca and Juan and Ramon Bernal of Las Vegas, New Mexico Territory. The sheriff from Trinidad, along with soldiers and armed citizens, trailed the sheep and surrounded Coe and his men while they were playing cards at a ranch on the Purgatoire about twelve miles above Boggsville, Colorado. The prisoners were sent to Fort Lyon but escaped within two weeks. Since no one knew Coe was one of the men, the search for him resumed.

Coe had the habit of stopping at ranches and making himself at home, knowing no one dared oppose him. More than a week after he escaped from Fort Lyon, Coe stopped at such a ranch near Madison, New Mexico Territory, and asked that his horse be fed. He then told the woman in the ranch house to prepare a meal for him. Once he finished eating, he went to the bunkhouse and lay down for a nap. The woman who kept the ranch sent her son to catch soldiers who earlier in the day had stopped there looking for Coe. The soldiers soon returned and took the sleeping Coe prisoner. The soldiers took him to Pueblo, Colorado, where Coe was jailed to await trial.

Luke Cahill, an old trapper, was one of the guards at the jail. He later recalled that after the sun set on July 20, 1868, a small party of soldiers called at the jail and said it was necessary to move Coe to new quarters. The jail was opened and the men put Coe in a wagon. Coe protested when the men put a rope around his neck and drove under a large cottonwood tree not far away on the bank of Fountain Creek. Charles W. Bowman, a Pueblo newspaperman wrote in 1881, that Coe was "privately hung by a committee of soldiers—it was believed at the instigation of their superior officer. Certain it is, they were not court marshaled, nor was there any public demonstration of sorrow for the deceased."

On July 23, 1868, the *Colorado Chieftain* reported that the morning after the execution Coe's body was found hanging from the tree, still handcuffed and in leg irons. The paper reported that the body was cut down and buried beneath the tree. Many years later when Pueblo officials were excavating for a new road in the vicinity of Fourth Street, workers found the skeletal remains of what was believed to be Coe.

After Coe's death, his gang members were dealt with and lawlessness in the region declined. The stone structure that was Robbers' Roost remained and may have been used in later years by other outlaws as a hideout. Today, however, only what appears to be the foundation of Coe's hideout remains. It is located on private property in the Oklahoma Panhandle, and permission must be obtained to visit the site.

Bass Reeves,
the Most Feared U.S. Deputy Marshal

ON THE SPRING DAY OF May 10, 1875, a six foot, two inch, two-hundred-pound former slave stood in front of Judge Isaac Parker at Fort Smith and was sworn in as a deputy U.S. marshal. The man was Bass Reeves. He was destined to become the most feared lawman in Indian Territory.

Born a slave in 1838 in Paris, Texas, Reeves took the surname of his master, George Reeves, a farmer and politician. When he got into a fight with his master in the early 1860s, Bass Reeves fled north into Indian Territory and lived with Seminole and Creek Indians. He became a crack shot with a pistol and so skilled with a rifle that he was barred from competitive turkey shoots. When the Emancipation Proclamation of 1863 freed him, Reeves moved to Arkansas and homesteaded near Van Buren. Once he got his farm going, he married Nellie Jennie from Texas. They began raising a family, and in time they had ten children—five boys and five girls.

Reeves and his family farmed until 1875, when Isaac Parker was appointed federal judge in Fort Smith. Parker appointed James F. Fagan as U.S. marshal. It was Fagan's job to hire two hundred deputy U.S. marshals. Fagan heard about Bass Reeves, who knew Indian Territory and could speak several Indian languages, and he recruited Reeves as a deputy U.S. marshal. Reeves was sworn in and began riding through Indian Territory. Parker's court covered 75,000 square miles, then the largest district of any U.S. court in the nation. Reeves made several eight-hundred-mile roundtrips from Fort Smith to Fort Reno, Fort Sill, and Anadarko. When Reeves was given a stack of warrants for outlaws, he would get someone to read them to him because he could neither read nor write. He would memorize the warrants and then leave Fort Smith taking a wagon, a cook, and a posse man.

Bass Reeves. Courtesy of Western History Collections, University of Oklahoma Libraries.

Reeves rode a large red stallion with a white blaze. He carried two Colt pistols and always wore a black hat, nice clothes, and polished boots. He had the look of a lawman and was soon known throughout Indian Territory. He often would be gone for months, tracking down outlaws. When he returned to Fort Smith he was paid in fees and rewards, usually one thousand dollars but sometimes more. After paying his expenses, he might make four hundred dollars in profit, unless he collected a large reward. Reeves would then visit his family before setting out again in search of outlaws.

There are countless stories about Reeves. He liked people, but he was fearless. Once, after learning where two outlaws were hiding in the Red River Valley near the Texas border, he took a large posse to a spot twenty-eight miles from where they were hiding. He told his posse to wait in camp. Reeves disguised himself as a tramp, wearing old clothes and a floppy hat with three bullet holes; hid his pistols, handcuffs, and badge in his clothes; and walked the twenty-eight miles to the home of the outlaw's mother. Reeves told the woman that his feet hurt and that he had been chased by lawmen who shot him but only hit his hat. She invited him in and gave him water and food. She told Reeves her two sons were also outlaws and suggested he wait for them to return and join up with them.

When the two outlaws returned that night, the three men talked. The outlaws agreed that Reeves should join them. Everyone then went to sleep. Early in the morning Reeves quietly handcuffed the pair. At the first light of dawn, he kicked the outlaws, made them get up, and marched them outside. As they walked away from the house, their mother cussed Reeves until the party was out of sight. Reeves walked the outlaws many miles to where his posse was waiting.

Among the many outlaws Reeves tracked down was Bob Dozier, wanted for murder, robbery, and a long list of other crimes. In 1878, Reeves located him in the Cherokee Hills, and Dozier was killed by Reeves in a gunfight.

When Oklahoma became a state in 1907, Reeves's duties as a deputy U.S. marshal ended. During his thirty-two years as a marshal, he arrested more than three thousand outlaws and killed at least fourteen people in gun battles. Reeves joined the Muskogee police department but saw little action during his two years on the force. In 1909, he became ill and was diagnosed with Bright's disease. He retired and died January 12, 1910. Bass Reeves is buried at Muskogee in the old Union Agency Cemetery.

The Misadventures of Al Jennings

THE NAME AL JENNINGS has faded from the memory of many Oklahomans. This outlaw claimed to have killed eighteen men; however, no record can be found proving that he killed anyone during his career as a cowboy, lawyer, gunman, train robber, convict, evangelist, politician, movie actor, and consultant to Hollywood westerns.

Alphonso J. Jennings was born November 25, 1863, in Virginia. His father, J. D. Jennings, moved to Missouri following the Civil War, and later the family moved to Oklahoma, where the father served as probate judge in Woodward and Tecumseh. Exactly when Jennings arrived in Oklahoma is something of a mystery. He was in Kansas about 1884, where he supposedly was admitted to the bar in Comanche County at the age of twenty-one.

After the run of 1889, he served as a prosecuting attorney in Canadian County at El Reno, Oklahoma Territory, from 1890 to 1894. The next year he moved to Woodward, where his two brothers, Ed and John, had opened a law practice. A few months after Jennings arrived in Woodward, his brother Ed was killed and John was wounded in a shootout with Temple Houston, son of Texan Sam Houston and a rival attorney in Woodward.

After Houston was acquitted in 1896, Jennings left Woodward and went to work as a ranch hand in the Creek Nation. Near Bixby in Tulsa County, he joined a gang of outlaws, and by late 1897, the outlaw gang was frequently referred to as the Jennings Gang. They robbed a post office, one or two trains, and a general store. Exactly how many robberies they pulled is still debated. Robbing was not very profitable. In one train robbery, they fled with only three dollars. Some say they also took a jug of whiskey.

The Jennings Gang lasted only a few months. In late November 1897 Jennings was wounded by lawmen, captured, and sentenced to life in prison, where his cellmate for a time was reportedly William

Sidney Porter, better known as O. Henry, the well-known writer. Jennings's lawyer brother John got Al's sentence reduced to five years, and he left prison in 1902 and received a presidential pardon from Theodore Roosevelt in 1907.

Two years later Jennings married a woman named Maude who had visited him in prison. Maude was at least six inches taller than Jennings, who was a small man. By 1911, the couple was living in Oklahoma City where Al entered politics. In 1912, he won the Democratic nomination for Oklahoma County attorney, but he lost in the general election. Jennings then turned to religion, became an evangelist, and went on the lecture circuit. He was not a success, and he returned to practicing law. Two years later, he ran unsuccessfully for governor of Oklahoma. When he lost, he was quoted as saying, "There's more honesty among train robbers than among some public officials."

Following his political failure, Jennings decided to capitalize on the fact that his name was known in every Oklahoma home. With the help of a professional writer, Jennings produced his autobiography about his days in Oklahoma. The New York City house D. Appleton published his book *Beating Back* in 1915. A movie producer liked the book and made it into a film starring Jennings as himself. The movie was filmed in New Jersey and had the same title as his book. It tells the story of a man who beat back at society until it recognized and honored him. The film was hardly the truth.

Jennings next formed his own film company in what is now Culver City, California. He produced and starred in *The Lady in the Dugout* in 1918. The film had only moderate success. Although Jennings soon sold his film company, he found acceptance among movie people in growing Hollywood. They were charmed to have a "real-life outlaw" in their midst. Jennings became an adviser to movie studios producing western pictures. He also acted in more than one hundred silent and early sound pictures including *Hands Up* (1917), *The Ridin' Rascal* (1920), *The Sea Hawk* (1924), and *Loco*

Al Jennings. Courtesy of Research Division, Oklahoma Historical Society (no. 2728).

Luck (1927). He usually played villains in the films.

With money earned from movies, Jennings and his wife purchased a small ranch in Tarzana, California, in the western end of the San Fernando Valley, and raised chickens. He found pleasure sitting on the front porch of his ranch house telling stories about his earlier life in Oklahoma to anyone who would listen.

In 1945, Jennings attracted national attention when he sued the producers of *The Lone Ranger* radio program. During the previous year they had mixed fiction with real people drawn from history. In an episode that aired on August 7, 1944, the Lone Ranger met Al Jennings, but Al did not like the way he was portrayed. Jennings claimed he was the "fastest gun on the range." Eighty-two at the time, he said, "They had this Lone Ranger shooting a gun out of my hand, and me an expert." Jennings lost his case. However, he was pleased in 1951 when Columbia Pictures produced the highly fictionalized film *Al Jennings of Oklahoma,* starring Dan Duryea as Jennings. Anything but a true biography, the film portrayed Jennings as a brave man of gallant deeds. It added to the myth that Jennings sought to create.

In 1961, Jennings's wife died. Heartbroken, he went to bed and died four weeks later. Al Jennings is buried in Oakwood Memorial Park at Chatsworth in Los Angeles County next to his wife. The simple gravestone reads "Al Jennings of Oklahoma, 1863–1961."

Bill Tilghman, Lawman

OLD WEST LAWMAN AND GUNSLINGER Bat Masterson referred to him as "the greatest of us all." Teddy Roosevelt once said, "He would charge hell with a bucket." Both men were speaking of Bill Tilghman, a frontier lawman who had more courage than most.

The story of William Matthew "Bill" Tilghman began in Fort Dodge, Iowa, where he was born on July 4, 1854. He left home by age fifteen and hunted buffalo on the southern plains with his older brother Richard. During the next several years, the two roamed the plains, reportedly killing hundreds if not thousands of buffalo for their hides. The Tilghmans sold the hides in Dodge City, Kansas. When nearly all of the wild buffalo on the southern plains had been slaughtered, the Tilghmans gave up hunting shaggies and moved to Dodge City. There in the spring of 1877 Bill Tilghman and Henry Garis became owners and operators of the Crystal Palace saloon.

The following year someone claimed Tilghman had been involved in a train robbery in a neighboring county. He was found not guilty. A few months later Tilghman was again arrested, this time for horse stealing, by Ford County sheriff Bat Masterson. Tilghman was found not guilty.

Tilghman and Garis continued to operate the Crystal Palace saloon. At some point, Bill Tilghman's father and younger brother Frank moved to Dodge City. At about the time they arrived, Tilghman was hired as a Ford County deputy sheriff at Dodge City. It was his first job as a lawman. He helped to capture a horse thief, but newspaper reports reveal little more about his life as a lawman during this time.

During the spring of 1878, Tilghman and his partner sold the Crystal Palace saloon. Soon Tilghman bought another saloon called the Oasis for his brother Frank to run. The *Dodge City Democrat* reported that the specialty of the Oasis would be "Methodist cocktails and hard-shell Baptist lemonades."

When Cheyenne Indians raided white settlements on the southern plains in the fall of 1878, Tilghman was hired as a scout by the U.S. Cavalry at nearby Fort Dodge. He was back in Dodge City within a few months and set his eyes on becoming city marshal. When George M. Hoover, a wholesale liquor dealer, became mayor, Tilghman got the job and Thomas C. Nix was hired as assistant marshal. Tilghman also continued as a deputy sheriff.

Tilghman soon became ill with the bacterial infection erysipelas, commonly called St. Anthony's Fire, which caused bright red blotches on his face and lower extremities. Assistant Marshall Nix took over his duties. When Tilghman recovered within a few weeks, the *Dodge City Globe* reported that his friends presented him with a forty-dollar gold badge to welcome him back. Whether or not the new badge helped, Tilghman and Nix kept law and order in Dodge City until March 1886. Tilghman resigned as city marshal one month before his term was to end. He became a cattleman, but he retained his commission as a deputy sheriff and occasionally performed law enforcement duties. He also was hired to police voting polls in newly organized Wichita County, located northwest of Dodge City. Settlers there were arguing over which new settlement should be the county seat.

On Tilghman's thirty-fourth birthday, he shot and killed Ed Prather, a saloonkeeper who threatened him. The killing was ruled self-defense. Six months later Tilghman was asked to help several other deputies charged with transporting county records from Cimarron after the Kansas Supreme Court made Ingalls, Kansas, the county seat. The lawmen were carrying out a court order when some Cimarron men started shooting. One man was killed and eight others were wounded in the gunfight that followed. Soon after the battle, Tilghman decided to leave Kansas and what he considered the "game of law and disorder." He was attracted to Oklahoma's first land run and on April 23, 1889, arrived in the new town of Guthrie. When

Guthrie's town marshal, Bill Grimes, asked Tilghman to serve as deputy town marshal, he accepted. After the Organic Act was passed in 1890 and a federal court was established at Guthrie, Grimes and Tilghman were appointed deputy U.S. marshals.

Tilghman and other deputy U.S. marshals, especially Heck Thomas and Chris Madson, set out to bring law and order to Oklahoma Territory. Thomas, a native of Georgia, was first a police officer in Georgia and Texas before becoming a deputy U.S. marshal in Isaac Parker's court in 1886. Madson, a native of Denmark, came to the United States in 1876 and joined the U.S. Cavalry. After serving at Fort Reno and elsewhere in Indian campaigns, he left the army in 1891 and became a deputy U.S. marshal in Oklahoma Territory. Outlaws called Tilghman, Thomas, and Madson The Three Guardsmen. They are credited as being largely responsible for cleaning up nearly all of the horse-riding outlaws in Oklahoma.

Tilghman became well known when he captured the notorious Bill Doolin in Eureka Springs, Arkansas, in January 1895. Thomas later killed Doolin near Lawton. In 1910, three years after Oklahoma became a state, Tilghman retired as a deputy U.S. marshal. Soon he was elected to the Oklahoma state senate. He resigned that position in 1911 to become chief of police in Oklahoma City.

Tilghman enjoyed watching silent motion pictures, especially westerns, but when he viewed a film produced by former outlaw Al Jennings in 1913, Tilghman said the film's portrayal of lawmen was slanderous. Tilghman and some associates produced their own film, the five-reel *The Passing of the Oklahoma Outlaws,* to correct the misconceptions in Jennings's film. Tilghman and other former marshals appeared in the film. After it was edited, Tilghman took a print and began touring Oklahoma towns to show the film and give lectures, where a 151-page book written by Richard Graves (his real name was Capt. Lute F. Stover) was offered for sale. Stover had also written the script for Tilghman's film. The book related Tilghman's experiences as a lawman.

Bill Tilghman. Courtesy of Western History Collections, University of Oklahoma Libraries (Rose Collection, no. 1756).

After the discovery of oil in Oklahoma, Tilghman was asked to come out of retirement and clean up the boomtown of Cromwell, Oklahoma, and put a stop to the gambling, prostitution, and other criminal activities. On Halloween night, 1924, the seventy-year-old Tilghman was killed by a federal prohibition officer, Wiley Lynn, who was arrested and tried for the crime. The jury accepted Lynn's account of the shooting that he fired at Tilghman in self-defense.

Citizens and lawmakers paid tribute to Bill Tilghman's memory when his body was taken to the state capitol in Oklahoma City. His final resting place is in Oak Park Cemetery at Chandler in Lincoln County, where a large stone marks the grave.

Tilghman has not been forgotten. On October 18, 1994, the United States Postal Service issued its Legends of the West series of twenty-nine-cent postage stamps. They also released the series on postcards.

Each stamp features the likeness of one of several prominent figures in the Old West. They included Buffalo Bill, Annie Oakley, Chief Joseph, Bill Pickett, Charles Goodnight, Wild Bill Hickok, and Bill Tilghman. Eight years later the Oklahoma State Senate Historical Preservation Fund commissioned and later dedicated a portrait of Tilghman painted by Harold T. Holden that may be viewed today in the state capitol.

Al Spencer, Forgotten Outlaw

THE NAME AL SPENCER WAS once well known in Oklahoma. Countless newspaper stories told of his exploits as a bank and train robber, but, because he plied his trade toward the end of the era of horseback-riding outlaws, Spencer is mostly forgotten today.

Ethan Allen "Al" Spencer was born the day after Christmas in 1887 near Lenapah in modern Nowata County. He came from a law-abiding farm family. Like many other young men, he married early, and he soon was the father of a baby girl. Why he turned to crime in his early thirties is not known, but in 1916 he was arrested in Nowata County on four counts of cattle theft.

In 1919, he and two other badmen burglarized a clothing store in Neodesha, Kansas. The Burns Detective Agency was hired to track down the criminals. Detectives recovered most of the stolen goods and arrested Spencer in La Junta, Colorado. He was returned to Kansas, where a court convicted him of the crime and sentenced him to five years in prison. Before Spencer was sent to the Kansas penitentiary, Oklahoma authorities gained custody so they could try him on charges of cattle theft. Spencer pled guilty and was sentenced to three to ten years in the Oklahoma penitentiary at McAlester, where he was taken in March 1920.

Spencer became friends with another convict named Henry Wells, a veteran outlaw born in Virginia who grew up in Wheaton, Missouri. Wells left home after trouble with a girl and went to Indian Territory and found a job as a cowboy. He married and lived in a cabin in Lost Creek Canyon southwest of Okesa. His minor troubles with the law grew around 1914 when he began robbing banks, perhaps a dozen. He was arrested in 1915, convicted of bank robbery, and sentenced to ten years in the McAlester prison. From Wells, Spencer learned a great deal about robbing banks.

In the 1920s, when it was not unusual for Oklahoma governors to grant convicts leaves of absence, Spencer was given leave on July 26, 1921, to attend to family business. He returned to McAlester a month later, where he became a trustee and was trained to be an electrician. Early in 1922, he was assigned to do electrical work outside the prison in someone's home. He completed the work, packed up his tools, and fled McAlester. Within a month, Spencer made contact with Silas Meigs, who had earlier fled the prison in a similar fashion. The pair robbed the American National Bank at Pawhuska, escaping with $147. Soon the two men robbed a bank at Broken Bow, taking between $7,000 and $8,500. They forced a motorist to drive them three miles north of town, where they had left two horses. The robbers rode away.

A few days later Meigs was killed in a gun battle with lawmen northwest of Bartlesville, where he had gone to visit his brother. In the meantime, Spencer hid in the Osage Hills, a vast stretch of country with timber, rocky canyons, and thickets of almost impenetrable scrub oak. Friends and relatives brought him food.

Spencer then joined up with Henry Wells and two other outlaws and robbed a bank at Pineville in southwestern Missouri. A few days later lawmen spotted the robbers. One of them was wounded, but Spencer and the others escaped. Spencer hopped a freight train bound for Oklahoma. He soon found three other men to help him burglarize a store in Ochelata south of Bartlesville. They were surprised by the town's night marshal, who was shot and killed by the outlaws. They fled in a car. On June 16, Spencer and another man robbed the Elgin State Bank in Chautauqua County, Kansas, escaping with about $2,000 in cash and $20,000 in bonds. Spencer returned to the Osage Hills.

Soon more banks were robbed. On July 26, 1922, four masked men held up the Citizens' National Bank in Spencer's hometown of Lenapah, fleeing with $1,339. On September 8, they held up the First State Bank at Centralia north of Vinita. The robbery netted them nearly $3,000 in cash and $200 worth of bonds.

Exactly how many banks were robbed by Al Spencer during the eighteen months following his escape from prison in McAlester is not known. Evidence suggests he probably robbed at least twenty banks in Oklahoma, Kansas, Missouri, and Arkansas. While rewards for his capture totaled only $500 early in 1923, by July of that year they climbed to nearly $2,000. Spencer's desire for fame grew, and he began comparing himself to earlier Oklahoma outlaws like Bill Doolin and Cherokee Bill.

On August 21, 1923, Spencer and his hired outlaws robbed the Katy Limited, train No. 123, at Okesa in Osage County and stole registered mail packages from the postal express car. The search for Spencer intensified.

The end came on a Saturday evening, September 15, 1923, when he was shot and killed. How and where he was killed, however, remains something of a mystery. U.S. marshal Alva McDonald, a veteran lawman and personal friend of Teddy Roosevelt's, claimed he and other lawmen waited along a dark road in northern Oklahoma just south of Caney, Kansas. Lawmen yelled, "Hands Up!" when he appeared, but Spencer fired at the lawmen and they shot him dead. Another account found in the *Bartlesville Daily Enterprise* reported that Spencer was not killed in Oklahoma but about five miles north and a half mile east of Coffeyville, Kansas, near a schoolhouse. A third account can be found in outlaw Henry Wells's autobiography, in which he claims that Stanley Snyder, a friend of Spencer's, killed the outlaw with a shotgun while Spencer was eating supper with his back to Snyder. The only thing certain is that outlaw Al Spencer was shot and killed on September 15, 1923.

Two days later his body was displayed at a funeral home in Bartlesville and viewed by 15,000 curious people. His body was then taken by train to Nowata. Burial was in Ball Cemetery near Childers in Nowata County. Only his widow, twelve-year-old daughter, and two or three other people attended the burial.

Al Spencer's outlaw days were over, but a new breed of badmen soon took his place using only automobiles. Spencer was the last major Oklahoma outlaw to use horses in his crimes.

Pretty Boy Floyd, Bank Robber

THE DEPRESSION 1930S WERE not easy for most Oklahomans. Many people were poor, and, if stories in newspapers and on radio were to be believed, the only easy money was being made by bank robbers who escaped in automobiles.

The story of Charles Arthur Floyd, better known as Pretty Boy Floyd, is part of Oklahoma's colorful history of the period. Floyd, however, was not an Oklahoma native. He was born February 3, 1904, in Bartow County, Georgia, the son of a farmer and one of seven children. The family moved to eastern Oklahoma about 1912 and settled near the small town of Hanson in the Cookson Hills. Times were tough, and to make ends meet Floyd's father became a bootlegger.

Charles attended school and picked cotton to help the family keep food on the table. In 1921, at the age of seventeen, Charles married sixteen-year-old Ruby Hargraves. Finding it difficult to support his wife, Charles left home to find work in the wheat harvest. He located a few jobs and often spent nights sleeping in hobo camps. Soon he gave up looking for work, returned home, and bought his first gun. At eighteen, he held up a post office and got away with pennies. Police arrested him on suspicion, but his father gave him an alibi.

Charles and his wife took a train to St. Louis, where he robbed a grocery store of about $16,000. He bought a new Ford and new clothes. Suspicious of Floyd's sudden wealth, police searched his home and found some of the stolen money. He was sentenced to five years in the Missouri State Penitentiary at Jefferson City. While in prison, his wife gave birth to their son Jack Dempsey Floyd. She then divorced Charles. When he was released, Charles returned to his parents' farm in eastern Oklahoma only to learn that his father had been killed in a family feud with J. Mills, who was acquitted of the crime. Charles took his father's rifle and looked for Mills, who reportedly was never seen again.

By the mid-1920s, Charles was living in East Liverpool, Ohio. He was a hired gun for bootleggers and rumrunners along the Ohio River. A few years later Floyd left Ohio for Kansas City, Missouri, a town that attracted other hired guns and gangsters. Charles made friends among the criminal element and learned how to shoot a machine gun. Charles acquired the nickname "Pretty Boy" from Beulah Baird Ash, a Kansas City madam in a house of prostitution. When police suspected Floyd and some criminal friends of trying to kill a fellow officer, he left town with the friends and headed east to Akron, Ohio.

On Charles's twenty-sixth birthday, February 3, 1930, he robbed a bank in Sylvania, Ohio. It was the first of about thirty banks that Floyd would rob, including several in Oklahoma. Late in 1932 Floyd decided to rob his hometown bank in Sallisaw. A few relatives were tipped off in advance and were in town when Floyd and two other

Pretty Boy Floyd. Courtesy of Library of Congress.

outlaws drove into town. Before robbing the Sallisaw State Bank, Floyd stopped by the barbershop across the street. His seventy-two-year-old grandfather was sitting outside waiting for a haircut. They spoke as Floyd went inside and said "Howdy" to two friends. He told them that he was going to rob the bank and that they should lay off the telephone. Floyd, Aussie Elliott, and George Birdwell then robbed the bank of more than $2,500, forced the cashier to go with them, and left. The cashier was released a few blocks away. The Sallisaw police chief was sitting in his car just around the corner from the bank and did not know the bank was being robbed until he was told afterwards. The sheriff and deputies chased the outlaws by car but failed to catch them. No one was killed in the Sallisaw robbery, but before Floyd's career in crime ended, he killed at least ten people.

On the night of June 16, 1933, Floyd and Adam C. Richetti returned to Kansas City. Richetti had served time in the Oklahoma State Penitentiary for robbing a bank at Sulphur. When Floyd and Richetti learned that some gunmen friends planned to free Frank Nash, another criminal, the following day, Floyd and Richetti offered to help. Nash, who earlier served time for murder in the Oklahoma penitentiary at McAlester, had escaped from the U.S. Penitentiary at Leavenworth, Kansas. Officers soon captured Nash at Hot Springs, Arkansas. He was being returned to Leavenworth when the gunmen tried to free him from lawmen at Kansas City's Union Station. The gunmen killed four officers but accidentally killed Nash.

Floyd and Richetti fled Kansas City for Toledo, Ohio, where they met Beulah Baird and her sister Rose Baird. They traveled to Buffalo, New York, where they rented an apartment. Floyd was living in Buffalo when FBI agents killed John Dillinger in Chicago on July 22, 1934. After Dillinger's death, Charles "Pretty Boy" Floyd immediately became the FBI's public enemy number one. He became a national figure with a price on his head.

Floyd decided to return to Oklahoma. Driving a newly purchased Ford sedan, Floyd, Richetti, and the two women headed west. Near

Wellsville, Ohio, their auto skidded and struck a telephone pole. The women took the vehicle into Wellsville for repairs while Floyd and Richetti hid in some nearby woods with their weapons. When two suspicious men were reported in the woods, Wellsville police went to the area. In a gun battle that followed, Richetti was wounded and captured. Floyd escaped and stole a car. Police and FBI agents converged on the area. They spotted an auto behind a corncrib on a farm. As officers approached, Floyd jumped from the car and ran. Shots were fired and Floyd fell to the ground.

When FBI agents asked him if he was "Pretty Boy" Floyd, he supposedly replied, "I am Charles Arthur Floyd." He soon died; it was October 22, 1934. Floyd's body was taken to a funeral home in East Liverpool. Within hours, perhaps 10,000 people viewed the body before it was returned to Oklahoma. About 20,000 people attended the funeral held in Sallisaw. Floyd was buried in the Akins Cemetery.

Floyd's grave was marked with a headstone, but souvenir hunters desecrated it. In 1985, someone stole it. Today, a new headstone marks his grave of Charles Arthur "Pretty Boy" Floyd, who died at the age of thirty.

Part VI

~

People, Events, and Things

Everyone has his day and some days last longer than others.

Winston Churchill

Will Rogers's Last Interview

IT WAS THE SUMMER OF 1935. At about 3:15 P.M. on a Wednesday afternoon, Wiley Post's large plane flying from Fairbanks dipped out of the sky and flew over a small and rough landing field at Palmer, Alaska Territory. Concerned that Post's plane was too large to land, Joe Crosson, the airport manager, waved them on. They flew on to Anchorage and landed. There, another flyer, Chet McLean, offered to fly Post and his passenger, humorist Will Rogers, back to Palmer in his small plane. It landed in Palmer that Wednesday afternoon, August 14, 1935.

Before Post and Rogers could squeeze out of the small plane, newly arrived settlers—nearly all men—in the Matanuska Valley swarmed around. One asked Rogers how he felt. Rogers replied, "Wait'll I get out, will ya?" When his feet touched the ground, he told the crowd, "I came to look around, not to report on my health." Rogers then said, "Where you boys from? Anybody here from Claremore?" That tickled the crowd, and as they roared with laughter, Rogers grinned. Standing on the fringe of the crowd was Wiley Post, who said, "I thought it was about time for something funny."

Rogers was then given a quick driving tour of the new settlement. It was a New Deal project of President Franklin Roosevelt's. Only weeks before, 203 families from Michigan, Minnesota, and Wisconsin had arrived to establish the Matanuska Colony. Each family drew lots for forty-acre tracts where they were to establish farms. We know the details of Rogers's visit because Arville Schaleben, a twenty-eight-year-old newspaper reporter in the crowd, had been sent by the *Milwaukee Journal* for four months in 1935 to report on the colony and especially on a large contingent of settlers from Wisconsin.

After officials gave Rogers a tour, they returned him to the waiting plane, where Schaleben then interviewed him. When asked how the Matanuska Valley looked, Rogers said, "It looks fine, fine! You got a mighty nice place here. We saw some colonists and caught one guy moving his stove in." Rogers said he would "just as soon be moving in with him." Rogers noticed Schaleben making notes and asked, "Say, you're a newspaper man, ain'tcha? I kinda thought there'd be one looking around here." Schaleben told Rogers that he was correct and that he had been a reporter with the *Milwaukee Journal* since 1929.

A bystander interrupted and asked Rogers if it was true that he and Wiley Post were thinking about flying to Russia and Asia. Somewhat surprised, Rogers asked, "Russia?" Apparently not wanting to answer the question, he said, "Say, I saw a Communist here a minute ago." He turned and pointed a finger toward a man on the fringe of the crowd who had a full red beard that reached down to the third button on his blue work shirt. "There, there he is!" cried Rogers in glee. Everyone laughed.

Will Rogers, shorty before he took off with Wiley Post (right) from a lagoon near Point Barrow, Alaska, on August 15, 1935. Post's experimental Lockheed Explorer sea plane crashed when its engine failed. Courtesy of Western History Collections, University of Oklahoma Libraries (Keith Collection, no. 28).

About then, a construction crew cook rushed up and presented Rogers with six fat, brown cookies just as the humorist was climbing back into Chet McLean's small plane. Rogers took a bite from one and brushed the crumbs from his lips with the sleeve of his coat. "They're good," he exclaimed, "but I'll toss them out if we can't get off the ground." The door closed and the plane began to taxi down the runway.

As soon as the plane was in the air, Arville Schaleben went to where he was staying and wrote his story. At the time, it was a routine report on the humorist and his pilot friend. When Rogers and Post were killed less than twenty-four hours later when their plane crashed near Point Barrow, Schaleben's interview with Rogers became news. It was Rogers's last interview with a newspaper reporter. Schaleben's story was transmitted around the world. It was another contribution to the legend of Will Rogers that has become bigger than life in the minds of people who still remember him. For many young people, it is just a name. They never saw him in the movies, heard him speak, or read his newspaper columns. If they had, his humble and folksy personality and common sense philosophies would have won them over.

At heart, Will Rogers was an Oklahoma cowboy. He was born November 4, 1879, the youngest of eight children, on the family ranch in the Cherokee Nation near modern Oologah. His father was Clement Vann Rogers and his mother was Mary Schrimsher. Both were part Cherokee. As a boy he learned from a freed slave how to use a rope to lasso Texas longhorns on the family ranch. He learned to ride a pony soon after he was old enough to sit in the saddle. He attended several schools, including Kemper Military School at Boonville, Missouri, in 1897 and 1898; however, he dropped out after the tenth grade to be a cowboy. He regretted not finishing school, but in the years that followed he kept learning by reading books and by thinking and talking to educated people.

In August 1898, Rogers was working for Jack Mulhall, a well-known rancher from Oklahoma Territory, who had hired twenty cowboys. They went to Kansas City, Missouri, to participate in the Priests of the Palace parade. During the downtown parade, Rogers roped a large policeman directing traffic. The incident stopped the parade until Rogers untangled his rope around the policeman. That day Rogers earned twenty dollars, reportedly the first show money he ever earned.

In 1902 and 1903, he traveled with Texas Jack's Wild West Show, where he was billed as "The Cherokee Kid," and he was with Wirth Brothers Circus in Australia and New Zealand. Returning to the United States in 1904, Rogers appeared at the World's Fair in St. Louis and in New York City.

His hard-earned roping skills paid off. He became a vaudeville performer, touring the United States, Canada, and Europe between 1905 and 1915. His roping skills and his enjoyment in talking to people while he roped made him a star. In May 1916, he gave his first presidential performance for Woodrow Wilson and two months later joined the Ziegfeld Follies in New York as a comedian and emcee. Two years later, he made his first motion picture, a silent film titled *Laughing Bill Hyde*. It was the first of more than seventy movies he would appear in during his career. By 1933, Rogers was the highest paid film star in Hollywood. While he never won any awards for his acting, he apparently was satisfied in knowing that he created a timeless quality in his film characters, which is still apparent to people viewing his films today.

Rogers moved his family to California in 1919 to be close to the motion picture business. There he and his wife, Betty, made their home and raised their children—Will Rogers, Jr., Mary Rogers, and Jim Rogers. Their youngest son, Fred, died of diphtheria when he was two. The year 1922 saw Will begin writing a syndicated newspaper column. Before his life ended, Rogers would also write six books, penning in all more than two million words. Americans liked Rogers's wit, and he was frequently quoted. He also became a radio commentator; his talks on Gulf Oil radio broadcasts reached millions of listeners.

Many of his remarks are still quoted. One is "Diplomacy is the art of saying 'Nice doggie' until you can find a rock." Other favorite quotations by Rogers include:

"When the Okies left Oklahoma and moved to California, they raised the average intelligence levels in both states."

"An ignorant person is one who doesn't know what you have just found out."

"Ancient Rome declined because it had a senate; now what's going to happen to us with both a Senate and a House?"

"Live in such a way that you would not be ashamed to sell your parrot to the town gossip."

"On account of being a democracy and run by the people, we are the only nation in the world that has to keep a government four years, no matter what it does."

"The best doctor in the world is the veterinarian. He can't ask his patients what is the matter—he's got to just know."

"There's no trick to being a humorist when you have the whole government working for you."

"The more you read and observe about this Politics thing, you got to admit that each party is worse than the other. The one that's out always looks the best."

"The income tax has made more liars out of the American people than golf has."

When the Depression and Dust Bowl hit Oklahoma, Rogers decided to raise money for people back home in need of help. In February 1931, he began a whirlwind tour of Oklahoma at the Shrine auditorium in Oklahoma City, putting on his one-man show. When he was met with a thunder of applause, he strolled on stage and said, "Shut up." All the money from the tickets went to helping Oklahoma people in need. During five days, Rogers flew from town to town to perform at different times of the day. Before the week ended, he had visited twenty Oklahoma towns, having been flown from town to town by well-known pilot Capt. Frank M. Hawks. By the time Rogers did his last one-man show at Tulsa, he had raised more than $100,000 to help rural residents and Indians, the chief sufferers from the drought and Depression. Rogers gave his time free and required that there be no overhead in connection with any of his appearances. Rogers was described as "The greatest farm relief Bill yet."

Since he was a boy Rogers had loved horses, but after taking his first plane ride at Atlantic City in 1915, he added flying to the list, only to die two decades later with his friend Wiley Post. Arville Schaleben went on to cover news from six continents and eventually became associate editor of the Milwaukee paper before his death in 1999 at the age of ninety-two, sixty-four years after he was the last newspaperman to interview Will Rogers.

Oklahoma Symbols and Emblems

FROM THE STATE'S EARLIEST DAYS, the pioneers sought to adapt the trappings of long-established states, including symbols and emblems, to show they were progressive. One newcomer was Frank H. Greer, a newspaperman who worked on his brother's paper, the *Winfield Courier*, in southern Kansas. There Greer learned the newspaper business and soon was determined to have his own paper. He learned from Santa Fe Railroad executives where new towns would be established when the Unassigned Lands were opened to settlement in Oklahoma Territory on April 22, 1889.

The day before the opening, Greer hid in a railroad freight car loaded with telephone poles before it headed south into Oklahoma Territory. With twenty-nine dollars in his pocket, Greer reached the site of future Guthrie the evening of April 21. The next day he jumped out of the railroad car and staked his claim at ten minutes past noon, the hour when the lands were opened for settlement.

Greer immediately established a newspaper, the *Daily State Capital*. He gathered news and returned by train to Winfield, where the first issues of the paper were printed at his brother's press. The paper promoted Guthrie's good qualities to encourage outside investment. Greer wanted Guthrie to become the territorial capital. Although Greer had snuck in the night before the land was officially opened and was a Sooner, his paper criticized others who made illegal land claims. His newspaper became the organ for the dominant Republican Party. Greer helped to found the Oklahoma Historical Society and the Oklahoma Territorial Press Association, and he was elected to the territorial legislature, serving on the Labor, Manufactories, and Home Industry Committee.

Greer was strongly partisan in his desire to make Guthrie the territorial capital. One friend later described Greer as a "vigorous, aggressive, courageous editor." He did everything he could to make

Oklahoma Territory one of the most colorful and picturesque commonwealths the West had ever seen. As a journalist, he understood the importance of symbols and emblems in establishing the desired image. As a lawmaker, he promoted the passage of legislation creating a Grand Seal of the Territory of Oklahoma in March 1893. The description of the seal reads in part:

> Under the motto "Labor Omnia Vincit" [Labor Conquers All Things] shall be Columbia, as the central figure, representing Justice and Statehood. On her right is the American pioneer farmer, on her left is the aboriginal American Indian. These two representatives of the white and the red races are shaking hands beneath the scales of Justice, symbolizing equal justice between the white and the red races of Oklahoma, and on the part of the Federal Government. Beneath the trio group is the cornucopia of plenty and the olive branch of peace, and behind is the sun of progress and civilization. Behind the Indian is the scene depicting the barbarous, nomadic life of the aborigines—teepees, emigrant train, grazing herds, etc., representing Oklahoma in her primeval wildness. Behind the white man is a scene depicting the arts of civilization—farmer plowing, rural home, railroad train, compress, mills, elevator, manufactories, churches, schools, capitol and city. The two scenes are symbolic of the advance of the star and empire westward. The peaceful conquests of the Anglo-Saxon and the decadence of the red race. Under all shall be the words "Grand Seal of the Territory of Oklahoma."

In 1905, the Latin motto on the Grand Seal of the Territory of Oklahoma was incorporated into the official Great Seal of the State Oklahoma at the constitutional convention for the proposed state of Sequoyah that never became a reality. The new seal's center has a five-pointed star within a circle. In the center of the star is the original seal of Oklahoma Territory, and on each of the star's five rays is the seal of one of the Five Tribes—the Cherokee, Chickasaw, Choctaw, Creek, and Seminole nations. The seal also has forty-five small stars representing the U.S. states existing before Oklahoma statehood. The seal's name is labeled around the border with the date 1907 at the bottom.

The story of Oklahoma's state flower is a bit more complicated. It begins in 1893 when officials at the Chicago World's Fair decided that each state should select a unique flower to go in a national wreath. Although not yet a state, Oklahomans wanted to participate and decided on the passionflower; however, when they learned that Arkansas had already selected it, they had to choose a new flower. Mistletoe—or "Christmas flower," as some people call it—has a long tradition of bringing luck to those who kiss under its small branches. It grows on trees in southern Oklahoma, has dark-green leaves and white berries, and is clearly visible during the fall and winter months after trees shed their leaves. The territorial legislature made mistletoe the official flower of Oklahoma in 1893, and three years after Oklahoma became a state, the legislature made it the new official floral emblem.

Even so, by the 1930s many Oklahomans—especially gardeners and garden clubs—objected to mistletoe, pointing out that it is a parasite that survives by attaching itself to trees or shrubs and drawing nutrients from the sap of its host. Gardeners said they wanted a state plant they could cultivate in their home gardens; however, their pleas were ignored. Oklahomans did get a new state wild flower in 1996 when the legislature selected the Indian blanket with its red flowers and yellow tips. It was selected because it symbolizes Oklahoma's Indian heritage and scenic beauty. Another official state flower was added to the list in 2003 when a hybrid tea rose called Oklahoma was selected.

Greer's dreams for Oklahoma were contagious during the state's early years, and many other pioneers joined in establishing other symbols and emblems to help Oklahoma's image. The first Oklahoma flag was adopted in 1911 and was mostly red with a large centered white star with the number forty-six reflecting on Oklahoma as the forty-sixth state. In the early 1920s, however, red flags were closely associated with communism, and in 1924 the Daughters of the American Revolution held a contest to replace the red flag. The winning entry had a blue field and an Indian (Osage) war shield and peace pipe in the center. It was designed by Mrs. George Fluke, Jr., and became the official flag of Oklahoma in 1925. A few years later the word "Oklahoma" was added to the bottom of the flag. The official flag salute, adopted in 1982, proclaims, "I salute the flag of the State of Oklahoma. Its symbols of peace unite all people."

The colors green and white are the official state colors adopted by the legislature in 1915 by concurrent resolution of the House and Senate on recommendation of the Ohyohoma Circle, an organization made up of the wives of members of the Fifth Legislature.

In 1937, the legislature selected the eastern Redbud that grows wild in valleys and ravines as the official state tree. It is colorful in early spring with its reddish-pink blossoms that brighten the countryside. The barite rose rock became the official state rock in 1969. The reddish-brown stone that resembles a rose in full bloom is found only in a streak of rock that runs north and south through the middle of Oklahoma.

The official state bird, adopted in 1951, is the scissor-tailed flycatcher. It has a long, sleek, deeply forked tail that resembles a pair of scissors. Meantime, on the ground is the state's official reptile, commonly called the Mountain Boomer. It is the eastern collared lizard, and it can grow to more than a foot in length and is capable of running on its two back legs. The lizard can be various colors, including blue, green, brown, and yellow and is identified by the distinctive black and white collar around its neck. The American buffalo, or bison, became the official state animal in 1972, and in 1974 the white bass—sometimes called the sand bass—became the official state fish.

In 1990, the raccoon became the official state furbearing animal, and the black swallowtail became the state butterfly in 1996.

Oklahoma also has an official state dinosaur (*Acrocanthosaurus atokensis*), a lizard-eating monster, a genus of allosaurid dinosaur from the Morrison Formation of Jurassic North America. A large skeleton of this dinosaur can be seen in the Hall of Ancient Life of the Sam Noble Oklahoma Museum of Natural History in Norman. Oklahoma also has an official state fossil—*Saurophaganax maximus*, a large, carnivorous dinosaur that roamed modern Oklahoma, preying on small dinosaurs about 150 million years ago. A restoration of the creature is also on display at the Sam Noble Museum.

Most Oklahomans know the state song, "Oklahoma," from Rodgers and Hammerstein's musical (adopted in 1953). Less well known is the official state waltz, "Oklahoma Wind," by Dale J. Smith (adopted in 1982), or the official state country-and-western song, "Faded Love," a blues fiddle swing tune, written by Bob Wills, his father John, and his brother Billy Jack Wills (adopted early in 1988). The official state children's song is "Oklahoma, My Native Land" by Martha Kemm Barrett (adopted in 1996). Also in the realm of music, lawmakers established the fiddle as the state musical instrument in 1984. While the fiddle and violin are essentially the same musical instrument, the fiddle is used in folk music, accounting for why lawmakers chose to identify it as the state instrument.

The legislature made milk the official state beverage in 1985. In 1988, the legislature decided that the official Oklahoma meal is fried okra, squash, cornbread, barbecue pork, biscuits, sausage and gravy, grits, corn, strawberries, chicken fried steak, pecan pie, and black-eyed peas. In 2005, strawberries became the official state fruit, and on November 1, 2007, watermelons became the state's official vegetable.

One wonders if the legislature will proclaim an official medicine to treat heartburn.

David Payne, Boomer

DAVID L. PAYNE WAS AN adventurer, scout, soldier, politician, and Boomer—someone who wanted to settle in Indian Territory, a region set aside only for Indians. Some people call Payne the "Father of Oklahoma," but others oppose the title because Payne died six years before Oklahoma Territory was formed in 1890 and because his actions as a Boomer ignored the rule of law.

David Payne was born on a farm in Grant County, Indiana, on December 30, 1836. He attended a rural school near his home. In the spring of 1858, Payne and his brothers left Indiana intending to fight in the Utah Mormon War. As they headed west across Illinois and Missouri, David Payne's desire to fight waned. Crossing the Missouri River into Kansas Territory, David Payne found beautiful wooded country in Burr Oak Township, Doniphan County, in northeastern Kansas. At age twenty-two, he acquired some land and built a sawmill; however, his business soon failed. He turned to hunting wild game to survive. He became a good hunter and learned to read signs. Impressed with his skills, neighbors hired him to do their hunting. In time, the federal government hired him as a scout on several expeditions. One of them took Payne into present-day Oklahoma in the 1850s.

When the Civil War began, Payne enlisted in the Fourth Kansas Volunteers created to protect settlers from Indians. In April 1862, Payne's regiment was consolidated with another unit, creating the Tenth Kansas Infantry, which saw action in Kansas, Missouri, Arkansas, and Indian Territory. Payne and 386 other men in the Tenth joined more than nine thousand other Union soldiers in the Army of the Frontier participating in the Battle of Prairie Grove that secured northwestern Arkansas for the Union.

Payne left the army in August 1864 and returned to Kansas, where he was elected to the Kansas legislature, serving in the 1864 and 1865 sessions. In March 1865, he enlisted as a private in Company G, Eighth Regiment of Western Volunteers to protect settlers from Indians in western Kansas. After serving a year, he got out and some months later became postmaster at Fort Leavenworth, Kansas, in 1867. In the fall of that year, he reenlisted again as captain of Company D in the Eighteenth Kansas Cavalry and served until October 1868, when he became a captain in the Regular Army's Company H, of the Nineteenth Kansas Cavalry. His service ended in late 1869 after a winter campaign against the Indians on the western plains. For a time, Payne served as a scout for Gen. Philip Sheridan. Payne left the military in 1870 and moved to south-central Kansas, where he again was elected to the Kansas legislature. Later, in 1875 and 1879, Payne served as assistant to the Doorkeeper of the U.S. House of Representatives in Washington D.C.

There Payne became friends with Elias C. Boudinot, a Cherokee attorney working as a lobbyist for the railroads that wanted to lay tracks through Indian Territory. President Rutherford B. Hayes opposed white settlement in Indian Territory, declaring it unlawful for whites to enter the territory. Hayes's action gave supporters of settlement a chance to rally. Attracted to the movement, Payne returned to Kansas, where he learned that another Boomer, Col. C. C. Carpenter, had taken a party of settlers from Coffeyville, Kansas, into Indian Territory. After they reached the North Canadian River, soldiers escorted the group back to Kansas.

Payne organized his own party, entered Indian Territory, and laid out a townsite where Oklahoma City stands today. Soldiers arrested Payne and his group, took them to Fort Reno, and then escorted them back to Kansas. Payne resented the fact that federal law prohibited the military from interfering in civil matters. Payne took another party back to Indian Territory in July 1879. Again soldiers arrested them and this time took them to federal court at Fort Smith, Arkansas. Judge Isaac Parker ruled against Payne and fined him one thousand dollars.

David L. Payne (seated second from left) and other Boomers. Courtesy of Western History Collections, University of Oklahoma Libraries (Phillips Collection, no. 3065).

Payne did not give up. He organized other parties in southern Kansas that tried unsuccessfully to settle in Indian Territory. He even founded a newspaper, the *Oklahoma War Chief*, to promote the cause. On one of his stays in Indian Territory, soldiers seized his printing press, burned the building it was in, and again took Payne and his group to Fort Smith. Soon the public began to complain about the military's treatment of Payne and the others. The case was turned over to the U.S. District Court in Topeka, Kansas. Judge Cassius G. Foster quashed the charges and ruled that settling in the Unassigned Lands was not a criminal offense. Payne's group cheered, but the government did not immediately accept the court's ruling.

Although he did not live to see white settlement occur, Payne continued to work for opening Indian Territory to settlement—an event that did not happen until 1889, over four years after Payne died. His last speech was in Wellington, Kansas, on November 27, 1884. The next day he died of heart failure at age forty-eight. Thousands of people attended the funeral in the Methodist Episcopal Church at Wellington and visited his grave in a local cemetery. His grave remained in Kansas until 1995, when his remains were moved to Oklahoma. A monument was dedicated over the new grave in Stillwater, Payne County, named in his honor.

Kate Barnard, First Woman Elected to State Office

KATE BARNARD WAS ONCE described as an army of one. Early in the twentieth century, she was the most influential woman in Oklahoma during the Progressive Era. She was a pioneer politician, social reformer, and something of a folk figure in the state's early history.

The story of Kate Barnard begins in the small town of Geneva in Fillmore County, Nebraska, where she was born on May 23, 1875. Her family moved often, and she spent much of her childhood in Kansas, where financial problems plagued her parents. During the late 1890s, she and her father, attorney John Barnard, moved to Oklahoma Territory. As a young woman, she became a schoolteacher and worked as a stenographer. Having experienced poverty, she was sympathetic to the suffering of others. Kate Barnard discovered her calling was politics and social reform.

Barnard soon became an officer in the Provident Association of Oklahoma, a benevolent organization maintained by business leaders and local churches in the state. It quickly became obvious to her associates that she had no intention of limiting herself to the dispensing of charity. She supported compulsory education and the abolition of child labor. She also campaigned to raise wages for city workers and urged the employees to join a union. At the Oklahoma constitutional convention in 1906, her lobbying on progressive issues attracted the attention of others. The following year at the age of thirty-two, Barnard was elected to the Oklahoma state office of commissioner of charities and correction. Barnard became the first woman anywhere in the world to hold such a post; however, it was the only position that the 1907 constitution permitted a woman to hold. She was a key player in enacting compulsory education laws, state support of poor widows who were dependent on their children's earnings, and statutes banning child labor. Barnard also advocated

Kate Barnard. Courtesy of Western History Collections, University of Oklahoma Libraries (Ferguson Collection, no. 202).

legislation removing unsafe working conditions for Oklahomans and eliminating the blacklisting of union members.

Her most important work came, however, when she discovered that Oklahoma convicts—jailed in Kansas under contract because there were no prisons in Oklahoma—were being treated badly in Kansas prisons. The prisoners were forced to work in coal mines and were often tortured. Barnard put pressure on Charles N. Haskell, Oklahoma's first governor, who got the state to construct the Oklahoma state penitentiary at McAlester. The prisoners in Kansas were returned to Oklahoma. Meantime, Barnard got legislation enacted that established a three-tiered prison system separating young offenders from more hardened criminals.

Barnard's political downfall began in 1913 after she took up the cause of Indians who were being cheated out of their lands. William H.

Murray, who had been Speaker of the Oklahoma House of Representatives in 1907 and 1908, and other prominent Oklahoma businessmen and officials, got the legislature to deny funding for her office of charities and corrections. During her two terms in office from 1907 to 1914, Barnard got thirty statutory laws passed in the Oklahoma legislature. She realized, however, that Oklahoma politicians had become less reform oriented. She learned that getting legislation enacted was much easier than forcing bureaucrats to implement reforms.

Unfortunately, Barnard was a solitary woman. She never considered marriage, and, unlike other women activists of her time, she refused to align herself with women's organizations and their issues, believing such associations would restrict her efforts to compete with men on equal ground. Her approach worked for a time. When she experienced setbacks, however, she was alone and had no network of sympathetic friends.

After Barnard left public office in 1915, she moved to Colorado to recuperate from a nervous breakdown. Ten years later, in 1925, she returned to Oklahoma and threatened to stir up the state "from a stretcher." She said that the legislature's call to rewrite the state's convention was nothing more than putting the farmers of Oklahoma on the auction block to provide cheap labor to build up industries. She declared that Oklahoma was facing a "moral and spiritual crisis."

By then Barnard's health was declining, and she lived quietly in an Oklahoma City hotel. On Sunday, February 23, 1930, Kate Barnard was found dead in her room at the Egbert Hotel on North Broadway. She was fifty-four. The next day Governor Holloway ordered the flag on the state capitol to be lowered to half-mast during her funeral the following Thursday. In his proclamation, the governor described Barnard as "one who served well and faithfully in the cause of human welfare and who committed this commonwealth in its infancy to the call of the unfortunate and afflicted." Barnard was buried in Fairlawn Cemetery in Oklahoma City next to the grave of her father, a former Oklahoma City attorney. Her grave was not marked until the 1980s.

In the spring of 2001, a bronze statue of Barnard by Sandra Van Zandt of Claremore was unveiled in a ceremony on the first floor of the state capitol. During the ceremony, state senator Enoch Kelly Haney of Seminole called Barnard an "extraordinary woman who was elected at a time when women could not even vote, and she took on some very unpopular issues. But they were issues that continue to have tremendous impact on our state." Today the statue of Kate Barnard stands as a tribute to the many contributions she made to early Oklahoma history.

The Night Boise City Was Shaken
~

It was about half past midnight on July 5, 1943. The heat of the day had given way to the usual cooling that occurs during the summer at Boise City, located in the far western end of the Oklahoma Panhandle. Most of its 1,400 residents had gone to bed when an airplane began dropping bombs on the sleepy town. The town's residents awoke to a series of six bangs and booms that sounded more like large firecrackers they had heard a day earlier as they celebrated Independence Day.

A few minutes earlier Fred Kreiger, band director in the local school and also editor of the weekly *Boise City News*, had gone to bed when he heard the drone of a plane, a whistle, a crash, and an explosion. He quickly got up, dressed, and ran outside. "My first thought was an enemy plane," he recalled, but wondered why Boise City would be bombed. "After I saw how deep the bombs bored into the pavement, I was glad I hadn't hid under that big paper cutter at the office," said Kreiger, who added, "What this place needs are some searchlights and anti-aircraft guns."

When the bombs began falling, F. L. Bellew, the town's night watchman, was near the post office. He flattened himself on the sidewalk, watched the sky, and wished he had his high-powered rifle as the plane made a second pass over Boise City. Not far away near the Cimarron County Courthouse, Coleen Jones and four girlfriends had just left the local movie theater. Their dates were soldiers from the U.S. Army Air Force base at Dalhart, Texas, about thirty miles south of Boise City. When a bomb hit the ground, Jones asked a soldier what it was. "By God, it's a bomb!" he quickly replied. They ran away as fast as they could for safety.

At the Liberty Café, located on the highway, seven oil company truckers hurriedly put down their coffee cups and sandwiches and ran to their loaded tanker trucks and drove out of town as fast as they could. Not far away, Pastor R. D. Dodds found the front door on his white frame church blown open and some of the rainbow-colored windows broken. Later he told a reporter, "If one-fourth of the people who came to see the hole the bomb made would only attend church." By the next day, nearly every resident of Boise City had learned that their town had been bombed by the U.S. Army Air Force. Lt. Max Siegel, public relations officer at the Dalhart base arrived in Boise City and made the announcement. He added that no one had been hurt and that property damage amounted to less than twenty-five dollars. The B-17 Flying Fortress that dropped the bombs was one of a group that had taken off from Dalhart to bomb an army range near Conlen, Texas, northeast of Dalhart. One of the planes got off course, and the navigator spotted the lights of Boise City and especially one light in the Cimarron County Courthouse square that had the general pattern of the bombing range. Maj. C. E. Lancaster, commanding officer of the Dalhart base, described the bombing as accidental, caused by "a mistake of navigation." Lancaster explained that the crew believed the lights in the courthouse square were those of the bombing range.

The B-17 made six passes over Boise City, dropping one bomb on each run. Fortunately, they were practice bombs containing just over ninety-seven pounds of sand and about three pounds of gun powder. In reconstructing the events of the early morning hours of July 5, investigators determined that the first bomb landed in an alley northwest of Court Avenue near an apartment where several people were sleeping. It hit an empty garage, blowing open the door and leaving a twenty-by-forty-inch crater. The B-17 made another pass over Boise City, aiming at four lights. The bomb they dropped missed the First Baptist Church by inches and left a crater three feet deep. On the plane's next pass, its third bomb hit the earth in front of the Style Shoppe building. The fourth bomb hit only yards from the McGowan Boardinghouse and missed a parked tanker truck full of fuel. The fifth bomb hit some eighty feet from a small house, and the sixth bomb fell near the railroad tracks on the southeastern edge of town.

About then Frank Garrett of Boise City's power company ran to the Southwestern Public Service building and pulled the town's master light switch. He hoped the townspeople would not mind. To the crew of the B-17, starting on another pass over the town, the sudden darkness suggested the bombing practice was not succeeding. The B-17 made no further passes over Boise City and returned to its air base at Dalhart.

As the bombs were falling on Boise City, John Atkins, the town's air raid warden, hurriedly phoned a report to the FBI in Oklahoma City. Atkins then sent the Oklahoma adjutant general a telegram that read, "Boise City bombed one A.M. Baptist Church, garage hit." Before the sun rose on Boise City the following morning, FBI agents, U.S. Army officials, and the Oklahoma Highway Patrol had men on the scene investigating what had happened.

In the next weekly issue of the *Boise City News*, editor Fred Kreiger wrote that the bombing was "mortifying" and "horrifying." But the anger felt by most Boise City residents soon gave way to pride as news of the bombing focused national attention on their town. *Time* magazine carried a story on July 19 headlined "The Bombing of Boise City" and noted that the citizens of Boise City acted the way most civilians do who have never been bombed before. The magazine said, "Most of them ran like hell, in no particular direction." *Newsweek* magazine observed that Boise City was one of the most unlikely targets for an air raid. By the end of World War II, *Ripley's Believe it or Not*, a syndicated cartoon for newspapers, was describing Boise City as the only town in the continental United States to be bombed during WWII.

In 1993, fifty years after the bombing, the citizens of Boise City sent letters to military magazines and otherwise sought to locate the B-17's crew members to invite them to the town. In time, they located some the members, most of whom remained tight-lipped. The crew members did not want to go to Boise City, preferring to remember their outstanding record in Europe rather than their blunder in the Oklahoma Panhandle. The crew apparently had the choice of disciplinary action after the incident at Boise City or immediate transfer to the European theater of war. They chose war and left for England. Most of them remained together and became one of the top B-17 crews in the Eighth Air Force before the war ended.

One crew member, Henry Garringer, a former sergeant in the U.S. Army Air Force, did agree to tape a message over the telephone from his home in California. He blamed "motivation" as the cause of the accident and admitted the crew "screwed up," but he added that the crew members spent the rest of their military careers being the best. Garringer's message was played over a public address system on July 4, 1993, at the dedication of a bronze plaque near a bomb crater and a replica bomb protruding from cement, memorializing the night Boise City was bombed half a century earlier.

Roscoe Dunjee, Oklahoma's Little Caesar

AFTER LANGSTON UNIVERSITY was founded at Langston City, forty miles northeast of Oklahoma City, fifteen-year-old Roscoe Dunjee was one of eighty-one black students who enrolled in the school's first classes in 1898. At Langston, Roscoe majored in printing and worked on the weekly *Langston City Herald*.

Dunjee was the son of Rev. John William Dunjee, a prominent Baptist minister. Roscoe was born in 1883 at Harpers Ferry, West Virginia, where his father founded the *Harper's Ferry Messenger* and helped to establish Storer College and other black educational institutions. In 1892, Reverend Dunjee was appointed general missionary over the Baptists of Oklahoma by the American Baptist Home Missionary Society, then one of the nation's largest black organizations. Dunjee, his wife, and their five children moved to Oklahoma Territory where their first home was a dugout at Choctaw. Reverend Dunjee's son Roscoe later often said his father was the son of John Tyler, the tenth president of the United States, and a female slave. Tyler had more children than any other president—eight children with his first wife and seven with his second wife.

After his father died in 1903, Roscoe Dunjee moved to Oklahoma City. He bought a small printing press and opened a print shop. In 1915, he started the *Black Dispatch*, a weekly newspaper in Oklahoma City that served about seven thousand blacks in the area. He selected the paper's name because whites used the phrase "black dispatch" as a slang term.

Because the first state legislature in Oklahoma separated the races in public places, a black community grew and prospered in the area around modern Bricktown in Oklahoma City. The black community, first called Sandtown and later Deep Deuce, stretched from what is now called the Oklahoma River north to Second Street east of downtown.

From the start, Roscoe Dunjee adhered to high standards of journalism in the *Black Dispatch*. He wrote editorials about racist attitudes and sought to instill pride in black heritage. The newspaper's banner was a black angel with a horn protruding from its shoulder containing the words "5 Cents Per Copy." The paper's nameplate or flag also included the phrases "Mouthpiece for All Better Thinking Colored People" and "A Message from the Black Fold."

Gradually, the paper's circulation grew. In time, as blacks left Oklahoma to take jobs in other parts of the nation, they kept up their subscriptions. Within a few years, the paper gained a national following and at its peak had more than 26,000 subscribers.

Roscoe Dunjee used his paper to train black journalists. He became well known for his fiery editorials. He attacked discrimination and encouraged blacks to fight for civil rights. He wrote editorials criticizing blacks who did not vote. When the National Association for the Advancement of Colored People (NAACP) was organized in Illinois in 1910, Dunjee was among the first to join the Oklahoma City branch.

During the exodus of blacks from the South in 1915, Dunjee wrote many columns containing advice for blacks moving north. During World War I, he wrote editorials demanding recognition of black soldiers. When racial tensions exploded in a riot at Tulsa in 1921 and claimed the lives of up to three hundred blacks and destroyed the black community called Greenwood, Dunjee provided complete coverage of how a minor incident sparked the violence. Dunjee reported that white business interests hired agitators to rouse whites.

In 1941, Dunjee supported a newly formed organization called the Oklahoma Federation for Constitutional Rights when it started an investigation into discrimination. Governor Leon Phillips called the organization "the height of folly." Dunjee responded with a long editorial that cited court cases and the activities of the NAACP. It began with the words: "Surely the governor belongs to that class spoken of in the Bible; 'which has eyes and see not; which have ears and hear not.'"

Roscoe Dunjee, Oklahoma's Little Caesar. Portrait by Simmie Knox. Courtesy of Oklahoma State Senate Historical Preservation Fund.

Dunjee noted that blacks were denied their civil rights on every train and bus in Oklahoma. He also participated in federal lawsuits against the state seeking equal rights for blacks. In each case, the state lost. Using the Oklahoma cases, the U.S. Supreme Court eventually dismantled the entire system of segregation in America.

The Federal government investigated the loyalty of Dunjee's newspaper during World War II, but the *Black Dispatch* survived the scrutiny. Financial problems soon developed, however, forcing Dunjee, then in his seventies, to sell the newspaper in 1955 to a nephew. The family continued to run the paper until it closed in 1982.

Roscoe Dunjee remained active in community and civil rights matters until his death in 1965 at the age of eighty-two. In 1969, he was inducted posthumously into the Oklahoma Journalism Hall of Fame. In 2005, his portrait—painted by Maryland artist Simmie Knox—was unveiled on the fourth floor of the state capitol. Today, Roscoe Dunjee is remembered for the newspaper he founded in Oklahoma City and for helping to shape American history as a spokesman and leader in the civil rights movement. During his life, his work helped to change discriminatory practices in Oklahoma and the nation.

The Miller Brothers' 101 Ranch

THE 101 RANCH IS LEGENDARY, almost larger than life; nevertheless, it was real. Take away its romance and color and it is the story of enterprise, imagination, and the hard work of George Washington Miller and his three sons.

Miller was born near Danville, Kentucky, on February 22, 1842. He married Mollie Carson of Louisville, Kentucky, early in 1866. Around 1868 Miller moved his family west to Newtonia, Missouri, and one year later they moved to Baxter Springs, Kansas, close to the border of northeastern Indian Territory.

Miller was twenty-eight in 1871 when he established a ranch near modern Miami, Oklahoma. He acquired about four hundred Texas longhorns and hired a few cowboys to watch the animals. Gradually he built his cattle business by making cattle-buying trips to Texas and trailing the herds north to his ranch before shipping them to market. Miller adopted the 101 brand in the early 1870s. Tradition says he borrowed it from the name of a saloon in San Antonio, Texas. On buying trips south, his cowboys often drank too much in the saloon. Miller decided that if the cowboys had to see 101 on the rumps of the cattle being trailed north, they would be reminded of their excesses.

About 1878 Miller leased Indian land on the Salt Fork River near modern Ponca City. In 1881, Miller bought a house in Winfield, Kansas, north across the border of Indian Territory. Winfield had schools, churches, and conveniences not found in Indian Territory, where whites could not settle. By the late 1890s, Miller's operation became known as the 101 Ranch, and it grew and prospered. When Miller died at the age of sixty-one on April 25, 1903, his three sons took over the reins of the ranch.

Thirty-five-year-old Joseph, twenty-five-year-old Zachary, and twenty-two-year-old George each had his own area of expertise. Joe was an expert in grains and plants; Zack was a cattleman; and

George was a whiz at finance. The Miller brothers made the 101 Ranch perhaps the largest farm and ranch operation in America. It attracted countless visitors and much attention. In its heyday, the ranch had fifteen departments, each with its own manager. The ranch bred beef and dairy cattle, grew wheat and corn, and raised Arabian horses, polo ponies, hogs, geese, chickens, turkeys, and other animals. Eventually the ranch had its own meatpacking plant, tannery, saddle-making shop, creamery, ice plant, post office, school, laundry, saloon, phone system, ranch store, café, and bank. The ranch even issued its own currency called Miller Scrip, which could be spent at the ranch store and which was generally accepted within a hundred-mile radius of the ranch.

While Joe and George concentrated on running the farm and ranch, Zack sought to capitalize on the public's fascination with the Old West. He held annual rodeos featuring riding, roping, shooting, bulldogging, and Indian dancing. Bill Pickett, who began bulldogging using his teeth, was hired to perform the feat at the 101 Ranch. Jumping from his horse, he would sink his tenth into the steer's lip, reportedly dropping the animal every time. The ranch gave Pickett his start as a rodeo performer. The Millers hosted conventions of many national organizations at their ranch. In the 1920s one such group was the National Editorial Association. According to most accounts, visitors arrived in thirty regular and special trains. Perhaps 60,000 people were fascinated by the 101 entertainment.

The Miller brothers had put on Wild West shows on their ranch for several years, but in 1907 they began touring the nation with what was called the 101 Ranch Wild West Show. It annually toured from spring to fall throughout the United States, Mexico, and Canada. The show traveled in its own train with freight cars and Pullmans. The show went to England in 1915, and the 101 Ranch cowboys were the stars of the show. Several of them became western film stars, including Hoot Gibson, Tom Mix, Buck Jones, and Ken Maynard.

In 1923, the Salt Fork River flooded, destroying crops, drowning

Geronimo (at the wheel) and other Indian performers at the Miller Brother's 101 Ranch. The Miller brothers were able to attract Geronimo to their ranch during a special show put on for countless newspaper editors and reporters on June 11, 1905. The car is a Locomobile. The Miller brothers advertised the event as the last buffalo Geronimo would kill. Cowboys herded a buffalo to bow-and-arrow range. Geronimo's arrows were not fatal, and a cowboy had to shoot the animal. Courtesy of Western History Collections, University of Oklahoma Libraries (Ferguson Collection, no. 745).

livestock, and damaging buildings and equipment at the ranch. The financial loss was at least $250,000. The 101 Ranch survived, but by the late 1920s public interest in Wild West shows began to fade with the arrival of radio and motion pictures.

In 1927, Joe Miller died, and two years later George Miller died in an automobile accident. The ranch began to decline. Zack Miller, the surviving brother, tried to keep the ranch profitable, but legal and financial problems developed even before the Depression arrived. In 1932, he filed bankruptcy and tried to raise money with the 101 Ranch Wild West Show. It closed in 1939 after the New York World's Fair. The U.S. government seized the show's remaining assets, and Zack Miller was broke. In 1941, the Federal Farm Security Administration bought eight thousand acres of the ranch land and divided it into thirty-four farms. Miller managed to buy and operate the 101 Ranch Store but then moved to Texas, where he died in 1952.

Today the 101 Ranch is only a memory. The large white house that was a ranch landmark is gone. Crumbling foundations are all that remain south of Ponca City of the once-fabulous empire. But George W. Miller and his sons left an enduring legacy that is a colorful page in Oklahoma history.

The Man from Bugtussle

THE STORY OF CARL BERT ALBERT is that of an Oklahoma boy who fulfilled his childhood dreams and much more. It is the story of a man who chose a career in politics and rose to hold the highest national political office of any Oklahoman in U.S. history.

Albert was born on May 10, 1908, in a mining camp just north of McAlester, about a year after Oklahoma became a state. He was the oldest of five children born to Ernest and Leona Albert, who were neither poor nor wealthy. When young Albert was about three, his parents moved to Bugtussle, a small community six miles northeast of McAlester. (Three years earlier the town had been renamed Flowery Mound, but many locals still called it Bugtussle.)

As a young boy, Albert marveled that there was meaning on a page of printed letters. He soon learned to read and entered the school at Bugtussle determined to learn. When Albert was about six and in the first grade in 1914, local congressman Charles D. Carter visited the school. He told the students that the United States was a great country and that any of the children could grow up to be a congressman from that district. Young Albert was certain that Carter was speaking directly to him. Tradition suggests that Albert made up his mind that day to be a congressman. Years later, he remembered that "from early on, everything I did was calculated to being elected to Congress."

After completing the eighth grade, Albert dropped out of school to help his father on the farm, but he continued to read and study. When his parents moved into McAlester a year later, he entered McAlester High School and excelled. There Albert received the nickname "The Little Giant" because he stood only five feet and four inches in height. Albert was a member of the school's debate team that won a state championship. He became a public speaker, student body president, and class valedictorian.

With ten dollars in his pocket, Albert entered the University of Oklahoma at Norman in the fall of 1927. To pay his way, he immediately landed three jobs—waiting tables, working as a soda jerk, and tutoring. As a freshman at OU, Albert won the National Oratorical Contest with a speech about the U.S. Constitution. He won $1,500 in cash and a trip to Hawaii. Albert majored in government at OU and impressed his teachers and fellow students. Graduating in 1931 with a key in Phi Beta Kappa and numerous other awards, he received a Rhodes Scholarship and studied at Oxford University in England for three years, earning two degrees.

When he returned to Oklahoma, he worked as a legal clerk and was admitted to the bar. In 1937, he began practicing oil law in Oklahoma, Illinois, and Ohio. In June 1941, as war clouds hung over Europe, he enlisted in the U.S. Army as a private. In 1942, soon after World War II began, he received a direct commission as a second lieutenant and was assigned to the Judge Advocate's office in Washington, D.C. During the war, he was stationed in Australia, New Guinea, the Philippines, and Japan with the Third Armored Division. He was awarded a bronze star, and when the war ended Albert's rank was lieutenant colonel.

Albert returned to McAlester to practice law. When he learned that the local congressman would not run for reelection, he became a candidate, won on the Democratic ticket, and headed to Washington to represent Oklahoma's Third Congressional District, which he did for thirty years until 1977. Between 1955 and 1961, he served as majority whip in the House of Representatives. In 1961, he became majority leader, and in 1971 he became Speaker of the House, the third-highest elective office under the Constitution. Twice he was second in line of succession to the presidency. At one point, Albert summed up his personal political views by saying that he "very much disliked doctrinaire liberals—they want to own your minds. And I don't like reactionary conservatives. I like to face issues in terms of conditions and not in terms of someone's inborn political philosophy."

Carl Albert. Courtesy of the Carl Albert Congressional Research and Studies Center, University of Oklahoma.

Albert was sixty-eight years old when he retired. An editorial in the *New York Times* described him as "a conciliator and seeker of consensus, a patient persuader . . . trusted for his fairness and integrity." He returned to Bugtussle, where for the next twenty-four years he maintained an office in nearby McAlester, lectured at the University of Oklahoma, and made speeches across the nation and overseas. His legacy in Oklahoma includes Carl Albert State College in Poteau, the Carl Albert Indian Health Facility at Ada, the Carl Albert Center established at OU to study his life and the Congress, and Carl Albert Park, located south of Durant.

On February 4, 2000, at the age of ninety-two, Carl P. Albert died in McAlester, only a few miles from where he had been born and where as a boy a congressman had challenged him to be great.

Oklahoma Inventors

During the state's first century, innovative Oklahomans created numerous inventions that are today used around the world. Probably best known is the shopping cart, invented in 1937 by Sylvan Goldman of Oklahoma City, where they were first used in the Standard Food and Humpty Dumpty supermarkets. Goldman created the first shopping cart by attaching wheels to a folding chair. Each cart had room for two shopping baskets, and when not in use the carts could be folded and stacked against a wall and the baskets stacked on the floor. The shopping cart was patented on March 15, 1938. The original cart is on display at the Oklahoma History Center.

Another Oklahoma invention is the parking meter, invented by Carl C. Magee of Oklahoma City and first installed there on July 16, 1935.

The story of the yield sign is longer. Oklahoma highway patrolman Clinton Riggs got the idea for a yield sign while attending a traffic institute meeting in 1939 at Chicago. The war years slowed its development, but in 1959 the first yield sign was used at a dangerous intersection in Tulsa. It reduced the number of accidents. Soon the keystone-shaped yield sign became popular and was adopted by cities and states across the nation. Riggs, who also had a successful career with the Tulsa Police Department, is credited with designing the Tulsa Police shoulder patch in the same shape as the yield sign.

Because of the many successful inventors in the state, Oklahoma governor Henry Bellmon established by decree the Oklahoma Inventors Congress in 1966 during his first term in office. All succeeding administrations have supported the group, which is believed to be the oldest continuously functioning organization in the nation dedicated to inventors and the inventive process.

The list of inventions produced by Oklahomans and persons with ties to the state is long. One such story is that of Ed Roberts.

While he was in the air force, he finished his bachelor's degree in electrical engineering at Oklahoma State University. A native of Miami, Florida, Roberts was later stationed in San Antonio, Texas. In 1970, he and a few friends founded an electronics company called Micro Instrumentation and Telemetry Systems (MITS) to produce and sell electronic kits. The company's first successful product was an electronic calculator kit that was featured on the cover of *Popular Mechanics* in November 1971. The calculators sold well, and sales were more than one million dollars in 1973. As other companies started building calculator kits, there was a price war that left Roberts's company in debt by 1974. Meantime, Roberts created the Altair 8800 computer and wrote about it in the January 1975 issue of *Popular Electronics*.

One undergraduate student at Harvard University got excited about the article. His name was Bill Gates. Gates and his friend Paul Allen contacted Roberts and went to work for him to write a BASIC interpreter for the machine. Gates dropped out of Harvard. Later, Gates and Allen left Roberts's company to form their own, a company called Microsoft.

Roberts sold his company for six million dollars in 1977. He changed careers and went off to medical school, later becoming a country doctor in Cochran, Georgia, until his death in April 2010. However, Roberts is still remembered as the inventor of one of the very first hobbyist personal computers.

Most Oklahomans know of flyer Wiley Post, who died in a plane crash in Alaska with Will Rogers. However, many do not know that Post had a hand inventing the modern-day flight suit and the autopilot.

Likewise, Oklahomans are unaware that another native son, Gordon Matthews, invented voice mail and got it patented on February 1, 1983. Born in Tulsa, Matthews later moved to Texas, where he earned the title the Father of Voice Mail. Matthews has at least forty other patents, including a device called Automatic

Marshal. It tracks how long each player plays on the golf course and sets off an alarm when they dawdle.

The story of another Oklahoma invention began in 1902, when German immigrant Carl Frederick Malzahn moved from Minnesota to Perry, Oklahoma Territory, and opened a blacksmith shop. His two sons, Charlie and Gus, soon joined their father's business, and in time Charlie was running it. When the oil boom occurred, the business became a machine shop to serve the oil industry. Following World War II, Charlie's son, Ed Malzahn—who had a mechanical engineering degree—realized that there was a need for a piece of equipment to dig ditches for gas, electric, and plumbing lines. Until then, picks and shovels had been used. He invented a compact trencher that today is known as the Ditch Witch. Today, the Perry company designs and manufactures a wide range of high-quality underground construction equipment.

These and countless other inventions have strong ties to Oklahoma as do their inventors. They add much to the rich history of the state.

Oklahoma Storms, Fires, Floods, Train Wrecks, and Other Disasters

EVERY OKLAHOMAN KNOWS THAT tornadoes can be a threat in the state. Most readers will remember May 3, 1999, when a large tornado moved though areas of southwestern Oklahoma City and Moore, demolishing or damaging more than eight thousand homes and causing more than one billion dollars in damage. Forty-eight people died. The tornado was part of an outbreak of seventy-four tornadoes that affected parts of Oklahoma and southern Kansas. The warning system undoubtedly saved the lives of many Oklahomans.

Warning systems did not exist in the state's early years. There certainly were tornadoes in the area, even before the Five Tribes made their homes in the region, but no detailed accounts have been found. After white settlers arrived, a growing number of newspapers provided stories on storms, floods, fires, train wrecks, and other disasters. In 1950, Oliver Asp of the U.S. Weather Bureau office, then located in Oklahoma City, wrote that between 1875 and 1949, 496 tornadoes claimed 924 lives in Oklahoma. These tornadoes injured more than four thousand persons and were responsible for more than $51 million in property damage. Asp noted that the first tornado of record occurred in 1875, but its location was not reported. Two more tornadoes occurred in 1882, killing two persons and injuring forty-eight others; the years 1884, 1885, and 1892 recorded one tornado each without deaths, but Asp did not indicate where they struck. The following year, on April 25, 1893, a tornado that set down in Cleveland County southwest of Moore killed thirty-one people and caused considerable damage.

By 1896, Oklahomans began paying more attention to tornadoes after a funnel dropped from the clouds on October 29, 1896, about twenty miles east of Guthrie. The funnel was at least one hundred yards wide, and its path was several miles long. When it first touched ground, it destroyed a farmhouse, killing the farmer; next it destroyed the general store and post office, killing the postmaster and his wife in the community of Mitchell. Continuing on its path, it did more damage in Payne County, where several people were killed. Apparently, the same tornado then struck Wewoka, injuring several people as it destroyed a store, a church, and four other buildings. It killed perhaps eight people as it destroyed a store and more homes near Krebs, before lifting back into the clouds. Details of this storm have been found in wire service reports sent from Oklahoma Territory to the Associated Press.

As the population of Oklahoma Territory grew and more newspapers were established, severe weather reports increased. When a large tornado formed on May 10, 1905, over Snyder in Kiowa County, it became big news because it killed 105 people and injured more than 100 others. As news reached Oklahoma City, the *Daily Oklahoman* reported that nearly one hundred corpses had already been buried. It noted that three carloads of coffins had been delivered by train from Oklahoma City, together with a dozen undertakers who had been attending a convention there. A heavy rain with some hail and high winds hampered rescue and cleanup efforts as groups of engineers from the Oklahoma National Guard rushed to Snyder from Lawton. They helped with searching for missing people and maintaining law and order.

As with any disaster this large, there were numerous stories of miraculous escapes from death, but other accounts of tragedy. In one account carried nationally by the Associated Press, Kansas City, Missouri, attorney A. W. Farrar was traveling to Snyder from Quanah, Texas. He saw the tornado forming and arrived in Snyder just after it struck. "The sight was appalling. A path 900 feet wide extended through the town. . . . In this space there was not a trace of buildings left standing, and the ground was short of grass. Splinters, beams, and heavy timbers were driven into the soil and marked the course. . . . The survivors, including many injured, seemed dazed by the terrible experience. I never heard a sob, a cry, nor a groan from the crowd. . . . Even those who had lost members of their families, wives, husbands, parents or children were dry-eyed and talked dully and calmly of their loss."

One account of the Snyder tornado published by the *Philadelphia Inquirer* reported the sad story of a man who grabbed a woman he thought was his wife and hurried to a place of safety, only to realize that the woman was not his wife. He later identified his wife's body in a temporary morgue. Her head had been severed from the body.

Snyder was still recovering from the tornado when a year later on June 22, 1906, a small tornado followed the same path as the 1905 tornado and swept through the town. It did considerable damage, but no one was hurt. The residents of Snyder were in storm shelters.

During the next few decades, other especially damaging tornadoes occurred in the state. The U.S. Weather Bureau (renamed the National Weather Service in 1970) says that a tornado struck Peggs, a small community northwest of Tahlequah in Cherokee County, on May 2, 1920, killing seventy-one people. Another tornado touched down in Creek County southwest of Tulsa on November 4, 1922, killing six persons and causing half a million dollars in property damage. Then, on June 16, 1928, a tornado struck the communities of Blair and Headrick, located in Jackson County in southwestern Oklahoma. The storm killed four people, and property damage totaled $1,500,000. In 1930, a tornado struck Bethany, just west of Oklahoma City, killing twenty-three people and causing considerable property damage.

Soon after Congress created the U.S. Weather Bureau as part of the Department of Agriculture in 1890, the new government agency established an office in Oklahoma City. From its beginning, it was the bureau's policy not to forecast severe local storms or even to use the word "tornado" in its weather forecasts. Weather forecasting was in its infancy. Many citizens then called tornadoes cyclones, but this changed in 1938 when forecasters were allowed to say "tornado." Few forecasts mentioned the possibility of tornadoes because the science of understanding such storms was only beginning. During World War II, the study of weather began to mature in the military and continued after the war when several deadly tornadoes occurred. Sixty-nine people died and 353 were injured in a tornado at Antlers in Pushmataha County on April 12, 1945. That same day, another tornado killed 13 and injured 113 people at Muskogee.

Then, in 1947, came the infamous tornado that cut a 221-mile path from White Deer, Texas, northeast across Oklahoma and into Kansas. The tornado killed 169 people and injured 890. Six people died in Gage and Shattuck, but 93 died in Woodward in northwestern Oklahoma, where the tornado struck at about 9 P.M. It cut a path almost two miles wide, destroying more than one hundred city blocks on the western and northern sides of the city, and damaged portions of southeastern Woodward. One-third of the city was destroyed. Some residents of Woodward still date events in their community as having occurred before or after the tornado struck.

A damaging tornado struck Tinker Air Force Base in Oklahoma City on March 20, 1948. Air force weather officers E. J. Fawbush and R. C. Miller at Tinker observed the storm and learned much. Five days later, they successfully forecast another tornado that struck Tinker. Their experience led to the establishment three years later of the Severe Weather Warning Center, a new Air Weather Service unit responsible for forecasting severe weather for all air force bases on the U.S. mainland. Since then, the study of weather forecasting has greatly matured, and the National Weather Center has been constructed on the campus of the University of Oklahoma in Norman to house the institution's meteorology studies. The center also houses the National Weather Service's Storm Prediction Center and the National Severe Storms Laboratory, plus a local office of the National Weather Service that was once located in nearby Oklahoma City.

Rainstorms without tornadoes have also earned a few places in the history books because of flooding. Since the state's territorial days, heavy rains have often caused serious flooding in many areas. Remnants of the deadly hurricane that struck the Texas coast in 1896 brought rains that caused flooding on the Arkansas River and its tributaries, affecting more than half of modern Oklahoma and causing millions of dollars in damage. When another hurricane struck Galveston, Texas, in 1900, it brought rains that produced widespread flooding in eastern Indian Territory.

Unusually heavy rains and snow are not uncommon in Oklahoma. Some more significant reports found in the files of the National Weather Service include the following:

OCTOBER 13–16, 1923: Severe flooding along the North Canadian River caused a breach in the Lake Overholser Dam, forcing the evaluation of about 15,000 residents in Oklahoma City.

MARCH 1924: Heavy snowfall over much of the state with Alva reporting thirty-seven inches for the month. Norman had twenty-four inches and Oklahoma City more than twenty inches.

FEBRUARY 21–22, 1971: A blizzard struck northwestern Oklahoma, dumping thirty-six inches of snow on Buffalo, then a state record.

OCTOBER 11, 1973: Over fifteen (15.68) inches of rain fell on Enid in thirteen hours. Twelve inches of the rain fell in only three hours, causing severe flash flooding.

DECEMBER 1987–JANUARY 1988: In December, a snowstorm dropped eight to fourteen inches of snow with drifts up to four feet in northwestern Oklahoma. Before the storm ended, a severe ice storm occurred along a forty-mile-wide stretch from Duncan to Norman to Tulsa. Ice accumulations of one to two inches on trees and power lines caused most of the $10 million in damages. In early January, another snow storm dropped ten inches over large areas of the state.

While nature is usually blamed for tornadoes, floods, and winter storms, it cannot be blamed for major fires that destroy property and cause death and injury. Sometimes humans are responsible, as was the case when arson destroyed seven buildings in Sapulpa, putting eleven firms out of business in April 1908. Another fire of undetermined origin in May 1910 destroyed all of the businesses on the western side of the square at Beaver. Among the buildings lost was the old courthouse, one of the most historic structures in town.

One of the more tragic fires in Oklahoma during the twentieth century occurred in April 1918, when thirty-eight boys and men confined as patients at the Norman state mental hospital, now Griffin Memorial Hospital, died in an early-morning fire. A night watchman discovered the fire in a linen closet. When he opened the door, the fire quickly spread through the frame structure. The *Norman Transcript* later reported that fire investigators concluded that either an electrical defect or spontaneous combustion started the fire.

About one year after the Norman fire, eight people were killed and more than twenty were injured when a wagon carrying two quarts of nitroglycerin exploded in the residential area of Big Heart, a town located northwest of Bartlesville in Osage County. The Associated Press reported that the explosion "broke every window in the town and shook the ground for hundreds of yards around." All telephone and telegraph communication in Big Heart was destroyed.

Another accidental explosion occurred in September 1915 at Ardmore when a spark from a hammer ignited 250 gallons of gasoline in a tank car at the Santa Fe yards. News reports say the explosion set off a large quantity of dynamite stored in a nearby freight shed. The explosions killed about fifty people and injured two hundred others; buildings on Ardmore's main street were damaged either by the explosions or fires that followed.

Accidents involving trains often made news in early Oklahoma. News reports concerning one of the earliest train wrecks describes an accident on July 15, 1901, near Wymark, Indian Territory, where two freight trains on the Missouri, Kansas and Texas line collided head-on while crossing a bridge over the Arkansas River. Both engines fell into the river, and the collision started a fire that burned up the bridge and the train cars. Five men were killed in the accident, and three others died from their injuries. Poor railroad communication caused the wreck.

Another head-on train wreck occurred on December 2, 1912, at Ninnekah, seven miles south of Chickasha. Two Chicago, Rock Island and Pacific passenger trains collided after the engineer on the south-bound train spotted the north-bound train coming around a curve. The south-bound engineer was trying to back his train into a siding at the time of the accident, which killed one man and injured twenty persons.

In 1904, the Meteor, a fast passenger train on the St. Louis and San Francisco line (the Frisco), was traveling from Dallas to St. Louis when it derailed near Vinita, Indian Territory, in what is now northeastern Oklahoma. The engine, baggage car, mail car, and two chair cars left the track. Fourteen passengers were seriously injured, and twenty others received slight cuts and bruises. The injured were transported to the railroad's hospital at Springfield, Missouri.

In shallow coal mines in McCurtain, in Haskell County, eight men were killed and four others were seriously injured in an explosion on October 20, 1922. The blast wrecked mine No. 2 of the Progressive Coal Company. Fortunately, fire did not follow the explosion. Four men buried in coal were found alive, given first aid, and rushed to the hospital. Some survivors said that the mine gas was ignited by the flame in a lamp worn by the mine's fire boss, who was killed in the explosion.

These are a sampling of stories about late nineteenth and twentieth century disasters that are a part of Oklahoma history. Fortunately, modern technology, including better weather forecasting, helps Oklahomans cope with the unexpected. The human factor, however, is often unpredictable.

Part VII

∼

Artists, Writers, and Entertainers

All that is gold does not glitter,
not all those who wander are lost.

J. R. R. Tolkien

Washington Irving's Oklahoma Visit

When Oklahoma celebrated its centennial in 2007, it was the 175th anniversary of Washington Irving's circular tour in Indian Territory. His visit might have been simply another page in Oklahoma history had Irving not been the best-known author in America in the early 1830s.

Forty-nine-year-old Irving returned to America in 1832 after spending nearly fifteen years in Europe. While in England, he wrote two stories that became very popular. When they were published in the United States, Americans greeted them with great enthusiasm, and almost overnight Irving was viewed as the greatest writer in American literature. The stories were "Rip Van Winkle," a tale about a man who falls asleep for twenty years (1819), and "The Legend of Sleepy Hollow," the story of schoolmaster Ichabod Crane, who meets a headless horseman (1820).

Soon after returning to the United States in 1832, Irving met Henry L. Ellsworth, the newly appointed commissioner charged with overseeing the move of eastern tribes to Indian Territory. Ellsworth invited Irving and a friend to join him on a trip to Fort Gibson in present-day eastern Oklahoma. Fort Gibson was then the westernmost military fort in the United States. Irving and his friend Charles J. Latrobe joined Ellsworth and traveled to western Missouri and then south to Fort Gibson, where Gen. Matthew Arbuckle, post commander, welcomed Ellsworth and his friends.

Arbuckle mentioned that three days earlier a troop of mounted rangers had left on a tour of the Plains Indian country between the Arkansas and Red rivers in country not yet explored by the military. When Commissioner Ellsworth said he would like to meet chiefs of the Plains Indians in the region, Arbuckle sent a messenger to the rangers telling them to stop and wait for the commissioner's party. Irving later wrote that they selected comfortable clothing to wear on

Washington Irving, painted in 1809 by John Wesley Jarvis. Courtesy of Historic Hudson Valley, Tarrytown, N.Y., SS.62.2 a-b.

their journey. Each member of the party took a bearskin and two blankets for bedding, plus flour, coffee, sugar, and salt pork; the group planned to rely on wild game for food. The party also took a tent should there be sickness or bad weather. The next morning they traveled northwest on the northern side of the Arkansas River through rugged country with thick undergrowth. Travel was slow, but a few days later they found the rangers waiting for them in camp a few miles south of modern Tulsa.

Ranger Capt. Jesse Bean greeted Ellsworth and Irving. The party decided to travel northwest and then go southwest before turning east to return to Fort Gibson. They left the next morning. That afternoon one of the Rangers killed an elk, and everyone had elk meat with his supper. The next evening they camped near where the Cimarron River flows into the Arkansas River in what is now southeastern Pawnee County. The following day some Osage Indians helped the rangers construct a bullboat made from a large buffalo hide. The bullboat transported Commissioner Ellsworth, Irving, and others safely across the Arkansas while the rangers forded the stream with the horses. Soon they made camp on the north side of the Cimarron River. It was October 15, 1832.

Travel was slow and difficult. Aside from animal and Indian trails, there were no roads and only scattered Indian settlements. After two days of travel, the party camped several miles south of modern Jennings. During the next three days, they traveled southwest across modern Payne County. The first night they camped near the present town of Yale, and the next night they camped on Stillwater Creek near modern Mehan, southeast of Stillwater. On October 21 their camp was a few miles west of modern Perkins. Earlier that day a ranger saw a wild horse and gave chase, but it got away. After camping, guide Pierre Beattie saddled a fresh horse, and, with his riata and rifle, he rode away. When he returned, he had in tow a young wild mustang. Irving noted that Beattie liked to hunt alone.

Leaving modern Payne County the following day, the group passed near the northwestern corner of present-day Lincoln County into what is now Logan County. They passed some miles east of modern Guthrie. The party headed southwest. At this point, there is some question as to their exact route. One account says that they camped northeast of modern Edmond near the head of Coffee Creek. Another account suggests that they crossed the southeastern corner of modern Kingfisher County. Regardless of the exact route, they did report that wild game was scarce and the men were hungry.

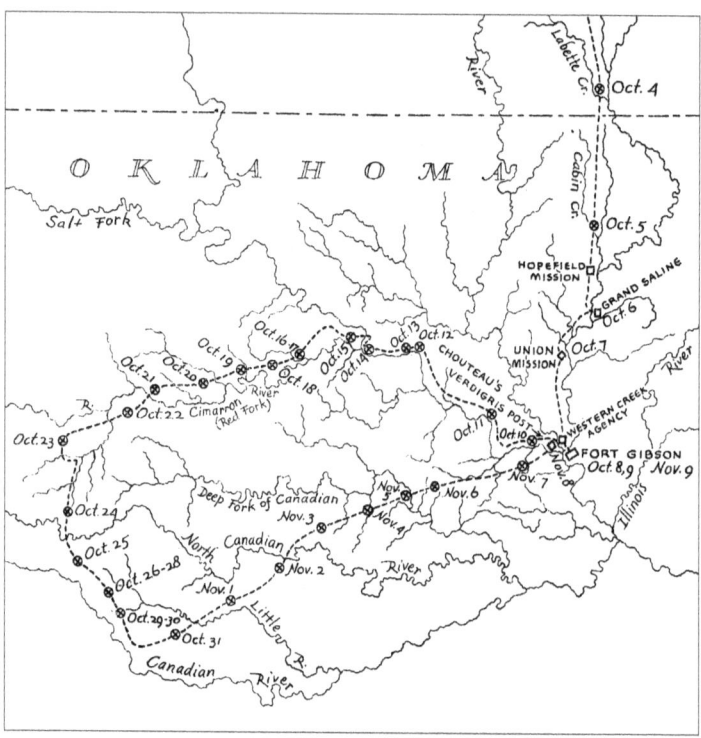

Approximate route of Washington Irving's 1832 tour of what would later be Oklahoma. From John Francis McDermott, ed., The Western Journals of Washington Irving (Norman: University of Oklahoma Press, 1944).

The next day, October 24, the party continued on and toward dusk made camp. Some of those who have tried to recreate the route suggest that the party passed the site of modern Jones and camped southeast of Spencer. Another account reports that the party traveled more to the west into what is now western Oklahoma County, camping northwest of modern Warr Acres. The next morning they moved their camp a few miles, and, according to Irving, rain fell and continued for the next three days. The party remained in camp. When the weather cleared on October 29, the group headed southeast looking for buffalo. They met some Osage Indians who told them where they could find buffalo. The party camped near the head of Little River near modern Moore in northern Cleveland County. There they spent two days hunting buffalo and chasing wild horses.

The party resumed their journey southeast, following Little River, which was flooding. They camped on high ground east of present-day Norman. Again, food was scarce for men and horses alike. The hardships soon caused the party to become disorganized and scatter. After continuing east and crossing the North Canadian River several times, some camped on November 4 near modern Okmulgee. The next night they camped in what is now eastern Okmulgee County. The half-famished parties came together when they found food at Creek settlements. The Creeks fed the men and their horses. Washington Irving reached Fort Gibson on November 8, one month after he first arrived at the post. He later wrote that everyone arrived "much battered, travel-stained and weather beaten." He added, however, that everyone was in "high health and spirits."

Two days later, Irving took passage on a small steamboat heading down the Arkansas River. We know of Irving's journey because he wrote about it in his book *A Tour on the Prairies* (1832). Commissioner Ellsworth and Charles J. Latrobe also wrote accounts of the journey that is remembered today because Washington Irving was there.

Artists in Indian Territory

EASTERN ARTISTS HAVE BEEN fascinated with what is now Oklahoma since the early nineteenth century. The first Anglo-American artists to come were Titian Peale and Samuel Seymour. They were members of Maj. Stephen H. Long's expedition to the Rocky Mountains in 1819 and 1820 that returned east through modern Oklahoma. Peale reportedly produced more than 100 drawings on the journey while Seymour is said to have made 150 sketches, of which 60 were completed as watercolors when he returned east. While many of the drawings from the expedition to the Rockies have survived, few have been identified as being made in Indian Territory.

The next American artist to come to Indian Territory was George Catlin in 1834. Born in Pennsylvania in 1796, Catlin was educated as a lawyer. He soon found he did not like practicing law and turned to painting. Catlin greatly admired Indians for living in harmony with nature, and he wanted to paint Indian life. He was the first painter to capture on canvas Plains Indians in their own territory, eventually becoming famous for some of these paintings. He was thirty-six years old when he arrived in 1834 with permission to join a military expedition at Fort Gibson in what is now east-central Oklahoma. Before the expedition left Fort Gibson, Catlin painted portraits of Osage Indians, including Chief Claremont, for whom the city of Claremore is named. Catlin also painted Chief Black Dog, who stood nearly seven feet tall; three young warriors who insisted on being painted together; and two young Kiowa children, captives of the Osages.

When the expedition left Fort Gibson under the command of Gen. Henry Leavenworth, it included nine companies of mounted dragoons. Aside from Catlin, others in the party were Col. Henry Dodge, Col. S. W. Kearney, and Lt. Jefferson Davis, who later became president of the Confederate States of America. The expedition traveled to Fort Holmes near modern Holdenville and south to where the Washita River flows into the Red River. Catlin later wrote that along the expedition's route he found an abundance of wild plums, grapes, currants, wild flowers, buffalo, and antelope.

At the mouth of the Washita River, many soldiers became ill with typhus fever, caused by hot weather and bad water. More than 150 soldiers in the expedition would eventually die. Meantime, Colonel Dodge, Catlin, and the healthy dragoons followed the divide between the Washita and Red rivers to a Comanche village near the base of the Wichita Mountains. Catlin marveled at the sight of wild horses, Arabian in appearance. He described the Comanches as low in stature, heavy and ungraceful except on horseback. Catlin praised their horsemanship and was impressed with their ability to protect themselves from atop their horses against enemy arrows. He painted what he saw, including a herd of buffalo running through a column of dragoons. Catlin painted Bow and Quiver, the Comanche head chief, and another chief called Mountain of Rocks. He also painted many Wichita and Kiowa Indians, and described the Kiowas as having "the fine and Roman outline of head."

The next eastern painter in Indian Territory was John Mix Stanley, a New Yorker, who traveled to Indian Territory in 1842 and set up a studio at Fort Gibson. Because Seminoles, Creeks, Osages, Chickasaws, and other tribes frequently visited the fort, Stanley found many subjects to paint. The following year, 1843, John Ross of the Cherokees called a grand council in Tahlequah. Stanley moved his studio to Tahlequah and was asked to design and paint a flag for the council. On it were two hands, one white and one red, on a background of white. During the council, Stanley painted many portraits. One was of Jim Shaw, a prominent Delaware Indian. He also painted Jesse Chisholm, a Cherokee, for whom the Chisholm Trail was later named. A few Indians feared having their portraits painted, but they soon lost this fear. It became an honor among the Indians to pose for Stanley.

In the fall of 1843, Stanley accompanied an Indian agent into what is now southwestern Oklahoma to attend a council with the Comanches. Stanley painted more portraits and landscape views. He remained in Indian Territory until about 1845 when he returned east. He first displayed his paintings in Cincinnati, Ohio, and then at the Smithsonian in Washington, D.C. Unfortunately, in 1865 a fire destroyed more than two hundred of them.

Next came Lt. James W. Abert, who led an eastbound reconnaissance party along the Canadian River to Fort Gibson in 1845. Abert, a native of New Jersey, and his party—consisting almost entirely of civilians—was attached to the third expedition of John C. Frémont, who took his main party to California. Abert made maps and produced written accounts of the journey. He also made several sketches and watercolors of native animals, activities at Bent's Fort in what is now eastern Colorado, and Indians including Kiowa chief Dohäsan, whose village they visited.

German artist Heinrich Balduin Möllhausen traveled to Oklahoma with Amiel Whipple's railroad mapping survey in 1853. He made drawings and watercolors. One watercolor shows the Canadian River near the town of Bridgeport. He also made a drawing of Camp Arbuckle near present-day Byars in McClain County. Möllhausen's other Oklahoma drawings portray Choctaws, Shawnees, Kiowas, Wichitas, and Indians belonging to other tribes.

Two French artists—Paul Frenzeny and Jules Tavernier—visited Oklahoma after *Harper's Weekly* sent them to illustrate the West. They rode the Missouri, Kansas and Texas Railroad from Kansas to Texas, stopping to make sketches at various points, including Fort Gibson. They made more drawings while traveling by train back across Indian Territory.

Rufus F. Zogbaum, a native of South Carolina, was also working for *Harper's Weekly* when he visited Indian Territory late in 1888. He made sketches of present-day Oklahoma City, Boomers, a crossing on the Canadian River, a relay house on the mail route between

Fort Reno and a military camp on the Cimarron River near modern Guthrie. He returned in 1896 to make additional sketches.

Three more eastern artists visited Indian Territory before 1900. A distant relative of George Catlin, Frederic Remington, sold his sheep ranch in Kansas in 1884 and traveled to Indian Territory in 1885 and again in 1888. His illustrations were published in *Century* magazine. Julian Scott, a native of Vermont and a Civil War artist, painted many Indian scenes in 1890. A native of Illinois who studied art in Chicago and Germany, Elbridge Ayer Burbank arrived in the late 1890s and was the only artist to paint Geronimo from life at Fort Sill in 1897.

Geronimo was a prisoner and reportedly had to be assured that Burbank was a "chief" before he would agree to be painted. According to one account, Geronimo figured a painting would be worth five dollars, so he charged Burbank a $2.50 sitting fee. Burbank had one problem with Geronimo. He could not get him to sit still; however, the artist succeeded in getting Geronimo's painting finished. When Geronimo saw it, he was so pleased that he signed it. He had only recently learned to sign his name.

Burbank remained in the Southwest and completed more than one thousand portraits of Indians during the years that followed. He even returned some years later to see Geronimo and was welcomed with open arms. Burbank recalled that Geronimo had acquired a taste for civilization, including apple pie. He demanded a five-dollar sitting fee when Burbank painted him again.

All of these artists documented Indian life in Indian Territory. Their art provides a visual record and valuable insights into Oklahoma history.

Artists Who Visited Indian Territory, 1820–1900

Titian Peale (1799–1885): A member of Long's expedition to the Rocky Mountains in 1819–1820. Although Peale reportedly produced more than one hundred drawings, it is not known if any were made in Indian Territory.

Samuel Seymour (1797–1882): Another member of Long's expedition. Seymour produced 150 landscape sketches, including two or three at Fort Smith. His drawings made in Indian Territory have not been identified.

George Catlin (1796–1872): The first artist to record the Plains Indians in their own territory. He arrived in Indian Territory in 1834, producing many paintings of Indians and Indian life.

John Mix Stanley (1814–1872): Came to Indian Territory in 1842 and reportedly remained until 1845. He produced countless Indian portraits and scenes.

James William Abert (1820–1897): Made a reconnaissance in Indian Territory in 1845 with guide Thomas Fitzpatrick. Abert made several sketches and watercolors.

Heinrich Balduin Möllhausen (1825–1905): Made three trips to the United States between 1849 and 1858. His drawings and watercolors included scenes in Indian Territory.

Vincent Coyler (1825–1888): Toured military installations in Indian Territory in 1868 and 1869. He represented Friends of the Indians, a Quaker organization concerned about humanitarian treatment of Indians. While he did not paint portraits of Indians, he did produce paintings of early forts in Indian Territory.

Paul Frenzeny (1840–1902): Hired by *Harper's Weekly* to illustrate the western frontier. Frenzeny came to Indian Territory in 1873, and many of his scenes were made at Fort Gibson.

JULES TAVERNIER (1844–1889): Hired by *Harper's Weekly* to go with Frenzeny to illustrate the West.

RUFUS F. ZOGBAUM (1849–1925): Hired by *Harper's Weekly* in 1888 to paint scenes in Indian Territory.

FREDERIC REMINGTON (1861–1909): Traveled through parts of Indian Territory in the springs of 1885 and 1888. The town of Remington in Osage County is supposedly named for the artist.

JULIAN SCOTT (1846–1901): Traveled west in 1890 as part of a census party and painted Indian scenes in Indian Territory now on display at the University of Pennsylvania Museum of Art.

ELBRIDGE AYER BURBANK (1858–1949): The only artist to paint Geronimo from life—in 1897 at Fort Sill. He completed more than one thousand Indian portraits. Burbank, located in Osage County, is named for the artist.

Angie Debo, Teacher and Writer

OKLAHOMA WRITER ANGIE DEBO became something of a controversial figure early in the twentieth century. She was a scholar who sought "to discover the truth and publish it." She did and not everyone liked it.

Angie Debo was not born in Oklahoma. Like so many early settlers, she came from somewhere else. Her birthplace was a farm about twenty miles south of Manhattan, Kansas. She was born January 30, 1890. When she was nine, her father bought a farm near Marshall, Oklahoma Territory. Her father and mother, Edward and Lina Debo, along with Angie and her younger brother, moved to Indian Territory in a covered wagon.

Debo attended a one-room school near her home. Three years later, at the age of twelve, she passed a territorial exam and received her common school diploma. The year was 1902. There was no high school for her to attend until one opened at Marshall. She rode her pony three and one-half miles to high school, but classes lasted only one year. As Debo later recalled, "there was no library, no magazines, and only the one book our parents managed to buy for each of us children as a Christmas present."

When Debo turned sixteen, the legal age to obtain a teacher's certificate, she took another territorial exam and became a rural schoolteacher. She taught in Logan and Garfield counties. When the town of Marshall started a new four-year high school, she went back and graduated with the first class in 1913. She was twenty-three years old. After teaching for two years, she entered the University of Oklahoma and majored in history. Professor Edward Everett Dale convinced her that she could have a career as a writer of history. After graduating in 1918, she worked as a principal but returned to teaching history in Enid.

In 1923, she decided to get more education. She went to the

Angie Debo. Courtesy of Western History Collections, University of Oklahoma Libraries (University of Oklahoma Press Collection, no. 14).

University of Chicago, but because women were then not allowed to enter the history field, she studied international relations. She earned her master's degree in 1924. Her master's thesis on the American policy of isolation was published a few months later. Debo became a member of the History Department at what is now West Texas State University at Canyon. She also worked on her doctorate at the University of Oklahoma and received it in 1933. The following year she became curator of the Panhandle-Plains Historical Museum in Canyon. Her doctoral dissertation was published that year by the University of Oklahoma Press.

The Rise and Fall of the Choctaw Republic won an award and was so well received that she stopped teaching and became a freelance writer, concentrating on Indian history. To make ends meet, she taught summers in Texas and Oklahoma and signed a contract with the University of Oklahoma Press to write a book on Indian history, *And Still the Waters Run*. She delivered the manuscript to the press, but its editors would not publish it. The manuscript describes the theft from Indians of their lands in Indian Territory. Her contract with the press was nullified. In 1940, however, the book was published by Princeton University Press. Debo was then fifty. She recalled that from that point on no state university in Oklahoma would hire her. She did find work for a year directing the WPA Federal Writers' Project in Oklahoma and edited the WPA guide to the state. She also wrote a chapter on Oklahoma history for the guide. When the guide was published, however, Debo was surprised to find a different chapter written by an unknown writer substituted for her own. Although her name appeared as the author of the chapter, she had not written it. It contained errors and was slanted toward the white settlers' view of Oklahoma history.

In 1941, she completed another book, *The Road to Disappearance: A History of the Creek Indians*, which was published by the University of Oklahoma Press. It was a carefully researched book telling the story of the Creeks from their aboriginal beginnings to the loss of their political independence during the first decade of the twentieth century. The book served as a basis for a landmark U.S. Supreme Court decision in which important land rights for the Creek nation were recognized.

Debo returned to teaching in rural Oklahoma schools. During World War II, she served as pastor of the Methodist church in Marshall. In 1947, Oklahoma State University hired Debo as curator of maps in its library, a position she held until 1955.

In 1949, the University of Oklahoma Press published her book *Oklahoma: Foot-Loose and Fancy-Free*, which was written at the invitation of the Rockefeller Committee. The book was a sweeping look at the forty-sixth state that concentrated on Debo's interpretation instead of on factual depth. She noted that in Oklahoma, "all the experiences that went into the making of the nation" were "speeded up" and "all the American traits have been intensified."

In her insightful look at education in Oklahoma, she noted that Oklahomans wanted schools but not scholarship. She wrote that the average grade school, high school, or college student "does not rank high in scholarship. The young people and their parents in country and city alike care more for 'activities' than for study." Thus scholarship and critical thinking were not emphasized at most levels. Scholarship, the body of principles and practices used by scholars to make their claims about the world as valid and trustworthy as possible, were pretty much ignored. Therefore—since citizens lacked critical thinking skills and as such were putty in the hands of the good ol' boys—it was easy for politicians, many with little education, to get elected to public office.

During her lifetime, Debo wrote nine books and edited many others. She also wrote numerous articles for magazines and journals, produced chapters and forewords in many books, and reviewed books for the *New York Times*. Her last book, *Geronimo: The Man, His Time, His Place,* was finished when she was eighty-three and still living in Marshall. It won a Wrangler Award from the National Cowboy Hall of Fame in 1978.

Although Debo received many honors and awards from individuals and groups in Oklahoma and elsewhere during her lifetime, the state of Oklahoma did not recognize her achievements until late in her life. Early in January 1988, Governor Henry L. Bellmon went to Marshall and presented Angie Debo with an Award for Scholarly Distinction. Her portrait was also hung in the state capitol next to those of humorist Will Rogers and other prominent Oklahomans. Angie Debo was ninety-eight. Less than one month after the governor presented her the award, Angie Debo died and was buried in North Cemetery at Marshall.

Woody Guthrie, Father of American Folk Music

SOME OKLAHOMANS STILL HAVE mixed emotions when they hear the name of their native son Woody Guthrie. Since his death in 1967, however, there has been greater appreciation of his life and legacy. Today, many people in Oklahoma and elsewhere consider him the father of American folk music.

The story of Woodrow Wilson "Woody" Guthrie began on July 14, 1912, when he was born in Okemah. He was the second son of Charles and Nora Belle Guthrie. As a boy, he was attracted to music and learned to play the guitar, mandolin, fiddle, and harmonica. His early childhood in Okemah was comfortable until his mother became ill and an older sister died. The family broke up. Guthrie spent winters in school, but during the summer months he worked as a migrant farmhand to make ends meet.

In 1929, the family came together again in Pampa, Texas, only to experience the Dust Bowl days of the mid-1930s. During this time, Guthrie spent his spare time singing and playing his guitar. When Guthrie was twenty-five in 1937, he went to Los Angeles wanting to be a singing western entertainer. He appeared on several radio programs acting like a hayseed and singing folk music and songs he had written, including "Do Re, Mi," "Oklahoma Hills" (Oklahoma's state folk song), and "Philadelphia Lawyer." Guthrie did not compose his own music but instead composed original lyrics for old tunes including traditional folk songs.

In California, he became sympathetic to the causes of the Communist Party. Seeing so many people down and out, he sought change to help them and began writing articles for leftist newspapers including the *Daily Worker*. In 1939, Guthrie moved to New York City, where the intellectual community embraced his authenticity and leftist philosophy. This period in Guthrie's life later became the

Woodie Guthrie and fellow singer Pete Seeger about 1943. Used with permission of the Woody Guthrie Archives (Photos-1, Box-2, Image-16), New York City.

source of much right-wing criticism of Guthrie. In 1940, Guthrie met Alan Lomax, who was going around the country recording folk songs for the archives of the Library of Congress. Lomax recorded Guthrie's ballads. They attracted the attention of RCA Victor, which released *Dust Bowl Ballads,* his first album of original songs. He gained more national attention for his music.

During the 1940s, Guthrie performed with many other popular musicians, including Burl Ives, the Almanac Singers, Huddie "Leadbelly" Ledbetter, Pete Seeger, and Josh White. Guthrie continued to write songs. During his lifetime, he wrote more than one thousand songs, many for children. Two of his well-known songs are "So Long, It's Been Good to Know You" and "This Land Is Your Land." They were written after he moved to New York.

"This Land Is Your Land" was written on a cold February day in response to the then-popular tune "God Bless America," sung by Kate Smith. Guthrie killed two bitter verses and rewrote his song in a patriotic tone. Otherwise, the song probably would not be the popular hit it is today. Many of Guthrie's songs expressed his deep love for Oklahoma and his country. His music reflected optimism for his fellow man and humor.

During World War II, Guthrie saw active duty with the Merchant Marine and was briefly in the U.S. Army. He found time to write *Bound for Glory*, a semi-autobiographical account of his Dust Bowl years, published in 1943. Guthrie also illustrated the book. Literary critic Clifton Fadiman praised the book and called Guthrie a national treasure. Guthrie also wrote poems and was praised as a fine poet. Some critics said he was more of a poet than a songwriter. He also was a talented artist. After his death, a large collection of his art ended up in the Library of Congress.

In New York, some of Guthrie's songs lost their folk flavor found in his earlier pieces. Guthrie borrowed the "illiterate" style of fellow Oklahoman Will Rogers in order to retain a folksy flavor to his performing. Guthrie once wrote, "I ain't a writer. I want that understood. I'm just a little one-cylinder guitar picker," but Guthrie, like Will Rogers, was educated and well read.

Guthrie continued to write songs and perform during the early 1950s. By the middle 1950s, his health was deteriorating. He had frequent mood swings, and his behavior was often unpredictable.

Alcoholism was suspected. So was schizophrenia. When he was correctly diagnosed by doctors, Guthrie was found to have Huntington's chorea, a degenerative nerve disorder that he had inherited from his mother. For thirteen years, he was in and out of hospitals until October 3, 1967, when he died in Creedmoor State Hospital, Queens, New York. He was fifty-five. His body was cremated, and his ashes were scattered in the ocean off Coney Island.

In 2004, the Oklahoma Senate honored Guthrie's memory by hanging his portrait painted by Charles Banks Wilson in the Oklahoma Capitol near Will Rogers's portrait. Guthrie is best remembered today for his ballads about a floundering America between the Depression and Dust Bowl days and World War II. His songs gave voice to what Americans were feeling, but they also roused a sense of patriotism across the land. His music lives on through his son Arlo Guthrie and other musicians, including Bob Dylan and Bruce Springsteen.

Gene Autry, Yodeling Cowboy

On September 29, 1907, Dr. Eugene E. Ledbetter traveled six miles west from Tioga, Texas, to the farm of Delbert and Elnora Ozment Autry to deliver their firstborn. The baby was named Orvon Gene Autry. His middle name was taken from the doctor's first name. He became Gene Autry, the singer and cowboy motion picture star.

Although most biographies of Autry's life list his place of birth as Tioga in southwestern Grayson County, Texas, the truth is that he was born on the family ranch in neighboring Cooke County about seventy miles northwest of Dallas. Gene Autry's father and mother were born in Cooke County during the 1880s. Gene's grandfather, a Baptist preacher, taught his grandson to sing when he was five, and soon Gene joined the church choir. His mother also encouraged his music and taught him hymns and folk songs. By the age of twelve, he was earning money by working on his uncle's farm bailing and stacking hay. He used some of the money to buy a mail-order guitar for eight dollars.

About two years later, when Autry was fifteen, his family moved to Achille, Oklahoma, and later homesteaded near Ravia in Johnston County northeast of Ardmore. By then, young Gene was already playing his guitar and singing when asked to do so. He found work as a baggage hauler at the local St. Louis & San Francisco Railway depot. There the station master gave him free lessons in telegraphy. Gene soon became a telegraph operator and was assigned to the railroad station at Chelsea in Rogers County. When not busy, he passed the time by strumming his guitar and singing.

Gene was twenty years old in the summer of 1927 when a man entered the railroad station at Chelsea as Gene was passing his time playing his guitar and singing. The man told him to continue and sat down to listen as he looked over a message he wanted to send. Presently, he asked Gene to sing another song, and Gene did. When the man gave Gene the message to send, he told the young man that with hard work he might have a future in radio. After the man left, Autry looked at the name on the message and realized the visitor was humorist Will Rogers, known around the world as a writer and movie star. Encouraged by Rogers, Autry worked on his music and saved his money.

In 1929, he went to Tulsa, auditioned, and landed a job on KVOO radio as "Gene Autry, Oklahoma's Yodeling Cowboy." A representative of a New York record company heard him sing and asked Autry to go to New York for an audition. They liked his voice but said he should stay away from popular hits. They urged him to find his own kind of songs and sound and get more experience. Autry did, and six months later he was back in New York making his first recordings—"My Dreaming of You" and "My Alabama Home." He soon signed a contract with the American Record Corporation. He was pleased, but soon after his first recordings were released, his forty-five-year-old mother died. His father left home, and Gene became head of the family, supporting himself, his two sisters, and a young brother.

His first recording hit came in 1931 with "That Silver-Haired Daddy of Mine." Autry had written the song with the help of a friend one night at the railroad depot in Chelsea. Within a month, the song sold 30,000 copies. By the end of the year, 500,000 copies had been sold. It eventually sold more than one million copies.

Autry joined the *National Barn Dance* program on WLS radio in Chicago. It was there that he became a major national star and soon attracted the attention of Hollywood, where sound pictures were new. Makers of western films, especially the cheaply produced B films, needed sounds. Autry soon went to California and appeared in the 1934 Mascot Pictures film *In Old Santa Fe*. He then had minor parts in a few other films and again found success. Audiences loved him. His first starring role was in Republic Picture's *Tumbling Tumbleweeds* in 1935. It was followed by *Melody Trail*, *The Sagebrush Troubadour*, and others. (A list of Autry's motion pictures is reproduced below.) Republic began producing one Gene Autry movie

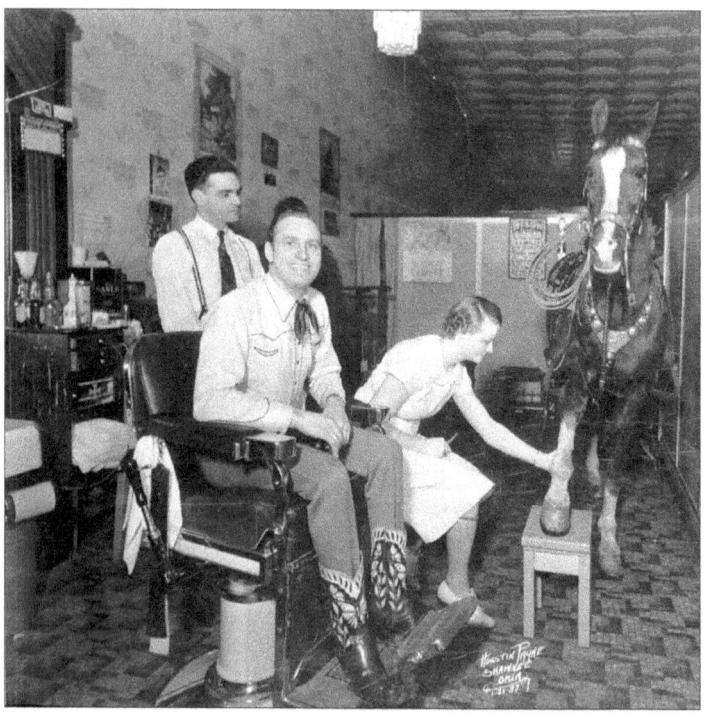

Gene Autry in a Shawnee barbershop, January 31, 1937. Courtesy of Western History Collections, University of Oklahoma Libraries (Babcock Collection, no. 28).

every six weeks. He was paid five thousand dollars for each. By the late 1930s, Gene Autry was one of the top box-office attractions in the nation behind Mickey Rooney, Clark Gable, and Spencer Tracy. Meantime, Autry's recording career continued. During his lifetime, he recorded 635 songs, including more than a dozen gold and platinum records. He wrote more than 300 of the songs.

With his wealth, Autry purchased twelve hundred acres of land just west of Berwyn, Oklahoma, north of Ardmore, to build a ranch to serve as a headquarters for a rodeo road show. A resident of Berwyn, Cecil Crosby, got the idea of changing the town's name to Gene Autry to honor the fast-rising recording, radio, and movie star. Residents of Berwyn signed a petition requesting the change. The Santa Fe Railroad and the Post Office Department gave their approval, and in November 1941 the Carter County Commission passed a resolution changing Berwyn's name to Gene Autry, Oklahoma. The official change took place on the state's thirty-fourth birthday, Sunday, November 16. More than 35,000 people were in the newly named town when Gene Autry and his crew broadcast his *Melody Ranch* on the CBS radio network from atop a railroad flatcar parked on a siding at the town's station.

The renaming of Berwyn to Gene Autry occurred just weeks before Pearl Harbor was bombed. World War II interrupted Autry's plans and career. In July 1942, during a live broadcast of his *Melody Ranch* radio program, he was inducted into the U.S. Army Air Force as a technical sergeant. He already had a private pilot's license and received basic training. Autry became a flight officer in 1942 with the Ninety-first Ferrying Squadron of the 555th Army Air Base Unit. He flew various types of planes, including C-104s and C-109s. Flying C-109s, he ferried fuel, ammunition, and arms to the China-Burma-India theater of war and flew over the Himalayas. He also made one flight to the CBI theater via the Azores off North Africa. Heading for the Azores, the plane he was copiloting had to turn around and retrace its course to avoid a typhoon. When his plane landed five hours later at Gander Bay, Newfoundland, one engine was out and the craft was low on fuel.

At the end of the war, Autry transferred to Special Services and took a USO troupe to the South Pacific before being honorably discharged in 1946. He then returned to his motion picture career. In 1950, he became the first major movie star to enter television with a weekly program on CBS called *The Gene Autry Show*. His success led him to produce other television westerns, including *Annie Oakley, The Range Rider, The Adventures of Champion,* and the first thirty-nine episodes of *Death Valley Days.*

Gene Autry was a sharp businessman. He invested in radio

and television stations during the 1950s. In 1961, he purchased the American League California Angels and held the title of vice president of the American League for the rest of his life.

Autry is also memorialized on the Hollywood Walk of Fame. Since 1960, the Hollywood Chamber of Commerce has honored celebrities and fictional characters by embedding five-pointed stars in a three-and-a-half-mile stretch of sidewalk along Hollywood Boulevard near Vine Street, each with a bronze emblem indicating the category for which he or she is honored. Autry is the only entertainer to have all five stars—for motion pictures, television, phonograph records, radio broadcasting, and live theater.

His longtime dream of preserving the heritage of the Old West came true late in 1988 when the Gene Autry Western Heritage Museum opened in Los Angeles. In 2004, it merged with the Southwest Museum, becoming the Autry National Center. Before he died in his California home on October 2, 1998, at the age of ninety-one, Gene Autry received numerous awards and honors. He had come a long way since he began his career as Oklahoma's Yodeling Cowboy.

GENE AUTRY FILMS

1934 *In Old Santa Fe • Mystery Mountain*

1935 *Sagebrush Troubadour • Melody Trail • The Phantom Empire • The Singing Vagabond • Tumbling Tumbleweeds*

1936 *Ride, Ranger, Ride • Oh, Susanna! • The Old Corral • Comin' Round the Mountain • Red River Valley • Singing Cowboy • The Big Show • Guns and Guitars*

1937 *Boots and Saddles • Round-up Time in Texas • Git Along, Little Dogies • Rootin' Tootin' Rhythm • Manhattan Merry-Go-Round • Public Cowboy No. 1 • Springtime in the Rockies • Yodelin' Kid from Pine Ridge*

1938 *Rhythm of the Saddle • Gold Mine in the Sky • Western Jamboree • The Old Barn Dance • Prairie Moon*

1939 *Mexicali Rose • South of the Border • Colorado Sunset • Home on the Prairie • Mountain Rhythm • In Old Monterey • Rovin' Tumbleweeds • Blue Montana Skies*

1940 *Gaucho Serenade • Shooting High • Carolina Moon • Ride, Tenderfoot, Ride • Rodeo Dough • Melody Ranch • Men with Steel Faces • Rancho Grande*

1941 *Down Mexico Way • Under Fiesta Stars • Sierra Sue • Back in the Saddle • Sunset in Wyoming • The Singing Hill • Ridin' on a Rainbow*

1942 *Stardust on the Sage • Heart of the Rio Grande • Home in Wyomin' • Call of the Canyon • Cowboy Serenade • Bells of Capistrano*

1946 *Sioux City Sue*

1947 *Robin Hood of Texas • Twilight on the Rio Grande • Saddle Pals • The Last Round Up • Trail to San Antone*

1948 *The Strawberry Roan • Loaded Pistols*

1949 *The Cowboy and the Indians • Rim of the Canyon • Riders in the Sky • Riders of the Whistling Pines • Sons of New Mexico • The Big Sombrero*

1950 *Indian Territory • Cow Town • Beyond the Purple Hills • Mule Train • The Blazing Sun • The Gene Autry Show* (TV series)

1951 *Valley of Fire • Whirl Wind • The Hills of Utah • Gene Autry and the Mounties • Texans Never Cry • Silver Canyon*

1952 *Apache Country • Wagon Team • Barbed-Wire • Blue Canadian Rockies • Night Stage to Galveston • The Old West*

1953 *Saginaw Trail • Pack Train • On Top of Old Smoky • Goldtown Ghost Riders • Last of the Pony Riders • Winning of the West*

1956 *Hollywood Bronc Busters*

1959 *Alias Jesse James*

1968 *Silent Treatment*

Patti Page, the Singing Rage

THE YEAR WAS 1946. World War II had ended. Oklahoma and the nation were adjusting to peace. In Tulsa, Clara Ann Fowler, eighteen, was singing on a fifteen-minute live program on KTUL radio. Clara was billed as Patti Page because the program was sponsored by the Page Milk Company. In a hotel room across town, Jack Rael, a dance band manager from Chicago, turned on the radio in his room. Clara Ann Fowler's singing caught his attention.

When the radio program ended, Rael telephoned the station and asked to speak to Patti Page. When she came on the line, he explained that he had heard her program and enjoyed her singing, and asked if she had ever thought about leaving Tulsa and singing in the big time. Fowler said, "No," that she wanted to be a commercial artist.

Rael explained that he was manager of the Jimmy Joy band from Chicago and that they were in Tulsa for a one-night stand. Rael persuaded her to send him some records of her singing. Less than two months later, the five-foot, four-inch singer from Oklahoma opened in Chicago for a six-week engagement with the band. She was billed as "The Singing Rage, Miss Patti Page."

The story of Clara Ann Fowler's quick rise to fame is like a fairytale. Born in Claremore on November 8, 1927, she was one of eleven children and grew up on a farm near Claremore where her parents tried to make ends meet. She enjoyed music and began singing at an early age at the Church of Christ in Tulsa.

At eighteen, she found a job singing on KTUL with Al Clauser and his Oklahoma Outlaws. When another singer with the band, her predecessor as Patti Page, left, Clara Ann Fowler was given the job and the stage name.

During the late 1940s, Patti Page toured with Jimmy Joy's band throughout the United States. She gained much experience and developed her silky voice and pure and simple singing style. Soon she was asked to make recordings. In 1948, she recorded the song "Confess" for Mercury Records. It required the singer to answer another vocalist. Because it was a low-budget recording, Rael suggested she sing the second part as well. She did. The novelty of one person singing two parts was a hit with listeners. The song became a Top 20 hit.

Patti liked the multiple-voice idea. She asked if she could sing an entire song as a quartet. When she approached Mitch Miller of Mercury Records with the idea, he was not sure it would work but let Patti record a song in multiple tracks. The song was "With My Eyes Wide Open I'm Dreaming." The 1948 record was her second hit and her first record to sell one million copies.

Two years later she recorded "All My Love." It was a bigger hit and remained number one in sales for five weeks. A few months later came an even bigger hit. "The Tennessee Waltz" was the top-selling record for about thirty weeks. In the following years the record sold nearly 10 million copies. At one point in her career she said, "I was a kid from Oklahoma who never wanted to be a singer, but was told I could sing. And things snowballed."

During the 1950s, Oklahoma's "Singing Rage" was the best-selling female vocalist in the nation. Many of her recordings became gold records. Early in the decade, she was selected favorite female vocalist in the first nationwide audience poll taken on Dick Clark's *Bandstand* program. In 1956, she married her first husband, Charles O'Curran, a Hollywood choreographer best known for staging the dance numbers of many Elvis Presley films. Patti and Charles adopted two children, Kathleen and Danny. The couple divorced in 1972.

Page's popularity continued during the 1960s. She received more national exposure in the new medium of television as a guest singer on such popular programs as *The Dean Martin Show*. In 1965, she recorded the title song from the Bette Davis film *Hush, Hush, Sweet Charlotte*. She performed the song at the Thirty-seventh Annual Academy Awards.

In 1990, she married Jerome J. Filiciotto. Until his death in 2009,

Patti Page. Courtesy of Miss Patti Page.

Patti and her second husband divided their time between a home near San Diego, California, and Hilltop Farm in New Hampshire, where they marketed Patti Page Organic Pancake mix and bottles of maple syrup.

Patti Page was still performing at age eighty. Thus far in her remarkable career she has sold about 100 million records and earned fifteen certified gold records. She rode on the Oklahoma Centennial float in the Tournament of Roses Parade in January 2007 and cherishes her Oklahoma roots. Page died January 1, 2013, in California.

Patti Page's Hit Songs

1948 "Confess"

1949 "With My Eyes Wide Open, I'm Dreaming" (Gold record)

1950 "I Don't Care If the Sun Don't Shine"
"All My Love (Bolero)" (Gold record)
"The Tennessee Waltz" (Gold-Platinum record)

1951 "Would I Love You (Love You, Love You)" (Gold record)
"Mockin' Bird Hill" (Gold record)

"Down the Trail of Achin' Hearts"
"Mister and Mississippi" (Gold record)
"Detour" (Gold record)
"And So to Sleep Again"

1952 "And So to Sleep Again"
"Come What May"
"Once in a While"
"I Went to Your Wedding" (Gold record)
"You Belong to Me" (Gold record)
"Why Don't You Believe Me" (Gold record)

1953 "(How Much Is That) Doggie in the Window" (Gold record)
"Butterflies"
"Changing Partners" (Gold record)

1954 "Cross over the Bridge" (Gold record)
"Steam Heat"
"What a Dream"
"Let Me Go, Lover!"

1955 "Go On with the Wedding"

1956 "Allegheny Moon" (Gold record)
"Mama from the Train"

1957 "Old Cape Cod" (Gold record)
"A Poor Man's Roses (or a Rich Man's Gold)"

1958 "Left Right Out of Your Heart
(Hi Lee Hi Lo Hi Lup Up Up)" (Gold record)

1962 "Go On Home"
"Most People Get Married"

1965 "Hush, Hush, Sweet Charlotte" (Gold record)

1968 "Gentle on My Mind"

1973 "Hello, We're Lonely" (with Tom T. Hall)

1981 "No Aces"

Kay Starr, Salon Singer

DURING THE MIDDLE TWENTIETH century, the name Kay Starr was well known in Oklahoma and across the nation. From the late 1930s into the late 1960s, she was one of the most prominent popular singers in the nation. Oklahomans were proud to claim her. Many still are even though she is not as well known today.

Kay Starr was born Katherine LaVerne Starks on July 21, 1922, in Dougherty, located along the Washita River in the Chickasaw Nation, Murray County. Her father was Harry Starks, a full-blood Iroquois Indian, and her mother, Annie, was Irish. When she was three years old, her parents moved to Dallas, where her father installed sprinkler systems in buildings. During the Depression, her mother raised chickens in a henhouse behind their home to help the family income.

Her publicist claims that when she was nine years old and living in Dallas, Katherine began singing to chickens as they sat on their roosts. Her parents paid little attention to their daughter's singing until an aunt recognized her talent. The aunt suggested that her mother enter Katherine in a weekly talent contest on WRR radio in Dallas. Her mother did, and Katherine won with the song "Now's the Time to Fall in Love." She returned each week and continued to win, until WRR radio gave her a three-day-a-week, fifteen-minute program on the station. Katherine sang popular songs and country music. She was paid three dollars for each program, and she received sacks of fan mail.

Three months after she started her radio program, her parents moved to Memphis, Tennessee. Katherine soon found work singing on *Starr Time,* broadcast by WREC radio in Memphis. She also appeared on the station's *Saturday Night Jamboree.* During this time, Katherine took the name Kay Starr because her name was often misspelled in her fan mail.

Her first big break came in 1937 when Joe Venuti and his band arrived in Memphis to play at the Peabody Hotel. Venuti's contract called for a female vocalist with his band. Hearing Kay Starr on the Memphis radio station, he was impressed and, with her parents' permission, hired her. She was so successful that she toured with the band for the rest of the summer and during the next two summers when she was not in school. Because she was a teenager, her mother accompanied her with the band.

During the summer of 1939, Joe Venuti recommended her to Bob Crosby, who had a well-known orchestra. Crosby was looking for a female vocalist. She got the job, and during her time with the group she sang regularly on the *Camel Caravan* radio program. That year, Kay joined the Glenn Miller Orchestra for two weeks, replacing Marion Hutton, who was ill. She and her mother then returned to Memphis, where in 1940 Kay was graduated from high school. She then rejoined Joe Venuti's orchestra in California.

The general draft call-up for World War II caused Venuti to break up his band. Kay joined Wingy Manone's New Orleans Jazz Band but was hired away in 1943 to sing with Charlie Barnet and his band to replace Lena Horne. With Barnet's band, she recorded many records that were distributed to the U.S. armed forces around the world. She also made five records on the Decca label with Barnet and his band. One of the records, "Share Croppin' Blues," was very successful and brought her new recognition.

Kay's career with the Charlie Barnet band ended suddenly when she caught pneumonia. She lost her voice. Instead of seeking surgery, she stopped speaking for six months in hopes her voice would return. It did, but now Kay's voice was deeper and huskier. Her new voice became her trademark.

Moving to Los Angeles, she began a career as a solo performer. Already well known, she had no difficulty finding work in night clubs. She also was invited to sing two songs on the Capitol label's all-star *Volumes of Jazz* series in 1945. In 1947, Capital Records signed

Kay Starr. Courtesy of Guy Logsdon.

her to a contract. Her song "I'm the Lonesomest Gal in Town" was well received. Enjoying even greater success was "So Tired," her first top ten hit in early 1949. In 1950, she recorded Perry Como's polka "Hoop-Dee-Doo," which climbed to number two on the charts.

On a visit to her hometown of Dougherty, she heard Pee Wee King's fiddle tune "Bonaparte's Retreat" and loved the simple melody. She recorded the song at Capitol, and it became a million-dollar best seller. She then recorded other songs, including a duet with popular country singer Tennessee Ernie Ford in 1952, and "Wheel of Fortune," a song that became an overnight hit and earned Kay another gold record.

During the next two years, Kay recorded many more single records in different genres—jazz, country, popular, spirituals, Broadway tunes, and rhythm and blues. By 1954, she had logged more than two dozen top-forty successes. After signing with RCA, she had another gold record with "The Rock and Roll Waltz" in 1956.

Although she became the first female vocalist with a top hit in the rock-and-roll era, her popularity as a recording star began fading with the advent of rock and roll.

During the 1960s, she turned to more solo concerts in the United States and England, including many performances in Las Vegas and Reno, Nevada. By the 1970s—she was then in her fifties—she cut back on her performances but occasionally did concerts and sang in nightclubs.

She married six times and has a daughter and grandchild. At last report, the girl from Dougherty, in her eighties, was living in Bel Air, California.

Notes on Sources

1. THE LAND, RIVERS, TOWNS, AND WILD CREATURES

THE CROSS TIMBERS

One of the earliest accounts of travel in what is now Oklahoma may be found in Washington Irving's *A Tour on the Prairies,* contained in *The Crayon Miscellany* (Philadelphia: Carey, Lea, & Blanchard, 1835). References to Dodge and Gregg may be found in Carolyn T. Foreman's *The Cross Timbers* (Muskogee: Star Printery, 1947). Marcy's material comes from Randolph B. Marcy and George Brinton McClellan, *Exploration of the Red River of Louisiana in the year 1852* (Washington, D.C.: A. O. P. Nicholson, 1854). See also Richard V. Francaviglia's *The Cast Iron Forest* (Austin: University of Texas Press, 2000) and "The Ancient Cross Timbers," produced by Tree-Ring Laboratory, University of Arkansas, and available on the Web. Of help was a brochure on the "Keystone Ancient Forest" prepared by The Nature Conservancy and available to visitors of the Keystone Ancient Forest Preserve in northeastern Oklahoma.

SOME WILD CREATURES

Much of the story of buffalo in Oklahoma may be found in my *The Buffalo Book, rev. ed.* (Athens: Ohio University Press, Swallow Press, 1989). Other helpful sources include C. J. Latrobe's *The Rambler in Oklahoma* (Oklahoma City: Harlow Publishing, 1955), C. N. Gould's *Travels through Oklahoma* (Oklahoma City: Harlow Publishing, 1928), Josiah Gregg's *Commerce of the Prairies* (two volumes) (New York: Henry G. Langley, 1845), Randolph B. Marcy's *Exploration of the Red River of Louisiana,* 32nd Cong., 2nd sess., 1853, S. Ex. Doc. 54, Washington, D.C., and F. S. Barde's *Field Forest and Stream in Oklahoma, 1912,* Annual Report of the State Game and Fish Warden (Guthrie, Okla., 1912.)

Another good source is *Mammals of Oklahoma* by William Caire, Jack D. Tyler, Bryan P. Glass, and Michael A. Mares (Norman: University of Oklahoma Press, 1989). Information on a recent report of black bears was found in Sheila Stogsdill, "Backyard Bear," *Oklahoman,*

July 28, 2007. See also, Jack D. Tyler and Wendy J. Anderson, "Historical Accounts of Several Large Mammals in Oklahoma," in *Proceedings of the Oklahoma Academy of Science* 70 (1990).

OKLAHOMA RIVERS
Source material included maps available at the Oklahoma Water Resources Board in Oklahoma City. Other bits and pieces came from the files of the Oklahoma History Society and the Western History Collections, University of Oklahoma Libraries.

NAMING AND PRONOUNCING OKLAHOMA TOWNS
The primary source for information was George H. Shirk's *Oklahoma Place Names* (Norman: University of Oklahoma Press, 1987). Other details were found in local historical sketches provided by chambers of commerce in several cities. Some information was found in *Chronicles of Oklahoma*.

WHEN OKLAHOMA GOT ELECTRIC LIGHTS
Much information was found in "The Story of Oklahoma Gas and Electric Co." (Oklahoma City: OG&E, 1983), the "History of the Public Service Company of Oklahoma" online at paoklahoma.com, and "History of OEC [Oklahoma Electric Cooperative]" online at okcoop.org. Additional material came from two undated booklets: "History of the Electric Power Industry" published by the Edison Electric Institute, and "History of Lighting and Lamps."

OKLAHOMA'S BLACK GOLD
Early historical material came from Muriel H. Wright's "First Oklahoma Oil Was Produced in 1859," *Chronicles of Oklahoma* 4, no. 4 (1926), and "Historical Tour of Oklahoma's Oil & Gas Industry," published by the Mid-Continent Oil and Gas Association of Oklahoma, Oklahoma City. Other material was found in the files of the Oklahoma Historical Society and the Western History Collections, University of Oklahoma Libraries.

II. On Trails and Rails

Early Trails
Helpful was Grant Foreman's "Early Trails through Oklahoma," *Chronicles of Oklahoma* 3, no. 2 (1925). Information on early trails linking Texas and modern Oklahoma was found in the *Handbook of Texas* online (tshaonline.org/handbook/online) and in the author's files on western trails.

Military Forts
The many sources consulted included the files of the Oklahoma History Society's *Chronicles of Oklahoma* and Vinson Lackey's *The Forts of Oklahoma* (Tulsa: Oil Capital Printing, 1963). Other publications used included Brad Agnew's *Fort Gibson: Terminal on the Trail of Tears* (Norman: University of Oklahoma Press, 1980), Edwin C. Bearss and Arrell M. Gibson's *Fort Smith: Little Gibraltar on the Arkansas* (Norman: University of Oklahoma Press, 1979), and Robert W. Frazer's *Forts of the West* (Norman: University of Oklahoma Press, 1977).

Trading Posts and Early Businesses
The bulk of the source material was found in *Chronicles of Oklahoma*, especially W. H. Clift's "Warren's Trading Post," *Chronicles of Oklahoma* 2, no. 2 (1924), and Harriette Johnson Westbrook, "The Chouteaus and Their Commercial Enterprises," pts. 1 and 2, *Chronicles of Oklahoma* 11, nos. 2 and 3 (1933). Other bits and pieces were found in the files of the Oklahoma Historical Society.

The Butterfield Overland Stage
Sources included Grant Foreman's "The California Overland Mail Route through Oklahoma," *Chronicles of Oklahoma* 9, no. 3 (1931), and Muriel H. Wright's "Historic Places on the Old Stage Line from Fort Smith to Red River," *Chronicles of Oklahoma* 11, no. 2 (1933). Other bits and pieces came from the files of the Oklahoma Historical Society and from the *Handbook of Texas* online.

Early Cattle Trails and Ranching
Much material came from the author's files and his *Cowboy Culture: A Saga of Five Centuries* (New York: Knopf, 1981). Bits and pieces came from the *Handbook of Texas* online.

When the Railroads Arrived
This story was taken from chapter eight in the author's *Entrepreneurs of the Old West* (New York: Knopf, 1986) and from the author's files.

"No Man's Land"
The files of the Oklahoma Historical Society and *Chronicles of Oklahoma* provided much source material, along with information contained in chapter eight of the author's *Entrepreneurs of the Old West*.

III. From Tipis and Lodges

Making Peace with the Plains Indians
The *Chronicles of Oklahoma* provided much background information, especially Howard F. Van Zandt, "The History of Camp Holmes and Chouteau's Trading Post," *Chronicles of Oklahoma* 13, no. 3 (1935), and Grant Foreman, "Historical Background of the Kiowa-Comanche Reservation," *Chronicles of Oklahoma* 19, no. 2 (1941). A popular version of Foreman's article, titled "100 Years Ago . . . Our First Treaty with Wild Indians," appeared in the *Daily Oklahoman* on August 26, 1938.

Mountains Named for the Wichita Indians
Randolph B. Marcy's *Exploration of the Red River of Louisiana* (1854) includes his material on the Wichita Mountains. Additional information came from the Oklahoma Geological Survey records and from the fourth edition of *Historical Atlas of Oklahoma* by Charles Robert Goins and Danney Goble (Norman: University of Oklahoma Press, 2006).

"Gopher John," Black Seminole
Sources for this story include Kevin Mulroy's "John Horse" entry in "African American History in the West," available online from the University of Washington. Also helpful was "Black Seminoles, Maroons and Freedom Seekers in Florida" in the files of the African Heritage Project, University of South Florida. Additional information was found in the *Handbook of Texas* online and from the Seminole Nation of Oklahoma, Wewoka.

Satanta, Kiowa Chief
Sources included Mildred P. Mayhall's *The Kiowas* (Norman: University of Oklahoma Press, 1962) and Wilbur S. Nye's *Carbine and Lance: The Story of Old Fort Sill* (Norman: University of Oklahoma Press, 1937). Some information was found in the *Handbook of Texas* online.

Cherokee William P. Ross, Father of Oklahoma Journalism
Ross's story is told in the author's *Red Blood and Black Ink: Journalism in the Old West* (New York: Knopf, 1998).

Jane Austin McCurtain
Much information on Jane McCurtain's life may be found in Dr. Anna Lewis's article "Jane McCurtain," *Chronicles of Oklahoma* 11, no. 4 (1933). Also helpful was an interesting article on her family—John Bartlett Meserve, "The McCurtains," *Chronicles of Oklahoma* 13, no. 3 (1935).

Quanah Parker, Last Comanche Chief
Clyde L. Jackson and Grace Jackson's *Quanah Parker* (New York: Exposition Press, 1963) is one of several publications consulted for facts about Parker. T. R. Fehrenbach's *Comanches: The Destruction of a People* (New York: Knopf, 1974) was also helpful. Additional material was located in the Western History Collections, University of Oklahoma Libraries.

Oscar Jacobson and the Kiowa Five
Material was located in the Western History Collections, University of Oklahoma Libraries, and in Peggy Samuels and Harold Samuels's *The Illustrated Biographical Encyclopedia of Artists of the American West* (Garden City, N.Y.: Doubleday, 1976).

IV. Oklahoma Treasure Legends

A Few Words about Treasure Legends
The opinions are the author's, and they are based upon more than four decades of collecting and studying western treasure legends from old-timers or old newspapers and other types of contemporary publications. Several guides to treasure legends were also reviewed. They include Jesse Rascoe's *The Golden Crescent: The Southwest Treasure Belt*

(Toyahvale, Texas: Frontier Book, 1962), Thomas Probert's *Lost Mines and Buried Treasures of the West* (Berkley: University of California Press, 1977), and Steve Wilson's *Oklahoma Treasures and Treasure Tales* (Norman: University of Oklahoma Press, 1976).

SPANISH LEGENDS

The legend of buried gold near Vici southwest of Woodward was told by Walter E. Smith in "Some Legends of Oklahoma," *Chronicles of Oklahoma* 4, no. 1 (1926). The legend of the gold bar and the earlier massacre of Mexicans came from an undated, unidentified newspaper clipping in the author's collection. Reference to the Cleveland County legend can be found in Howard F. Van Zandt's "The History of Camp Holmes and Chouteau's Trading Post," *Chronicles of Oklahoma* 13, no. 3 (1935).

WHY PIONEERS BURIED THEIR TREASURES

The first legend concerning John Hawkins was found in an old copy of the *Oklahoman* from November 30, 1907, with the headline "Money Buried Close To This Land Mark." The remaining stories were given to the author by a colleague who found them in old newspapers. Unfortunately, he failed to provide the dates and publication names.

BRYAN COUNTY TREASURES

As noted in the story, the source for the first treasure legend came from a story written by Paul Stephens and published in the *Oklahoman* on March 21, 1909. The tale about Jesse James's cave and story about the four kegs of gold coins both came from undated newspaper clippings.

HIDDEN TREASURES

Walter E. Smith's "Some Legends of Oklahoma," *Chronicles of Oklahoma* 4, no. 1 (1926), includes the tale of the Kansas bank robbers and others told here.

THE TRES PIEDRAS LEGEND

The family Bible of José Lopat appears to be the main source of this legend sometimes called "The Tres Piedras Legend," meaning the "Three Stones Legend," referring to three stone markers, each containing about fifteen large rocks and stretching over a distance of perhaps one-quarter of a mile. In about 1962, a fourth marker was found. Perhaps the earliest written version of the story was published under the headline "The Tres

Piedras Legend" in the *Oklahoman,* on September 27, 1903, about four years before Oklahoma became a state. A more comprehensive and up-to-date account was later compiled by Steve Wilson and appears in his *Oklahoma Treasures and Treasure Tales.* I borrowed this story from my book *True Tales of the Prairies and Plains* (Lawrence: University Press of Kansas, 2007).

THE TREASURE BELLE STARR SOUGHT
Most books on Belle Starr relate one form or another of this legend, but it is mostly speculation.

THE LEGEND OF CALIFORNIA GOLD
"The Legend of California Gold" came from Hazel Ruby McMahan (Mrs. James W. McMahan) in *Stories of Early Oklahoma: A Collection of Interesting Facts, Biographical Sketches and Stories Relating to the History of Oklahoma,* a 298-page work produced by the Oklahoma Society of the Daughters of the American Revolution in 1945. Only one copy has been located and is housed in the library of the Oklahoma Historical Society.

HE DID NOT KNOW THE TREASURE WAS THERE
This story appeared under the headline "Gold Found Under Rock in Hog Lot" in the *Oklahoman,* June 24, 1917.

V. OUTLAWS AND LAWMEN

THE MYSTIQUE OF OKLAHOMA OUTLAWS
The conclusions were reached by the author after years of studying outlaws in the American West and how they were viewed in many states and territories.

BILL DOOLIN, OKLAHOMA'S WORST OUTLAW
Some material on Doolin is contained in E. Bee Guthrey's "Early Days in Payne County," *Chronicles of Oklahoma* 3, no. 1 (1925). Other details were borrowed from Colonel Bailey C. Hanes's *Bill Doolin, Outlaw O. T.* (Norman: University of Oklahoma Press, 1980).

WILLIAM COE, OKLAHOMA'S LEAST-KNOWN OUTLAW
Coe's story was pieced together from various sources, including Albert W. Thompson's *They Were Open Range Days: Annals of a Western*

Frontier (Denver: World Press, 1946), Luke Cahill's "Recollections of a Plainsman," a narrative in the files of the Colorado State Historical Society, Denver, and Morris F. Taylor's "The Coe Gang: Rustlers of Robbers' Roost," in *Colorado Magazine*, Summer 1974 (reprinted in 1999 by the Carnegie Library Foundation in Trinidad, Colorado). Other details were found in Charles W. Bowman's *History of Bent County, Colorado* (Chicago: O. L. Baskin, 1881). Bits and pieces came from the files of the *Colorado Weekly Chieftain* (Pueblo) and the *Denver Daily Rocky Mountain News* (1868), plus J. Evetts Haley's *Charles Goodnight* (Boston: Houghton Mifflin, 1936).

BASS REEVES, THE MOST FEARED U.S. DEPUTY MARSHAL
Arthur T. Burton's *Black Gun, Silver Star: The Life and Legend of Frontier Marshal Bass Reeves* (Lincoln: University of Nebraska Press, 2006) is a worthwhile biography of Reeves.

THE MISADVENTURES OF AL JENNINGS
The files of the Oklahoma Historical Society and the Western History Collections, University of Oklahoma Libraries, contained helpful information. Also helpful was Duane Gage, "Al Jennings, the People's Choice," *Chronicles of Oklahoma* 46, no. 4 (1968). Newspaper articles from the *Daily Oklahoma* provided additional details. For more on the *Lone Ranger* episode depicting Al Jennings, interested readers can listen to *The Lone Ranger* program on the Internet at www.otrcat.com/lone-ranger-adventures-with-historical-western-figures-old-time-radio-show.html.

BILL TILGHMAN, LAWMAN
The works of the late Oklahoma author Glenn Shirley provided much material for this story. In addition, Theodore C. Humphrey, "The Frontier Lawman as Folk Hero: The Search for Bill Tilghman," *Journal of the Folklore Institute* 17, provided additional insights as did material in the files of the Oklahoma Historical Society.

AL SPENCER, FORGOTTEN OUTLAW
The sources for Spencer's story included a good summary of his life at "Find a Grave" online, plus early newspaper accounts, including one story from the *Shawnee Herald*, November 17, 1902 reporting

that Spencer was getting out of prison and another article in the *San Francisco Chronicle*, April 22, 1955.

PRETTY BOY FLOYD, BANK ROBBER
A few books have been written on Floyd, including Jeffery S. King's *The Life and Death of Pretty Boy Floyd* (Kent, Ohio: Kent State University Press, 1998) and Michael Wallis's *Pretty Boy: The Life and Times of Charles Arthur Floyd* (New York: St. Martin's, 1992). The FBI's official account of Floyd's life may be found online at the U.S. Department of Justice's website. In addition, many contemporary newspaper accounts of his exploits were found in the *Tulsa World* and in the *Oklahoman*.

VI. PEOPLE, EVENTS, AND THINGS

WILL ROGERS'S LAST INTERVIEW
Arville Schaleben's account of Will Rogers's last interview by a newspaper reporter was distributed by the North American Newspaper Alliance and was published in the *Oklahoman* on August 17, 1935. Other material came from the Will Rogers Memorial Museum in Claremore, Oklahoma, and early newspaper accounts found in the *Oklahoman* and *Tulsa World*.

OKLAHOMA SYMBOLS AND EMBLEMS
Information on the state's symbols and emblems was compiled from numerous sources, including the *Chronicles of Oklahoma*, files of the Oklahoma Secretary of State, Oklahoma Historical Society, and contemporary Oklahoma newspapers, especially the *Daily Oklahoman* and the *Tulsa World*. Information on Frank Greer was found in the files of the Oklahoma Historical Society.

DAVID PAYNE, BOOMER
A series of articles by William H. Osburn in *Chronicles of Oklahoma* (1929–1930) were helpful, as was Dan W. Peery, "Captain David L. Payne," *Chronicles of Oklahoma* 13, no. 4 (1935). Peery's article provided a great deal of documentation on Payne as a Boomer. Other information was found in the Western History Collection, University of Oklahoma Libraries.

Kate Barnard, First Woman Elected to State Office
One Woman's Political Journey: Kate Barnard and Social Reform, 1875–1930 (University of Oklahoma Press, 2003) by Lynn Musslewhite and Suzanne Jones Crawford is a fine biography. Additional information came from the *Daily Oklahoman,* including an account of Barnard's funeral in the February 25, 1930, and February 28, 1930, issues.

The Night Boise City Was Shaken
Newspaper accounts provided much of the source material, including the *Oklahoman,* July 5, 1943, and July 17, 1943. The bombing made national headlines through Associated Press and United Press reports. *Time* magazine carried a story on July 19, 1943, based upon press reports. Other bits and pieces were found in Norma Gene Butterbaugh Young's *The Tracks We Followed* (Amarillo: Southwestern Publications, 1991), a history of Boise City and Cimarron County; an article by Gene Curtis in the *Tulsa World,* February 17, 2001; Jeanne M. Devlin's "The Bombing of Boise City," *Oklahoma Today,* January–February 1991; and material from the Boise City Area Chamber of Commerce and Cimarron County Historical Society.

Roscoe Dunjee, Oklahoma's Little Caesar
A lengthy biography of Dunjee by Simmie Knox may be found online at "Art of the Oklahoma State Capitol." Also consulted was John Henry Lee Thompson's dissertation, titled "The Little Caesar of Civil Rights: Roscoe Dunjee in Oklahoma City, 1915–1955," completed at Purdue University in 1990.

The Miller Brothers' 101 Ranch
Two books detail the story of the 101 Ranch. They are Ellsworth Collings and Alma Miller England, *101 Ranch* (Norman: University of Oklahoma Press, 1937) and Michael Wallis, *The Real Wild West: The 101 Ranch and the Creation of the American West* (New York: St. Martin's, 1999). Bits and pieces were found in contemporary newspaper stories in the *Ponca City News, Daily Oklahoman,* and *Tulsa World.*

The Man from Bugtussle
Much source material can be found in the files of the Carl Albert Center at the University of Oklahoma. Additional information came from the *Biographical Directory of the United States Congress, 1774–present*

online at bioguide.congress.gov and Albert's biography written with Danney Goble titled *Little Giant: The Life and Times of Speaker Carl Albert* (Norman: University of Oklahoma Press, 1990).

Oklahoma Inventors
Source material included old issues of the *Daily Oklahoman* and information from the Oklahoma Inventors Congress, Oklahoma City.

Oklahoma Storms, Fires, Floods, Train Wrecks, and Other Disasters
There were numerous sources for these stories; some are included in the text. Several accounts on tornadoes and flooding came from the files of the National Weather Service. Of particular value were M. O. [Oliver] Asp's "Tornadoes in Oklahoma, 1876–1949," in *Monthly Weather Review* 20, no. 2 (Washington, D.C.: U.S. Weather Bureau, 1950), and Snowden D. Flora's *Tornadoes of the United States* (Norman: University of Oklahoma Press, 1953). Information on fires, train wrecks, and other disasters came from newspaper accounts. Helpful in locating these accounts was the website gendisasters.com.

VII. Artists, Writers, and Entertainers

Washington Irving's Oklahoma Visit
The principal source was Washington Irving's *A Tour on the Prairies* contained in *The Crayon Miscellany* (Philadelphia: Carey, Lea, & Blanchard, 1835). Other material came from "Centennial of the Tour of the Prairies," in *Chronicles of Oklahoma* 10, no. 3 (1932); Henry L. Ellsworth's *Washington Irving on the Prairie; or, a Narrative of a Tour of the Southwest in the Year 1832*, edited by Barbara D. Simison and Stanley T. Williams (New York: American Book Company, 1937); and Charles J. Latrobe's *The Rambler in Oklahoma: Latrobe's Tour with Washington Irving 1935*, edited by George H. Shirk and Muriel H. Wright (Oklahoma City: Harlow, 1955).

Artists in Indian Territory
Many sources were used, including "Early Oklahoma Artists" by O. B. Jacobson and Jeanne d'Ucel, a two-part series that began in *Chronicles of Oklahoma* 21, no. 2 (1953). The biographies of artists in Oklahoma were located in various modern biographical reference books.

Angie Debo, Teacher and Writer
Much information came from the files of Oklahoma State University's Special Collections and University Archives. In addition, several of Debo's books were consulted, including *And Still the Waters Run* (Princeton: Princeton University Press, 1940).

Woody Guthrie, Father of American Folk Music
Good biographical information came from the Woody Guthrie Foundation. Additional material came from the "Art at the Oklahoma State Capital" website and the "Find a Grave" website.

Gene Autry, Yodeling Cowboy
Several sources were used, including a detailed biographical sketch provided by the museum Autry established in Los Angeles before his death.

Pattie Page, the Singing Rage
Some information, including a helpful biography, was found on the Songwriters Hall of Fame online at www.songwritershalloffame.org and Page's official website, www.misspattipage.com.

Kay Starr, Salon Singer
The bulk of the source material came from Matthew C. Foley's "Who Is Kay Starr? A Short Biography," available online at members.tripod.com/~Kay_Starr/biography.html.

Index

This index is intended primarily as a reference guide to place-names and leading characters. It is not an index to subject matter, nor does it cover the introduction and notes.

Aaron, Okla., 20
Aaron, Calvin, 20
Abert, Lt. James W., 111, 216
Abilene, Kan., 59, 60
Achille, 228
Ada, Okla., 31, 195
Akins Cemetery (Sallisaw), 159
Akron, Ohio, 157
Alabama, 23, 26
Alaska, 197
Albert, Carl Bert, 193–95; death of, 195; as house speaker, 194
Albert, Ernest, 193
Albert, Leona, 193
Alfalfa County, 26
Allen, Okla., 40
Allen, Paul, 197
Alpha, Okla., 22
Altus, 18, 25, 46
Alva, 18
Anadarko, 22, 47, 79, 100, 141
Anchorage, Ala., 163
Anderson County, Texas, 94
Antelope, Okla., 25
Antelope Buttes, 11
Antelope Hills, 11, 25
Antlers, Okla., 202
Apache Indians, 8, 73, 74, 82
Appalachia, 24–25
Arapaho Indians, 28, 85, 106

Arbeka Trading Post, 122
Arbuckle, Gen. Matthew, 43, 44, 74, 209
Arbuckle Mountains, 113
Ardmore, 31, 32, 47, 59, 62, 204, 228, 230
Arkansas, 11, 17, 31, 48, 55, 57, 76, 141, 155, 171, 174, 175
Arkansas City, Kan., 12, 132
Arkansas Post, 49
Arkansas River, 14–19, 24, 33, 39, 41, 47, 49–53, 135, 203, 205, 209–12
Arkansas Territory, 49
Armstrong County, Texas, 18
Asah, Spencer, 99–100
Ash, Beulah Baird, 157, 158
Asp, Oliver, 199
Atlantic City, N.J., 168
Atoka, 25, 31, 56, 109
Atoka County, 12, 20, 25, 40, 56
Auchiah, James, 99–100
Austin, Lewis, 91
Autry, Orvon Gene, 228–33; death of, 232; list of films, 232–33

Baca, Juan, 139
Baca, Vicente, 139
Baird, Rose, 158
Bald Hill, 123

255

Baley Bridge, 124
Barnard, Kate, 178–80; death of, 180
Barnet, Charlie, 239
Barroum, B. A., 8
Bartlesville, 33, 154, 204
Bartow County, Ga., 156
Baxter Springs, Kan., 40, 189
Bean, Capt. Jesse, 211
Beard, Henry G., 26
Beattie, Pierre, 211
Beaver, Okla., 25, 204
Beaver County, 23, 25, 70
Beaver Creek, 69
Beaver River, 14, 17, 25
Beckham County, 20
Beer City, 23
Bel Air, Calif., 241
Bell Cemetery (Childers), 155
Bellew, F. L., 182
Bellmon, Gov. Henry, 196, 223
Bent's Fort, Colo., 216
Bernal, Juan, 139
Bernal, Ramon, 139
Berwyn, 26, 230–31
Bethany, Okla., 201
Big Head (outlaw), 120
Big Heart, Okla., 204
Big Tree (Kiowa), 86
Billings, Okla., 23
Birdwell, George, 158
Bixby, 144
Blackburn, Casper B., 56
Blackburn, Okla., 25
Blackburn, Sen. Joseph C. S., 25
Blackburn's Station, 56
Black Dog (Osage chief), 214
Blackface, Chief, 108–109
Black Hills, Wyo., 12

Black Mesa, 11, 135–40
Blain County, 22, 28
Blair, Okla., 201
Blue River, 14, 17, 47, 57, 110
Boggsville, Colo., 139
Boggy Creek, 56
Boggy Depot, 40, 41, 56
Bogy, Joseph, 49, 53
Boise, Idaho, 25
Boise City, 25, 115, 182–85
Bokchito, Okla., 46
Boone, Capt. Nathan, 40
Boone, Daniel, 40
Boonville, Mo., 165
Bordrick, Elmer, 22
Boudinot, Elias C., 28, 65, 195
Bow and Quiver (Comanche chief), 215
Bowlegs, Okla., 23
Bowman, Charles W., 140
Boyd Springs, 32
Boyles, Mrs. Frank, 119
Brevel, Jean Baptiste, 10
Briartown, 121
Bridgeport, 216
Broken Arrow, 25, 90
Broken Bow, 18, 154
Brookville, Kan., 60
Bryan County, 22, 28, 56, 57, 110–11
Buck, Rufus, 131
Buffalo, Okla., 203
Buffalo, N.Y., 158
Bugtussle, 193–95
Burbank, Elbridge Ayer, 217, 219
Burbank, Okla., 219
Burney, David C., 25
Burneyville, 25, 52
Burr Oak Township, Kan., 174

Busch, 20
Busch, Adolphus, 20
Bush Settlement, 56
Butterfield, John, 54–57
Byars, 44, 46, 216

Caballo, Juan. *See* Horse, John
Cache, Okla., 96
Cache Creek, 11, 52, 76, 77
Caddo, Okla., 61
Caddo County, 23, 79
Cahill, Luke, 139
California, 40, 42, 54, 122, 166, 185, 216, 224, 239
Caldwell, Kan., 60, 132
Calumet, Okla., 25
Camp Arbuckle, 44, 46
Camp Armstrong, 46
Camp at Boggy Depot, 46
Camp at Medicine Bluff Creek, 48
Camp at Purcell, 47
Camp Augur, 46
Camp Canadian, 47
Camp Cass, 46
Camp Chilocco, 46
Camp Choctaw, 46
Camp Comanche, 46
Camp Davidson, 46
Camp Frank, 47
Camp Guthrie, 47
Camp Holmes, 47, 51, 74, 107
Camp Leavenworth, 47
Camp Mason, 47
Camp McIntosh, 47
Camp Napoleon, 47
Camp near Cheyenne Agency, 48
Camp Neosho, 47
Camp Oklahoma, 47
Camp Osage, 47

Camp Radziminski, 47
Camp Recovery, 47
Camp Ross, 48
Camp Russell, 48
Camp Schofield, 48
Camp Starvation, 45, 48
Camp Steele, 48
Camp Supply, 45, 48, 52, 53, 62
Camp Washita, 48
Camp Wichita, 48, 78
Canada, 166, 190
Canadian County, 23, 25, 144
Canadian River, 11, 14, 16, 39, 40, 44, 47, 50, 53, 74, 75, 122, 216. *See also* North Canadian River; South Canadian River
Caney, Kan., 155
Caney River, 14, 16, 33
Cannon, Rufus, 130
Canton, 46
Cantonment, 46
Cantonment Davis, 47
Canute, Okla., 25
Canyon, Texas, 221
Captain Atoka, 25
Carson, Mollie, 189
Carpenter, Col. C. C., 175
Carrizo Creek, 136
Carrizo Valley, 136
Carter, Charles D., 193
Catlin, George, 214–15, 217, 218
Cavnar, Okla., 22
Cavnar, John, 22
Cayenne Mountains, 122
Chandler, Okla., 31
Chase, Owen G., 70
Chatsworth, Calif., 147
Chattanooga, Tenn., 88
Chautauqua County, Kan., 154

Chelsea, Okla., 228
Cherokee, Okla., 30
Cherokee Indians, 22, 27, 39, 40, 41, 44, 45, 49, 66, 77, 88–90, 171
Cherokee Bill. *See* Goldsby, Crawford "Cherokee Bill"
Cherokee Council, 64
Cherokee County, 21, 28, 201
Cherokee Hills, 143
Cherokee Trail, 41
Chesley, Frank, 33
Cheyenne Indians, 8, 48, 84, 149
Cheyenne, Okla., 106
Chicago, 77, 196, 217, 229, 234
Chickasaw Indians, 17, 25, 32, 44, 57, 63, 171, 215
Chickasaw Nation, 238
Chickasha, Okla., 25, 45, 46, 205
Chief's Knoll (cemetery), 96
Chihuahua, Mex., 115
Chikaskia River, 14, 17
Childers, Okla., 155
Chilocco, Okla., 46, 48
Chisholm, Jesse, 60, 62, 215
Chisholm Trail, 52, 60, 62
Choctaw, Okla., 186
Choctaw Agency, 22, 56
Choctaw Council, 58, 91
Choctaw County, 26, 39
Choctaw Indians, 22, 25, 28, 43, 50, 58, 61, 63, 74, 92–93, 171, 216
Choctaw Nation, 15, 33, 53, 91–93, 109
Chouteau, 114
Chouteau, A. P., 50, 75; family of, 49–50, 53
Chouteau Creek, 75, 106

Cimarron, Kan., 133, 149
Cimarron County, 25, 70
Cimarron County Courthouse, 182–85
Cimarron Cut-off, 67
Cimarron River, 14–15, 24, 48, 132, 136, 211, 217
Cincinnati, Ohio, 50, 215
Civil War, 8, 44, 52, 57, 59, 53, 82, 91, 111, 131, 135, 174
Claremont (Osage chief), 214
Claremore, 41, 114, 163, 181, 214
Clark, Dick, 235
Clauser, Al, 234
Cleveland County, 17, 28, 47, 51, 73–75, 106, 199, 213
Clinton, Okla., 113
Coal County, 109
Coalgate, Okla., 31
Cochran, Ga., 197
Cody, William F. "Buffalo Bill," 152
Coe, William, 135–40; death of, 140
Coffee Creek, 211
Coffee, Holland, 50, 52–53
Coffee's Station, 50, 52–53
Coffeyville, Kan., 19, 133, 155, 175
Colbert, Benjamin F., 57
Colcord, Charles F., 33
Colcord, Okla., 44, 48
Colorado, 15, 16, 59, 138, 139, 180, 216
Comanche County, 22, 112, 123, 144
Comanche County, Kan., 18
Comanche Indians, 8, 44, 45, 67, 73, 75, 76, 78, 82, 85, 94–96, 215, 216

Como, Perry, 240
Conlen, Texas, 183
Cooke County, Texas, 228
Cookietown, 23
Cookson Hills, 156
Coon, Joe, 80
Cooper, Col. Douglas H., 91
Coronado, Francisco Vasquez de, 39, 42, 76, 105
Cosden, Josh, 33
Cotton County, 11, 23, 52
Cowaya, John. *See* Horse, John
Coweta, Okla., 26
Coyler, Vincent, 218
Craig County, 28
Crane, Ichabod, 209
Creek County, 23, 201
Creek Indians, 23, 26, 33, 40, 50, 61, 63, 74, 82, 141, 171, 213, 215, 222
Creek Nation, 123, 144
Cromwell, 151
Crosby, Bob, 239
Crosby, Cecil, 230
Crosson, Joe, 163
Crowe, Okla., 20
Culver City, Calif., 145
Custer, 26
Custer County, 28
Custer, George Armstrong, 26, 45, 85, 113

Dale, Edward Everett, 220
Dak, J. E., 70
Dalhart, Texas, 182
Dallas, 112, 205, 238
Dalton brothers, 133
Danville, Ky., 189
Davis, Bette, 235

Davis, Jefferson, 214
Davis, Lewis, 131
Davis, Lucky, 131
Davis, Okla., 26, 44, 46, 113
Davis, Samuel H., 26
Debo, Angie, 220–23; death of, 223
Debo, Edward, 220
Debo, Lina, 220
Deep Deuce (Oklahoma City district), 186
Deep Fork, 14, 17
Delaware Indians, 215
Delaware, 70
Delhi, 125
Denison, Texas, 114
Denmark, 150
Denver, Colo., 118
Depot on the North Canadian River, 45
Dewey County, 12
Díaz, Porfirio, 83
Dill, W. H., 123
Dillinger, John, 158
Dill Ranch, 124
Doak, Josiah, 26
Doaksville, 15, 26, 91
Doan's Crossing, 62
Dobie, J. Frank, 129
Dodds, R. D., 183
Dodge, Col. Henry, 3, 73, 78, 214, 215
Dodge City, Kan., 60, 62, 148
Dog Ford, 122
Dohasan (Kiowa chief), 215
Doniphan County, Kan., 174
Doolin, William M. "Bill," 131, 132–34, 150, 155
Dougherty, 238, 241

Douthat, Okla., 23
Douthat, Zahn A., 23
Downing, Lewis, 90
Dozier, Bob, 143
Drake, Col. Edwin L., 32
Drumm, Maj. Andrew, 26
Drumm, Okla., 26
D'Ucel, Jeanne, 100
Duncan, Okla., 23, 60, 62, 203
Dunjee, John William, 186
Dunjee, Roscoe, 186–88
Durant, 20, 31, 40, 45, 57, 110, 195
Duryea, Dan, 147
Dutton, 22
Dutton, William R., 22
Dylan, Bob, 227

Eagle Pass, Texas, 82
East Liverpool, Ohio, 157, 159
Eden, Okla., 26
Edison, Thomas A., 29
Edmond, Okla., 211
Edwards, James, 50, 53
Elk City, 20
Elk River, 14, 20
Elizabethtown, N.Mex., 137
Elliott, Aussie, 158
Ellsworth, Henry L., 209–12
Ellsworth, Kan., 60
Ellsworth, Edith, 133
Elm Fork of the Red River, 14–19
Elmore, J. O., 26
Elmore City, 26
El Paso, Texas, 41
El Reno, 24, 45, 48, 60, 62, 66, 144
England, 29, 99, 190, 209
Enid, 203, 220
Eufaula, 40, 58, 62, 130
Eureka Springs, Ark., 150

Evans, Capt. L., 41
Evans, Neal, 8

Fadiman, Clifton, 226
Fagan, James F., 141
Fairbanks, Ala., 163
Fairfax-Blakeborough, Maj. J., 104
Fairview, 26
Farrar, A. W., 200–201
Faucett, H. W., 33
Fawbush, E. J., 202
Fayetteville, Ark., 41
Filiciotto, Jerome I., 235–36
Fillmore County, Neb., 178
Fisher, King, 27
Fisher's Station, 57
Fitzpatrick, Thomas, 218
Flagg Springs, 117–18
Florida, 80, 82
Flowery Mound, 193
Floyd, Charles Arthur "Pretty Boy," 131, 156–59
Floyd, Jack Dempsey, 156
Ford, Tennessee Ernie, 240
Ford County, Kan., 148
Fort Arbuckle, 44, 46, 113
Fort Beach, 46
Fort Blunt, 46
Fort Cobb, 45–48
Fort Coffee, 39, 44, 46
Fort Cooper, Fla., 94
Fort Dodge, Iowa, 148
Fort Duncan, Texas, 82
Fort Edwards, 47
Fort Elliott, 48
Fort Gibson, 39–42, 46, 47, 50, 53, 58, 62, 73, 89–90, 122–24, 209, 211–12, 214–18
Fort Holmes, 50, 53, 73–74, 215

Fort Leavenworth, Kan., 175
Fort Lyon, Colo., 135, 139
Fort Mann, Kan., 41
Fort Mason, 75
Fort McCulloch, 47
Fort near the Crossing of the Washita, 46
Fort Reno, 24, 45–48, 141, 150, 175, 217
Fort Sill, 8, 45–48, 55, 77, 86–87, 95–96, 114, 219
Fort Smith, Ark., 40–42, 44, 46, 48, 58, 62, 90, 130, 141, 175–77
Fort Supply, 45, 48, 52–53, 62
Fort Towson, 15, 26, 37, 42, 48, 91
Fort Union, N.Mex., 135, 137–40
Fort Washita, 40–42, 45
Fort Wayne, 44–45, 48
Foster, H. V., 33
Foster, Judge Cassius G., 177
Fountain Creek, 140
Fourmile, 26
Fowler, Clara Ann. *See* Page, Patti
Fowler, Jacob, 50
France, 117
Frazier, 25
Frémont, John C., 216
Frenzeny, Paul, 216, 218
Fulton, Robert, 15
Furr, Albert C., 26
Furrs, Okla., 26

Gable, Clark, 230
Gage, Okla., 202
Gainesville, Texas, 59, 62
Galbreath, Robert T., 33
Galveston, Texas, 203
Garfield County, 20, 30, 220
Garis, Henry, 148
Garrett, Frank, 184
Garringer, Henry, 185
Garvin County, 26
Gates, Bill, 197
Gates Creek, 39
Geary, A. G., 56
Geary's Station, 56
Gene Autry, Okla., 26, 230–31
Geneva, Neb., 178
Georgia, 150
Geronimo, Okla., 112
Geronimo (Chiricahua Apache), 217
Gesner, Abraham, 32
Getty, J. Paul, 33
Gibson, Hoot, 190
Glass Mountains, 26, 61
Glaze, Okla., 21
Glenn, Col. Hugh, 50
Glenn, Ida, 33
Glover, William, 17
Glover River, 14, 17
Golden, John, 88
Goldman, Sylvan, 196
Goldsby, Crawford "Cherokee Bill," 130, 155
Gopher John. *See* Horse, John
Goodnight, Charles, 138, 152
Gotebo, Okla., 26
Gould, Charles N., 20, 21
Grady County, 22, 25
Grandfield, 46
Grand River (Neosho), 14, 17, 32, 41, 49, 58, 62
Grand Saline River. *See* Salt Fork of the Arkansas River
Grant County, 27, 52, 53
Grant County, Ind., 174
Grant, Ulysses S, 130

Graves, Richard. *See* Stover, Capt. Lute F.
Grayson County, Texas, 228
Great Bend, Kan., 60
Greenville, Tenn., 88
Greenwood (Tulsa district), 187
Greer, Frank H., 169–70
Greer County, 13, 49, 126
Gregg, Josiah, 3, 10, 12–13, 40, 42
Grimes, Bill, 150
Guthrie, Arlo, 227
Guthrie, Charles, 224
Guthrie, Nora Belle, 224
Guthrie, Okla., 29, 31, 47, 48, 66, 149–50, 169, 199, 211
Guthrie, Woodrow Wilson "Woody," 224–27; death of, 227

Halsell, Oscar D., 132
Hammon, 26, 106
Hammond, J. H., 26
Haney, Enoch Kelly, 181
Hanson, Okla., 156
Hargraves, Ruby, 156
Harpers Ferry, W.Va., 186
Harrah, Okla., 21
Harrison, Benjamin, 21, 61, 66
Haskell, Okla., 10
Haskell, Charles N., 179
Haskell County, 27, 120, 205
Hawkins, John, 108
Hawks, Capt. Frank M., 168
Hayes, Rutherford B., 175
Headrick, 201
Henryetta, Okla., 26
Hickok, James Butler "Wild Bill," 152
Higgins, Okla., 56

Hobart, Okla., 20
Hokeah, Jack, 99–100
Holden, Harold T., 152
Holdenville, 17, 31, 40, 47, 50, 53, 73
Holloway, Gov. William Judson, 180
Holloway, William (stage agent), 56
Holloway's Station, 56
Hollywood, Calif., 166, 229, 232
Hoover, George M., 149
Hornaday, William T., 8–9
Horne, Lena, 239
Horse, John, 80–83; death of, 83
Hot Springs, Ark., 158
Houston, Texas, 77
Houston, Sam, 50, 53, 73, 144
Houston, Temple, 144
Hugo, Okla., 26, 43, 48
Hugo, Victor, 26
Hulbert, Okla., 88
Hunter, Charles, 23
Hunting Horse. *See* Tsatoke, Monroe
Huntington's chorea, 227
Huntsville, Texas, 86

Illinois, 174, 187, 194, 217
Illinois River, 14, 16, 48
Indiana, 174
Ingalls, Okla., 133
Ingals, Kan., 149
Insull, Frederick, 30
Iroquois Indians, 238
Irving, Washington, 3, 10, 209–12
Ivanhoe, Okla., 26
Ives, Burl, 226

Jacksboro, Texas, 86
Jackson, Andrew, 44, 77, 80
Jackson, Wyo., 79
Jackson County, 20, 25, 210
Jacobson, Oscar, 97–100; death of, 100
James, Jesse, 110
James Fork, 14, 17
Jefferson, Okla., 52, 53
Jefferson City, Mo., 156
Jefferson County, 27
Jennings, Okla., 114
Jennings, Alphonso J. "Al," 133, 144–47, 150; death of, 147
Jennings, Edward, 144
Jennings, J. D., 144
Jennings, John, 144–45
Jennings, Maude, 145, 147
Jesse, Okla., 47
Johnson, Grant, 130
Johnson County, 22
Johnson County, Ark., 132
Jones, Okla., 21
Jones, Buck, 190
Jones, Coleen, 182
Jones, Wilson Nathaniel, 61
Joseph, Chief (Nez Perce), 152
July, Maoma, 131
July, Susan, 80

Kansas, 8, 15–19, 26, 41, 52–53, 59–62, 64–66, 76, 84, 108, 120, 137, 144, 153, 155, 174–77, 178, 199, 202, 216–17
Kansas City, Mo., 59, 65, 157–59, 166, 200
Kay County, 27–28
Keahea, Zeb, 28
Kearney, Col. S. W., 214

Kenefic, Okla., 47
Kenton, 15, 136
Kentucky, 25
Kiamichi River, 14, 18, 39
King, Pee Wee, 239
Kingfisher, 27, 60, 62, 66, 133, 211
Kingfisher County, 22–28
Kingston, 47
Kiowa County, 26
Kiowa Five, 97–100
Kiowa Indians, 45, 73–75, 84–87, 97, 215–16
Kits Kait River. *See* Salt Fork River
Knox, Simmie, 188
Krebs, Okla., 200
Kreiger, Fred, 182, 184
KTUL radio (Tulsa), 234
KVOO radio (Tulsa), 229

LaFarge, Pierre, 115–18
La Harpe, Jean-Baptiste Bénard de, 9–10, 49, 53
La Junta, Colo., 153
Lake Texoma, 19, 42, 52
Lancaster, Maj. C. E., 183
Landon, Alfred M., 33
Langston, Okla., 27, 186
Langston, John M., 27
Langston University, 186
Las Vegas, N.Mex., 139
Las Vegas, Nev., 241
Latimer County, 56
Latrobe, Charles J., 209, 213
Lawrenceville, N.J., 88
Lawton, Okla., 9, 23, 48, 96, 105, 112, 150, 200
Lawton, Maj. Gen. Henry W., 23
Le Flore County, 17, 22, 28, 39, 56
Leavenworth, Kan., 158

Leavenworth, Gen. Henry, 40, 73, 214
Ledbetter, Huddie "Leadbelly," 226
Lee, William McDole, 52
Leeper, Okla., 27
Leeper, William P., 27
Lehigh, Okla., 31, 109
Lexington, Okla., 74–75, 106
Liberal, Kan., 23
Lincoln County, 151, 211
Lindsburg, Kan., 97
Little Big Horn River, 26
Little River, 14, 17, 47, 73, 213
Little Rock, Ark., 39, 42
Livingston, Robert R., 15
Logan County, 27, 211, 220
Lomax, Alan, 224
Long, Maj. Stephen H., 39, 42, 214, 218
Lookout Mountain, Tenn., 88
Los Angeles, Calif., 147, 224, 239
Lost Creek Canyon, 153
Louisiana, 59, 76, 117
Love County, 25, 52
Luther, Okla., 21
Lynn, Wiley, 151

Madill, 40
Madison, Kan., 19
Madison, N.Mex., 139
Madson, Chris, 150
Magee, Carl C., 196
Major County, 26–27
Malot, Harve, 123
Malzahn, Carl Frederick, 198
Mangum, Okla., 18
Manhattan, Kan., 220
Manone, Wingy, 239

Marcy, Capt. Randolph B., 3, 5, 11–13, 16, 40–42, 76–79
Marks, William, 122
Marland, E. W., 33, 35
Marlow, Okla., 27
Marlow Brothers Ranch, 27
Marshall, Okla., 220
Mason, Maj. Richard Barnes, 73, 74
Massachusetts, 52
Masterson, Bat, 148
Matamoros, Mex., 115
Matanuska Colony, 163–68
Matthews, Gordon, 197
Maynard, Ken, 190
Maysville, Mo., 58, 62
Mackenzie, Col. Ranald, 95–96
McAfee, Lee, 25
McAlester, Okla., 23, 41, 125, 153–55, 179, 193, 195
McAlester, John J., 23
McClain County, 27, 216
McCoy, Isaac, 39–40
McCoy, Joseph, 59–60
McCurtain, Okla., 205
McCurtain County, 18, 22
McCurtain, Jackson, 91–93
McCurtain, Jane Austin, 91–93
McDole, William, 53
McDonald, Alva, 155
McDonald, William C., 24
McLean, Chet, 163, 165
McMahan, Hazel Ruby, 124
Medicine Bluff, 78
Medicine Bluff Creek, 45, 78
Medicine Lodge, Kan., 14, 18, 85
Medford, Mass., 27
Medford, Okla., 27
Mehan, Okla., 211

Meigs, Silas, 154
Memphis, Tenn., 238–39
Mexico, 40, 74, 78, 82–83, 85, 110, 115–19, 190
Miami, Fla., 197
Miami, Okla., 20, 50, 53
Michigan, 163
Mill Creek, 113
Miller, George Washington, 189
Miller, Joseph, 189–92
Miller, Mitch, 235
Miller, R. C., 202
Miller, Zachary, 189–92
Miller Brother's 101 Ranch, 189–92; Wild West shows, 190–92
Millerton, 91
Mills, J., 156–57
Minnesota, 163, 198
Missouri, 18, 32, 54, 56, 58–62, 64, 67, 110, 137, 144, 155, 174
Missouri River, 174
Mitchell, J. O., 33
Mitchell, Okla., 200
Mix, Tom, 190
Möllhausen, Heinrich Balduin, 216, 218
Montague County, Texas, 60, 62
Moore, Okla., 199
Mopope, Stephen, 99–100
Morse, Samuel, 77
Mountain Fork River, 14, 18
Mountain of Rocks (Comanche chief), 215
Mountain Station, 56
Mount Marcy, 79
Mount Scott, 79
Mulhall, Jack, 165–68
Mulhall, Okla., 27
Mulhall, Zack, 27

Murray, William H. "Bill," 179–80
Murray County, 26, 238
Muscogee Indians, 74
Muskogee, Okla., 31, 43, 47, 90, 143, 202
Muskogee County, 9, 39, 120

Nacimiento, Mex., 82
Nail, Joel H., 57
Nail's Station, 56–57
Nash, Frank, 158
Nebraska, 39, 41
Neodesha, Kan., 153
Neosho Post, 50
Neosho River, 14, 18, 53. *See also* Grand River
Ne Shudse Shunga River. *See* Salt Fork River
New Jersey, 145, 216
Newman, Martin W., 27
Newman, Okla., 27
New Mexico, 11, 15–19, 24, 67, 115, 135, 139
New Orleans, La., 115–19
New Ponca, 27
New Springplace, 32
Newton, Kan., 60
Newtonia, Mo., 189
New York, N.Y., 54, 99, 166, 224, 226, 229
Ninnekah, Okla., 205
Nix, Thomas C., 149
Noble, Okla., 106
Noble County, 23
Nocona, Pete (Comanche chief), 94
No Man's Land, 67–70, 136. *See also* Oklahoma Panhandle
Norman, Okla., 24, 51, 66, 99, 194, 203, 213

Norman, Abner E., 24
North Boggy Creek, 56
North Canadian River, 14–19, 17, 29, 45, 124, 175, 203, 213. *See also* Canadian River; South Canadian River
North Cemetery (Marshall), 223
Nowata, Okla., 155
Nowata County, 153

Oakley, Annie, 152
Oak Park Cemetery (Chandler), 151
Oakwood Memorial Park (Calif.), 147
Oasis (saloon), 148–49
Ochelata, Okla., 154
O'Curran, Charles, 235
O'Curran, Danny, 235
O'Curran, Kathleen, 235
Ohio, 194
Ohio River, 157
Oil Creek, Pa., 32
Okarche, 22–23
Okay, Okla., 47, 49, 53
Okeene, 22
O'Kelley, C. T., 125–26
Okemah, Okla., 123, 234–37
Okesa, Okla., 153, 155
Oklahoma City, 9, 14, 29, 35, 47, 59, 62, 66, 145, 150, 168, 175, 186, 199, 201–205, 216
Oklahoma County, 7, 21, 145, 212
Oklahoma: Foot-Loose and Fancy-Free (Debo), 222
Oklahoma Panhandle, 10, 11, 15, 67–70, 103, 115, 125–26, 182–85. *See also* No Man's Land

Oklahoma River, 14, 16, 29, 186
Oklahoma Station, 47
Okmulgee, Okla., 22, 61, 213
Okmulgee County, 26, 213
Okmulgee Creek, 22
Omega, Okla., 22
Oologah, Okla., 27, 165
Orion, Okla., 27, 48
Osage County, 27–28, 155, 203, 219
Osage Hills, 154
Osage Indians, 27–28, 33, 49, 50, 73–75, 77, 132, 211, 214–19
Ottawa Indians, 40
Ottawa County, 23, 26–28
Otter Creek, 46–48
Ouachita Highlands, 12, 17

Page, Patti, 234–37; list of hit songs, 236–37
Palmer, Alaska, 163
Pampa, Texas, 224
Panther Creek, 113
Papin, Pierre M., 50, 53
Paris, Texas, 25, 141
Park Hill, 88
Parker, Cynthia Ann, 94
Parker, Isaac, 130–31, 141, 150
Parker, Quanah, 94–96; death of, 96
Parker's Fort, Texas, 94
Pawhuska, Okla., 9, 27
Pawnee, Okla., 134, 154
Pawnee County, 25, 154, 211
Pawnee Indians, 50, 132
Payne, David, 65, 131, 174–77; death of, 177
Payne County, 26, 28, 177, 200
Peale, Titian, 214, 218

Peggs, Okla., 201
Pennington, Okla., 21
Pennsylvania, 33, 214
Perkins, Okla., 211
Perry, Okla., 30, 198
Perryville, 41
Perryville Depot, 47
Peters, Susie, 97
Phillips, Gov. Leon Chase, 187
Phillips, Lee Eldas "L.E.," 33
Phillips, Waite, 33
Pickett, Bill, 152, 190
Pine Ridge, 23
Pineville, Ark., 154
Pirtle, Milton A., 22
Pirtle, Okla., 22
Pittsburg County, 23, 56
Pittsburgh, Pa., 91
Plunkettville, 22
Point Barrow, Alaska, 165
Ponca City, 18, 27, 30, 48, 59, 62, 189, 192
Porter, William Sidney "O Henry," 144–45
Post, Wiley, 163–68, 197
Poteau, Okla., 195
Poteau River, 14, 56
Pottawatomie County, 22, 122
Potter, William, 88
Pottsboro, Texas, 52
Prairie Dog Town Fork of the Red River, 14, 18
Prather, Ed, 149
Preston, Texas, 40, 52, 58, 62
Pryor, Nathaniel, 50, 53
Pueblo, Colo., 139–40
Purcell, 12, 47, 51, 74
Purgatoire River, 139
Pushmataha County, 22, 92, 202

Pusley, Silas, 56
Pusley's Station, 56

Quanah, Texas, 200
Quapaw, Okla., 27
Quapaw Indians, 15, 27, 74
Quivira, 76, 105

Rael, Jack, 234–35
Ravia, Okla., 228
Ream, Vinnie, 28
Red Fork, Okla., 24, 33
Red Fork of the Arkansas River, 8, 15
Red Oak, Okla., 56, 91
Red River, 14–19, 23, 39, 40, 48, 50, 52–53, 58, 60, 62, 76, 108, 209, 215
Red River Valley, 143
Reed, Jim, 120
Reeves, Bass, 130, 141–43; death of, 143
Reeves, George, 141
Remington, Frederic, 217, 219
Remington, Okla., 219
Remus, Okla., 22
Reno, Nev., 241
Reno City, 24
Revoir, Joseph, 49
Reynolds, Albert E., 52–53
Rhode Island, 70
Richetti, Adam C., 158
Richmond, 12
Riddle, John, 56
Riddle's Station, 56
Riggs, Clinton, 196
Ringling, John, 27
Ringling, Okla., 27
Rio Grande, 82, 110

Ritter, Ryan, 12
Robber's Cave, 103
Robber's Roost, 103, 136–40
Roberts, Ed, 196–97
Rock Bluff, 58, 62
Roger Mills County, 11, 25, 26, 27, 106
Rogers, Betty, 166
Rogers, Clement Vann, 165
Rogers, Fred, 166
Rogers, Ike, 130
Rogers, Jim, 166
Rogers, Mary, 166
Rogers, Will, 163–68, 197, 223, 226, 229
Rogers, Will, Jr., 166
Rogers County, 228
Romulus, Okla., 22
Rooney, Mickey, 230
Roosevelt, Franklin D., 31, 99, 163
Roosevelt, Theodore, 21, 96, 148, 155
Ross, John, 32, 48
Ross, William P., 88–90, 108; death of, 90
Rucker, Gen. Daniel H., 108
Russell County, Ala., 22

Salina, 40–41, 49, 50, 53
Sallisaw, 157–58, 159
Salt Fork River, 8, 14, 18, 190
Sampson, Sam, 131
San Antonio, Texas, 189, 197
Sand Springs, 3, 114
Sandtown (Oklahoma City district), 186
Sandzen, Birger, 97
San Fernando Valley, Calif., 147
San Francisco, Calif., 54, 57

Sans Bois Mountains, 103
Santa Fe, N.Mex., 23, 39–42, 74, 99, 105, 115–19
Sapulpa, 24, 28, 31
San Diego, Calif., 236
Satanta (Kiowa chief), 84–87; death of, 87
Saunders, George W., 8
Savanna, 47
Scaley Back Mountain, 114
Schaleben, Arville, 163–68
Schrimsher, Mary, 165
Scott, Julian, 217, 219
Sears, T. C., 65
Sedalia, Mo., 58
Sedalia Trail, 58, 62
Seminole, Okla., 31, 181
Seminole County, 23
Seminole Indians, 63, 80–83, 108, 141, 171, 215
Seneca Indians, 40, 74
Severs, Frederick B., 61
Sewell's Stockade, 52–53
Shaffer, C. B., 35
Shattuck, Okla., 202
Shaw, Jim, 214
Shawnee Indians, 40, 216
Shawnee Trail, 58, 62
Sheridan, Gen. Phillip, 78, 175
Sheridan's Roost, 48
Shreve, Capt. Henry Miller, 15
Siegel, Lt. Max, 183
Sill, Joshua W., 45
Sinclair, Harry, 33
Skelly, Bill, 33
Skiatook, 28
Skullyville, 22, 56
Slaughter, James, 28
Slaughterville, 28

Slick, Tom, 35
Smallwood, Benjamin Franklin, 109
Smith, Dale J., 173
Smith, Kate, 226
Smoky, Lois, 99
Snyder, 200–201
Snyder, Stanley, 155
South Canadian River, 16, 51, 107, 120. *See also* Canadian River; North Canadian River
Spavinaw Creek, 44
Spencer, Okla., 212
Spencer, Ethan Allen "Al," 131, 153–55
Springfield, Mo., 205
Spring River, 14, 18
Spring Valley, 12
St. Louis, Mo., 40, 54–57, 105, 156, 205
Stacks, Katherine LaVerne. *See* Starr, Kay
Stanley, John Mix, 215–16, 218
Starr, Belle, 120–21, 130; death of, 120
Starr, Kay, 238–41
Stephens, Paul, 110
Stephens County, 27, 46, 123
Stigler, Joseph S., 27
Stigler, Okla., 27
Stillwater, 28, 66, 133, 177, 211
Stillwater Creek, 28, 211
Stover, Capt. Lute F., 150
Stringtown, 20–21
Sulphur, Okla., 158
Summit View Cemetery (Guthrie), 134
Swann, Sir Joseph, 29
Sweeny, Okla., 21

Tahlequah, Okla., 21, 32, 89, 90, 108, 201, 215
Talihina, Okla., 28
Taos, N.Mex., 99, 115–16, 118
Tarzana, Calif., 147
Tavernier, Jules, 216, 219
Taylor, Gen. Zachary, 45
Taylor, Okla., 52
Taylor, Sister Olivia, 97
Tecumseh, Okla., 144
Tesla, Nikola, 29
Texas, 39, 40, 41, 48, 50, 56–57, 65, 67, 76, 78, 85–87, 94, 96, 129, 132, 135, 150, 222
Texas County, 70
Texas Panhandle, 16, 18, 40, 67, 86
Texas Road, 40, 42, 56
Thomas, Heck, 150
Three Forks Area, 49
Tilghman, William Matthew "Bill," 148–52; death of, 151
Tillman County, 13
Tipi, Red, 84
Tipton, Mo., 55
Tipton, Okla., 46, 47
Tishomingo, Okla., 22
Tishomingo (Chickasaw chief), 22
Titus, A. J., 30
Titusville, Pa., 32
Tonkawa Indians, 28
Tonkawa, Okla., 28
Topeka, Kan., 65
Tracy, Spencer, 230
Trapp, Martin Edwin, 21
Trinidad, Colo., 138–39
Tsatoke, Monroe, 99–100
Tulsa, 23–28, 31, 33, 46, 109, 196–98, 201, 203, 210, 229
Tulsey Town, 23

Tushka, Okla., 46
Tuskahoma, Okla., 22, 92
Tyler, John, 186

Union Agency Cemetery (Muskogee), 143
Ute Indians, 84
Utica, N.Y., 28
Utica, Okla., 28

Van Buren, Ark., 141
Van Buren, Martin, 77
Van Zandt, Sandra, 181
Venuti, Joe, 239
Verden, 47
Verdigris River, 14, 19, 41, 49, 50, 53
Vermont, 216
Vernon, Texas, 62
Vici, Okla., 105
Vinita, Okla., 28, 90, 154, 205
Virginia, 153

Waggoner, Tom, 132
Wagoner County, 26
Wakita, 31
Walker, Tandy, 56
Walker's Stage Station, 56
Walnut Bayou, 52
Walnut Creek, 52–53
Warr Acres, 212
Warren, Abel, 52, 53
Warren, Henry, 86
Washington, Okla., 97
Washington, D.C., 3, 21, 73, 96, 175, 194, 216
Washita Bend, 52
Washita County, 25
Washita River, 14, 19, 40, 42, 44, 48, 79, 113, 215, 238
Watie, Gen. Stand, 44
Watonga, Okla., 28
Watts, Okla., 44, 48
Wayne, Brig. Gen. "Mad" Anthony, 44
Weatherford, 28
Weatherford, William J., 28
Webbers Falls, 41
Webster, Mollie, 91
Wellington, Kan., 177
Wells, Henry, 153–54
Wellsville, Ohio, 158–59
Western Trail, 60–62
Wetumka, Okla., 122
Wewoka, Okla., 80, 82–83, 200
Wheaton, Mo., 153
Whipple, Amiel, 216
Whiskey Road, 41
White, Josh, 226
Whiteagle, Okla., 27
White Deer, Texas, 202
Whitefield, 121
White Shield Creek, 106
Wichita Indians, 73, 76–77, 215, 216
Wichita, Kan., 59–62, 64, 77, 78, 112
Wichita County, Kan., 149
Wichita Mountains, 10–13, 45, 73, 76–79, 105, 112
Wierman, Joe, 25
Wigwam Neosho, 50
Wilburton, 56, 103
Wills, Billy Jack, 173
Wills, Bob, 173
Wills, John, 173
Wilson, Charles Banks, 227
Wilson, Woodrow, 166

Winfield, Kan., 169, 189
Wisconsin, 163
WLS radio (Chicago), 229
Woodhouse, S. W., 11
Woodward, Okla., 23, 31, 105, 134, 144, 202
Woodward, Brinton W., 23
Woodward County, 12, 23, 53
Wouldbe (Noble Co.), 23
Wouldbe (Creek Co.), 23
WREC radio (Memphis), 238
Wright, Allen, 91

WRR radio (Dallas), 238
Wyoming, 12, 79
Wymark, I.T., 204

Yale, Okla., 211
Younger, Bruce, 120
Younger's Bend, 120

Zarrow family (Tulsa), 33
Zeb, Okla., 28
Zoghaum, Rufus F., 216, 219
Zybra, Okla., 20

www.ingramcontent.com/pod-product-compliance
Lightning Source LLC
Chambersburg PA
CBHW020833160426
43192CB00007B/626